PALGRAVE MACMILLAN
CHRISTIANITIES OF THE WORLD

Series Editors:

Dale Irvin is president and professor of World Christianity at New York Theological Seminary, in New York City.

Peter C. Phan is the inaugural holder of the Ignacio Ellacuría Chair of Catholic Social Thought, Theology Department, at Georgetown University.

In recent decades, there has been increasing awareness in the academy of a reality called World Christianity. The expression refers to the fact that today Christianity is no longer predominantly Western, but has become a more truly worldwide religion. This "catholicity," a hallmark of Christianity and a fruit of Christian missions, has resulted in a massive demographic shift in the overall numbers of Christians from the Global North (Europe and North America) to the Global South (Africa, Asia, and Latin America). Consequently, the twin forces of globalization and migration have simultaneously intensified the interconnections and amplified the differences among the various expressions of Christianity worldwide, radically transforming the character of Christianity as it finds expression in diverse forms all over the globe. In the twenty-first century, Christianity can only be expected to become even more multiple, diverse, and hybridized. Similarly, one can expect to find something that is recognizably Christian among all its diverse and autochthonous expressions to make a meaningful conversation possible. We call that conversation "Christianities of the World."

To help understand this phenomenon, Palgrave Macmillan has initiated a new series of monographs appropriately titled "Christianities of the World" under the general editorship of Peter C. Phan and Dale T. Irvin. The intention of the series is to publish single-authored or edited works of scholarship that engage aspects of these diverse Christianities of the world through the disciplines of history, religious studies, theology, sociology, or missiology, in order to understand Christianity as a truly world religion. To these ends, the editors are asking,

- How has Christianity been received and transformed in various countries, especially in Africa, Asia, and Latin America (the non-Western world) in response to their cultural practices, religious traditions (the so-called "world religions" as well as the tribal or indigenous religions), migratory movements, and political and economic globalization (inculturation and interfaith dialogue)? In particular, how have newer forms of Christianity, especially those that identify with the Pentecostal/Charismatic movement, changed the face of World Christianity? What are the major characteristics of Christianities both old and new? What new trajectories and directions can one expect to see in the near future?

- How should the history of Christian missions be narrated? How does one evaluate the contributions of expatriate missionaries and indigenous agents? How should one understand the relationship between missions and churches?
- How should theology be taught in the academic arena (be it in universities, seminaries, or Bible schools)? How should various Christian theological loci (e.g., God, Christ, Spirit, church, worship, spirituality, ethics, or pastoral ministry) be reformulated and taught in view of world Christianity or Christianities of the world, in dialogue with different cultures and different religions, or targeted toward particular ethnic or religious groups?
- How does the new reality of world Christianity affect research methods? How should courses on Christianity be taught? How should textbooks on Christianity, as well as on world religions, generally be structured? What should curricula, course work, required texts, faculty hiring, criteria for tenure and promotion, research, and publication look like in the academic world that is responding to the questions being raised by the Christianities of the world?

The issues are far-ranging, and the questions transformational. We look forward to a lively series and a rewarding dialogue.

Pentecostalism and Prosperity: The Socio-Economics of the Global Charismatic Movement
Edited by Katherine Attanasi and Amos Yong

Interfaith Marriage in America: The Transformation of Religion and Christianity
By Erika B. Seamon

Contemporary Issues of Migration and Theology
Edited by Elaine Padilla and Peter C. Phan

Theosis, Sino-Christian Theology and the Second Chinese Enlightenment: Heaven and Humanity in Unity
By Alexander Chow

Muslim-Christian Dialogue in Post-Colonial Northern Nigeria: The Challenges of Inclusive Cultural and Religious Pluralism
By Marinus C. Iwuchukwu

Christian Responses to Islam in Nigeria: A Contextual Study of Ambivalent Encounters
By Akintunde E. Akinade

Theology of Migration in the Abrahamic Religions
Edited by Elaine Padilla and Peter C. Phan

Christianities in World Migration
Edited By Peter C. Phan and Elaine Padilla (TK)

Theology of Migration in the Abrahamic Religions

Edited by

Elaine Padilla and Peter C. Phan

THEOLOGY OF MIGRATION IN THE ABRAHAMIC RELIGIONS
Copyright © Elaine Padilla and Peter C. Phan, 2014.
Softcover reprint of the hardcover 1st edition 2014 978-1-137-00103-0

All rights reserved.

First published in 2014 by
PALGRAVE MACMILLAN®
in the United States—a division of St. Martin's Press LLC,
175 Fifth Avenue, New York, NY 10010.

Where this book is distributed in the UK, Europe and the rest of the world, this is by Palgrave Macmillan, a division of Macmillan Publishers Limited, registered in England, company number 785998, of Houndmills, Basingstoke, Hampshire RG21 6XS.

Palgrave Macmillan is the global academic imprint of the above companies and has companies and representatives throughout the world.

Palgrave® and Macmillan® are registered trademarks in the United States, the United Kingdom, Europe and other countries.

ISBN 978-1-349-43353-7   ISBN 978-1-137-00104-7 (eBook)
DOI 10.1057/9781137001047

Library of Congress Cataloging-in-Publication Data

    Theology of migration in the Abrahamic religions / [edited by] Elaine Padilla and Peter C. Phan.
      pages cm.—(Christianities of the world)
    Includes bibliographical references and index.

    1. Christianity and other religions. 2. Abrahamic religions.
3. Emigration and immigration—Religious aspects—Christianity.
4. Emigration and immigration—Religious aspects—Judaism.
5. Emigration and immigration—Religious aspects—Islam.
    I. Padilla, Elaine, editor.

BR127.T476 2014
201'.7—dc23   2014014797

A catalogue record of the book is available from the British Library.

Design by Newgen Knowledge Works (P) Ltd., Chennai, India.

First edition: October 2014

10 9 8 7 6 5 4 3 2 1

Contents

Introduction: Migration in Judaism, Christianity, and Islam   1
Elaine Padilla and Peter C. Phan

Chapter 1
Theology, Migration, and the Homecoming   7
Dale T. Irvin

Chapter 2
"You Will Seek From There": The Cycle of Exile and
Return in Classical Jewish Theology   27
Devorah Schoenfeld

Chapter 3
Divine Glory Danced: Jewish Migration as God's
Self-Revelation in and as Art   47
Melissa Raphael

Chapter 4
Theology of Migration in the Orthodox Tradition   63
Kondothra M. George

Chapter 5
Embracing, Protecting, and Loving the Stranger:
A Roman Catholic Theology of Migration   77
Peter C. Phan

Chapter 6
Protestantism in Migration: *Ecclesia Semper Migranda*   111
Nancy Bedford

Chapter 7
The Im/migrant Spirit: De/constructing a Pentecostal
Theology of Migration   133
Amos Yong

Chapter 8
Migration: An Opportunity for Broader and Deeper Ecumenism   155
Deenabandhu Manchala

Chapter 9
Toward a Muslim Theology of Migration   173
Amir Hussain

Chapter 10
Challenges of Diversity and Migration in Islamic Political
Theory and Theology   187
Charles Amjad-Ali

Chapter 11
Signs of Wonder: Journeying Plurally into the Divine Disclosure   209
Elaine Padilla

Selected Bibliography   239

List of Contributors   249

Index   253

Introduction: Migration in Judaism, Christianity, and Islam

Elaine Padilla and Peter C. Phan

"Migration is a subject that cries out for an interdisciplinary approach." So declare Caroline B. Brettell and James F. Hollifield in the preface to their edited volume on migration theory.[1] In an effort to "reboot" migration theory through "interdisciplinarity, globality, and postdisciplinarity," they have assembled a team of specialists in anthropology, sociology, economics, geography, history, demographics, political science, and law to investigate the phenomenon of international migration. Conspicuously absent in this "talking across disciplines" on migration is religious studies/theology—an absence all the more poignant as both editors are professors at a Christian university with a large divinity school.

It is of course legitimate for methodological reasons to limit the discourse on migration to the social sciences, and Brettell and Hollifield deserve great credit for having brought together specialists in the above-mentioned disciplines for a common conversation on migration, as a result of which a richer understanding of this phenomenon was obtained. Nevertheless, in claiming a seat at the table of this interdisciplinary conversation on human mobility for theology, this book intends to draw attention to the fact that migration cannot be fully understood without a serious and rigorous examination of how religious factors have played an influential role in it. It is beyond doubt that throughout history, religion and religious freedom—or lack of it—have exerted a powerful "push" and "pull" in the dynamics of migration, whether internal or international/intercontinental, free or forced, temporary or permanent, documented or undocumented, planned or unforeseen. Furthermore, it is well documented that the migrants' religions have not only irreversibly changed the religious landscape of the countries of destination but have also forged the migrants into cohesive communities, providing them with effective means for physical survival, economic upward mobility, social stability, civil integration, cultural preservation, and of course, spiritual flourishing in the host countries.[2] On the other hand, migration is one of the key factors that has contributed immensely to the geographical expansion and internal diversity of religions across the globe.

While this reciprocal relation between migration and religion obtains in all the so-called world religions—religion fostering migration and migration expanding religion—the focus of this book is on the theology of migration in Judaism, Christianity, and Islam, as it is part of a trilogy entitled *Theology and Migration in World Christianity: Contextual Perspectives*.[3] That it is appropriate for a work on migration and world Christianity to include a discussion of Judaism and Islam requires no elaborate justification. It is common knowledge that there exist strong historical connections and theological commonalities among these three religions, so much so that they have been called the "Abrahamic Religions" or "Religions of the Book." As far as Christianity is concerned, since it stands in the middle, to understand it fully, it is necessary to place it in relation to the religious tradition that precedes it and that which follows it, though obviously its indebtedness to the former is much greater than to the latter. Conversely, to adequately understand Judaism and Islam in their historical developments, it is also necessary to place them in relation to Christianity and to each other.

Among the many features that link the three religious traditions, no doubt migration obtains pride of place. A migratory act marks a pivotal moment in the history of each of these three religions: Abram's journey (whose name will be changed to Abraham) from Haran to Canaan, Jesus' from Galilee to Jerusalem, and Muhammad's from Mecca to Yathrib (Medina). Though each of these migrations or journeys is invested by the followers of the three religions with different religious and theological meanings, they are all regarded as paradigmatic responses of faith and obedience to the divine command. Moreover, without frequent waves of migration, at times massive, with whole populations on the move, as part of exile and diaspora, wars of conquest, or missionary enterprise, these religions would not be what they are today.

This book does not, however, provide narratives of these migrations, which are readily accessible in any historical work on these Abrahamic religions. Rather it presents the *theology of migration* to be found in their sacred books, traditions, and sacred practices. Dale Irvin's opening essay shows the connection between migration and religion, illustrates the central place of Abraham's migration in the collective memory of the three religions associated with his name, and argues that from the religious point of view, migration is not only going forth but also "homecoming."

The next two essays discuss the meaning of migration in Judaism. Drawing on the Torah and the Talmud, Devorah Schoenfeld shows the multiple meanings of exile for Jews—as tragedy, punishment for sin, and places where God can be found. Melissa Raphael, reviewing Jewish art and dance and post-Holocaust Jewish thinkers, helps us see how migration is "a dance or series of rhythmic movements through space by whose progression Israel makes straight the path of the Lord."

The next five essays deal with the theology of migration from the Christian perspective and are divided chiefly along denominational lines. Kondothra M. George presents an Orthodox view of migration that demonstrates how historical events have positively contributed to the interpretation of Scriptures and the development of spirituality and liturgy in Orthodox churches in their host countries, and of an Orthodox theology cued by the trope of pilgrimage. Peter C. Phan surveys the teachings of modern popes, from Pius IX to Benedict, and three major documents of the Roman magisterium on migration, and sketches an outline of a Roman Catholic theology of migration. Nancy Bedford offers a Protestant view of the church as *ecclesia semper migranda*, with a particular focus on Latino and Latina Protestant migrants in the United States. From his personal experiences as a Chinese Malaysian migrant to the United States, Amos Yong outlines a Pentecostal theology of migration, drawing especially on Luke and Paul. Deenabandhu Manchala focuses on the thought of the World Council of Churches on migration, in particular on hospitality as an expression of inclusiveness.

The teaching of Islam on migration is presented in the next two essays. Adopting the concept of of his mentor, Wilfred Cantwell Smith, regarding "cumulative tradition," Amir Hussain highlights the migrations of the Prophet Muhammad and relates the Islamic teaching on migration to the experiences of Muslim migrants in North America. Charles Amjad-Ali surveys the complex political history of Islamic teaching and practices toward migrants, especially the *dhimmi* and *millat* systems, from the times of the Prophet to contemporary Europe, and argues for a view of Islam that respects its linguistic plurality (not only Arabic), its geographical multiplicity (not only the Middle East), and religious diversity, characteristics that have been greatly heightened by migration.

Elaine Padilla, in her concluding essay, develops a mysticism of migration or migratory spirituality. Drawing far and wide on the writings of prominent Jewish, Christian, and Muslim mystics, she presents a breathtaking vision of migration as the self's mystical journey with God as Mystery. The migration starts from divine love, is accompanied by God's self-disclosure in and through various visible signs, and after many waystations, arrives at the "Station of No Station." During this mystical migration, the self is never alone but travels in the company not only of the divine *Shekinah* but also of other human migrants. Furthermore, because the divine self-disclosure occurs in material signs, the migrating self develops a deep care for creation, and thus migratory spirituality flows into eco-ethics and spirituality.

At the end of this book on the theology of migration, the "talking across disciplines" about human mobility—it is hoped—has expanded immeasurably. Imagine this conversation taking place at a round table, where no participant needs to be removed to make room for others. One needs only enlarge the circle a little bit, and other people can join in the conversation. Furthermore, unlike at a rectangular table, which grants a place of honor to only one guest, at the round table anyone can be at the beginning, center, and end. Similarly, at this expanded interdisciplinary conversation on migration, no voice or discipline, not even the discipline that at one time was proclaimed the "queen of the sciences," is given preeminence. Every voice is listened to and taken seriously. Let the *symposium*— eating and drinking of ideas—on migration begin!

Notes

1. Caroline B. Brettell and James F. Hollifield, eds., *Migration Theory: Talking across Disciplines*, 2nd edition (New York: Routledge, 2007), viii. Brettell is the Dedman Family Distinguished Professor of Anthropology, and Hollifield is the Arnold Professor of International Political Economy and Director of the Tower Center for Political Studies at Southern Methodist University. The divinity school at Southern Methodist University is Perkins School of Theology.
2. The literature on religion and migration is burgeoning. Suffice it to cite here three works on immigration and the US religious situation: Diana Eck, *A New Religious America: How a 'Christian Country' Has Become the World's Most Religiously Diverse Nation* (San Francisco: HarperSanFrancisco, 2002); Karen I. Leonard, Alex Stepick, Manuel A. Vasquez, and Jennifer Holdaway, eds., *Immigrant Faiths: Transforming Religious Life in America* (New York: Roman & Littlefield, 2006); and Yvonne Yazbeck Hassad, Jane L. Smith, and John L. Esposito, eds., *Religion and Immigration: Christian, Jewish,*

and Muslim Experiences in the United States (New York: Rowman & Littlefield, 2003).
3. The three volumes are entitled *Contemporary Issues of Migration and Theology*, *Theology of Migration in the Abrahamic Religions*, and *Migration and Church in World Christianity*. The first appeared in 2013, and the third is scheduled for 2015.

Chapter 1

Theology, Migration, and the Homecoming

Dale T. Irvin

Migration and Religion: Beginning the Journey

The study of migration has expanded significantly over the past several decades in the academic world. The proliferation of programs, centers, journals, and monographs on the topic has been extraordinary. A search of the Internet for "migration studies programs" now turns up more than five million results. The increase in migration studies has been due in no small part to the explosive growth in human migration globally. According to the United Nations, more than two hundred million people, or more than 3 percent of the world's population, now live in a country other than the one in which they were born.[1] Even if all migration were to end tomorrow (which does not appear to be about to happen), the social, economic, political, and cultural impact of those living in new locations would continue to be felt around the world for generations to come.

Migration of course is not a new phenomenon. Human beings have been on the move for thousands of years. In some cases, the physical movement across borders into new social, political, and cultural locations has been temporary, as in the case of merchants who traveled great distances in the ancient world to sell their goods or services, but who intended eventually to return home. In other cases, the movement has been permanent, as when peoples have been taken captive into exile, or have been forced to resettle due to climatic conditions, or have moved in search of better material economic opportunities.

Over the past five centuries in the modern era, the pace of migration and the typical distances that migrants have traveled have both greatly increased. Migration in the modern period has been forced as well as voluntary. The mass movement of tens of millions of people of

African descent who were enslaved and sold into forced labor in North and South America is an example of the former, while the migration of European settlers who sought expanded material economic opportunities in America, Africa, and Asia is an example of the latter.

Even the most voluntary of migrations is seldom without a certain amount of ambiguity. Rarely is a move to a new country or cultural context undertaken without some underlying anxiety. Even in the most benign situations, migration has hardly ever been viewed as an entirely positive step by those embarking on such a journey. It is more often thought of as the least of several evils, as when approximately one million people emigrated from Ireland during the potato famine of the 1840s and 1850s to escape starvation. Anyone who migrates does so with a certain degree of hope and anticipation that reaches beyond whatever realistic expectations one might have.

In many cases over the past several centuries, those who migrated have successfully settled into the new territories into which they have moved, adjusting and even over time assimilating into the new social and cultural world where they had come to live. Even the most extreme forms of cultural assimilation hardly ever resulted in a total erasure of the natal identities, however. Some form of cultural retention could almost always be found even after several generations have passed, resulting in new mixed or hybrid forms of culture and identity.

For those who have undertaken migration, and often for their descendants who follow generations after them, the part of their memory and identity that reflects the place from which they migrated quite often continues to be configured in some manner or degree as the "homeland." Even when migrants have successfully assimilated into their new "home," they often retain some form of imagined image or memory of the "old home" from which they or their ancestors originally migrated. The transnationalism that migration brings about is structured along an axis of "home" and "away," of home land and foreign land.[2]

The field of migration studies in recent years has included a significant number of works exploring the role of religion in the phenomenon. Most of these efforts have focused on the historical and cultural aspects of religion, looking at how migration has created more complex or mixed cultural forms, at how religion has played a role in preserving a home identity among immigrants, or how religion has helped immigrants assimilate into a new civic environment.[3] Some of these studies have integrated other social factors such as gender and sexual orientation.[4] Several authors like Thomas A. Tweed have made migration a central aspect of their overall theory of religion.[5] Nonetheless, migration has not yet been a significant theme for Christian systematic or constructive theology, a somewhat surprising reality given the central role that migration has played not just in world Christian history and tradition over the centuries, but in the wider realm of Abrahamic traditions that links Christians with Judaism and Islam. Within all three of these Abrahamic faith traditions, migration is a trope for salvation. Thus the starting point for a theology of migration is fittingly in the story of Abraham himself.

Migration and Memory of Abraham

The figure of Abraham is significant in the religious traditions of Judaism, Christianity and Islam. The scriptures of all three remember Abraham and his family as having migrated in response to instructions from God. The earliest form of the story is found in the Tanakh, the book that Christians call the Old Testament or Hebrew Bible, in which Terah took his son, Abram (before his name was changed to Abraham), Lot, who was the nephew of Abram, and Sarai, the wife of Abram, and migrated from the city of Ur, in what is now southern Iraq, to settle in Haran, in what is now Turkey, where Terah died (Genesis 11:27–32). Settling in Haran proved to be profitable for the remaining members of the group, for Genesis 12:5b tells us that they amassed a significant amount of wealth, presumably in the form of livestock as well as other material goods, and acquired a number of "persons" (*nephesh* in Hebrew, often translated as "souls" in English), perhaps slaves they had purchased, or others from the city who attached themselves freely to the clan.

At some point, however, according to Genesis 12:1, God spoke directly to Abram and instructed him to leave his land, relatives, and patriarchal household in order to go to a new land that God would show him. The instruction to migrate was accompanied by a promise of blessing: "I will make of you a great nation, and I will bless you, and make your name great, so that you will be a blessing. I will bless those who bless you, and the one who curses you I will curse; and in you all the families of the earth shall be blessed" (Genesis 12:2–3).[6]

Genesis 12 tells us that Abram did as he was commanded, taking Sarai and Lot with him, and setting out for the land of Canaan. Shortly after arriving there, famine forced Abram and Sarai to journey with their livestock and slaves to Egypt, where they resided until the famine had subsided, allowing them to return to Canaan (Genesis 12:10–16). Even then, however, their migrating days were not over. Abraham and Sarah (their names were changed by God in Genesis 17:1), though quite wealthy, continued the nomadic life of wandering throughout Canaan with their flocks. At the end of their days, the only land they had come to own was the field in which they were buried (Genesis 23:17 and 25:7).

The story of Abraham's call and migration is remembered in the book of Acts in the scriptures that Christians generally call the New Testament. Stephen says in his speech that God first appeared to Abraham (not Terah) "when he was in Mesopotamia, before he lived in Haran, and said to him, 'Leave your country and your relatives and go to the land that I will show you.'" (Acts 7:2b-3). The memory of Abraham in the Second Testament is largely genealogical in character. The first followers of Jesus sought to identify themselves and their movement as having descended from Abraham and Sarah in order to lay claim to being legitimate heirs of the legacy of faith and salvation. But they also lifted up the promise of the blessing for all nations that Abraham and Sarah were to bring, as seen in passages such as Acts 3:25. The Apostle Paul in particular came to understand Jesus Christ to be the means by which that blessing would be realized among all nations (as seen in Romans 4:17–18 and Galatians 3:8–16). That horizon comes fully into view in the book of Revelation at the end of the New Testament, where representatives of all nations of the earth are depicted as coming up to worship in the New Jerusalem.

The Qur'an, the holy scriptures of Islam, also recalls Abraham's migration as part of the foundation of his faith. According to Surah 21, "The Prophets," Abraham's initial migration was actually an act of deliverance by Allah, who rescued the patriarch and his nephew from the hands of angry idolaters after Abraham had broken their idols. In rescuing them, Allah directed them to the land of promise (21:58–71; see also Surah 29, "The Spider," 16–26). According to the Qur'an, Abraham built the Sacred House or Kaaba in Mecca with Ishmael, his son, and instituted the pilgrimage (*al-hajj*) to it, a holy form of journeying that is closely akin to his initial migration in the manner in which it secured a promise (see Surah 22, "Pilgrimage," 26–27). Islam links Abraham's legacy with the Kaaba in Mecca most concretely and clearly with the universal aspects of the faith. It is in *al-hajj* that the universal aspects of Islam are most clearly experienced. Abraham's migration in Islam links deliverance with pilgrimage. The ongoing practice of *al-hajj* extends that to the ends of the earth.

Migration in Judaism, Christianity, and Islam

Abraham and his family set Judaism, Christianity, and Islam on the initial road to migration. Each faith tradition through the ages has, in its own way, continued the journeying. Several generations after

Abraham and Sarah first came to Canaan, their Hebrew descendents were forced by famine to take refuge again in the land of Egypt. This time they stayed, and grew strong in number. The Egyptians came to oppress them, however, forcing the Hebrews into slavery until God called Moses to lead the people to freedom.

The exodus was another kind of migration, as was the wandering in the wilderness for 40 years and the entrance into the land of Canaan that was led by Joshua. The last migration took on the form of conquest in the memory of the Hebrew people. Migration of a different sort was later forced upon this same people by another conquest, first by the Assyrian Empire against the northern kingdom of Israel, and then by Babylon with the fall of Jerusalem in the south. Ezekiel was a migrant who had been born in Jerusalem but forced into exile in Babylon, where he lived out his days in a foreign land. Ezra, on the other hand, was born in Babylon, according to Jewish texts and tradition, but he joined the migration back home to resettle and rebuild Jerusalem, the city not of his birth but of his ancestry.[7]

The majority of people of Hebrew descent did not return to Jerusalem in the days after Ezra and Nehemiah. Most continued to live in the *diaspora,* or "scattering." In Jewish history, *dispora* came to be understood as "wandering" as well. Wandering and exile were closely related, as seen in the story of Cain in Genesis 4:11–12. Following the destruction of the Temple in 70 CE, even the land of Israel itself became part of the exilic existence.[8]

By the first century CE, migration had taken the people of Israel and their religious and cultural identity not only around the Mediterranean Sea, but south into Egypt and Ethiopia, and east to India and along the Silk Road. Over the next 1,500 years, migration would continue to take Jewish communities into China, Central Asia, Arabia, Western Europe, and eventually South and North America. Jews living in these places continued to maintain their distinctive religious and cultural identity connected with text (the Torah) and tradition.

Within Western Europe, the dispersion of Jews was often conditioned by extreme forms of Christian anti-Judaism that were encoded in law.[9] Denied the right to own land within Christendom by European Christian law, Jews were by definition migrants and strangers. The myth of the "wandering Jew," which first appeared in print in 1602, told the legendary story of a first-century resident in Jerusalem named Ahasuerus who had joined in the mocking of Jesus as the latter was headed toward the cross, and as a consequence Jesus cursed Ahasuerus to roam the earth until Jesus's return.[10]

Over time, the dispersion of Jews gave rise as well to legends and myths regarding the "lost tribes of Israel" that spread beyond the boundaries of historic Jewish identity. Claims of Jewish descent came to be made for various peoples throughout the world for whom no historical or genealogical connection to the tribes of Israel could be reasonably traced or demonstrated.[11] British Israelism, for instance, which holds that the Anglo-Saxon "race" descended from members of the "lost tribes of Israel" who migrated to England from Mesopotamia, continues to find adherents among various Christians even today.[12]

If *diaspora*, or scattering, has been one aspect of the long history of Jewish migration, returning to the land of Israel and gathering the remnants to form "a people" again has been the other aspect through the centuries. Indeed, scattering and gathering are two sides of the same coin, or two sides to a single blade on the cutting edge of history in Jewish life.[13] Support for Jews returning to *Eretz Yisrael* is often associated with Zionism and described as a recent phenomenon, but it has deep and enduring precedents in Jewish life and thought. The thirteenth-century rabbi and scholar Moshe ben Nahman (also known as Nahmanides, or Ramban) is but one example.

Ben Nahman was originally from Spain. A generation younger than Maimonides, he shared with his better known colleague a vast knowledge of philosophy and Talmudic tradition. Ben Nahman is best known for his disputation in 1263 with the Dominican Friar Pablo Christiani before Jaime I de Aragón.[14] He wrote extensively on a number of other topics concerning Jewish life, however. Concerning the Torah, Ben Nahman argued that commandments kept in the land of Israel brought about a greater degree of holiness than commandments kept elsewhere. His sense of the importance of the land led him to migrate there to live in 1267. He settled first in Jerusalem but later moved to Acre, where he died in 1270. The Ramban Synagogue, which he founded in Jerusalem in 1267, still exists.[15]

Going forth and returning home, or scattering and gathering, have not only been powerful tropes for Jewish life and thought over the centuries but for Christian theological discourse and tradition as well. In the New Testament, in Acts 1:8, the Risen Christ tells his followers that they are going to be his "witnesses" (*martures*) to the "ends of the earth." In Matthew 28:19, the Risen Christ tells these same followers to go and teach "all nations." Their scattering began almost immediately as some from among these first followers journeyed to other cities and regions beyond Israel to spread the message of Jesus. Within decades of the resurrection event, Christian communities had formed in Damascus, Edessa, Antioch, Alexandria, and even Rome. Their scattering was not without a regathering, however. The book of Acts tells of the leaders coming from several other cities to confer in a council in Jerusalem over the conditions by which Gentiles would be admitted into their movement. Always on the horizon of the early movement was the belief that Jesus himself would come back soon, and that the scattered would be gathered together with him. Most often in the Second Testament the location of that gathering was literally or symbolically expected to be Jerusalem.

The first followers of Jesus clearly saw themselves as members of the household of Israel, known as the Nazarenes. The scattering of these disciples-turned-apostles ("sent ones") follows at first in the footsteps of the scattering (*diaspora*) of the rest of Israel. Within a decade or two, the apostolic horizon widened to embrace Gentiles in the "scattering." The book of James is addressed to the twelve tribes in the *diaspora*, while the book of I Peter is addressed slightly differently to the "strangers" (*parepidēmos*) in the *diaspora* of Asia Minor. Revelation 4:10, on the other hand, foresees the twelve tribes and twelve apostles being brought back together in the New Jerusalem and joined to form a combined leadership team of twenty-four "elders." The twelve tribes and twelve apostles are brought together again symbolically in Revelation 21:12–14, where they are inscribed in the walls and foundations of the New Jerusalem. Even as Christians began to separate their own identity from that of being Jewish, they continued to hold to going out and coming back, scattering and gathering, as central theological themes.

Christians were, for the first several centuries, without a homeland, without a place they could politically call their own. They began to find themselves politically at home in the fourth century, most notably in the Roman Empire. Over the next several centuries, Christianity within the Roman Empire and its various descendants in Europe became for the most part a settled faith. Yet even the most settled would find themselves from time to time taken up in an urge to travel for the faith, if not to migrate, then at least to go on pilgrimage.

Pilgrimages especially to the holy land of Israel began to be promoted by a number of prominent members of Roman society in the fourth century, the most important being Helena, mother of the emperor Constantine. Writings from pilgrims such as Egeria (or Etheria), a woman who spent three years in Jerusalem, were copied and circulated back home among those who could not travel, in order to communicate to them the spiritual benefits of such pilgrimages.[16]

Pilgrims tended to be persons who undertook temporary migrations for the purposes of faith. Most who set out on pilgrimage intended to return one day to their home community, bringing with them a blessing to be shared. Others considered migration and wandering to be a more permanent spiritual vocation. Many of the men and women who took monastic vows in particular considered wandering and holiness to be intrinsically connected. Germanic tribes had for several centuries been migrating into rural territories that had once been administratively under Roman law. By the sixth century, the territories they had come to occupy were providing fertile new lands through which these monastics could wander. A new form of spiritual migration called *peregrination* took hold throughout Western Europe. The *peregrini*, many of them Celts or Anglos from Ireland or England, were Christian monks and nuns who set out on a life of wandering throughout Europe. Wherever they went, they preached, established monasteries, and demonstrated signs and wonders associated with healing and salvation.[17]

Wandering was not confined to Christian monastics in the Roman Empire. It was also widely known among Christians in the Persian world and in India. By the seventh century CE, Christian monasteries were common along the Silk Road stretching across Central Asia. Christians had made their way alongside Buddhist and Manichaeans all the way to the imperial capital of China by the end of the seventh century. They were also accompanying merchants in the south of India and in other parts of Asia. By the fourteenth century, they were being joined by others from the Latin West who were in part riding the great new currents of migration that had been unleashed by the Crusades.

Modern Christian missions emerged from the spiritual efforts of Franciscans, Dominicans, and then Jesuits, who after the fifteenth century were being carried by the currents of Europe's new colonial ventures. Mercantilism might have been the driving engine, but mission and migration were thoroughly intertwined.[18] The entire modern missionary movement can be seen in one way as a movement for migration, and generated by a profound theological reimaging of migration. Missionaries were and still are migrants, some temporary but others permanent. Mission has to be understood as a theological practice intended to make the Christian message move: to make it migrate. The modern ecumenical movement, which was born from the missionary movement, likewise needs to be seen in light of a more profound theology of migration.

Christian spiritual understandings of migration have been matched through the century by those of Islam, for whom scattering and gathering are intertwined with religious belief and practice. As noted above, the Qur'an also recognizes the initial migration of Abraham and his subsequent journeys of pilgrimage to be foundational to true faith. As in Judaism and Christianity, Islam recognizes other migrations as central to its faith. The most important of these down through the ages was the migration that the Prophet Muhammad himself undertook from Mecca to Medina in 622 CE The *hijra* ("migration," often mistranslated into English as "flight") of the Prophet marks the beginning of the Islamic calendar. A previous round of migrations had taken place between 613 and 615 CE in response to the growing persecution the Prophet Muhammad and his followers were encountering in Mecca. Muhammad himself had organized their migration. By cover of night, various groups of the Prophet's followers, numbering more than one hundred, left Mecca and made their way by ship across the Red Sea to the city of Axum, where they were extended refuge by the Ethiopian king. Although these followers later returned to Medina, their journey is remembered in Islamic tradition as the first *hijra*.

Increasing opposition from the leadership of Mecca to the message of the Prophet led Muhammad and his closest followers to undertake the *hijra* of 622 CE / 1 A.H. That event was marked by miraculous occurrences, such as a spider weaving a web over the mouth of the cave where the Prophet hid in order to fool the pursing Meccans into believing that the Prophet was not to be found in there.

Eventually, the term *hijra* took on deeper spiritual meaning as well in Islam. Migration or exile in the cause of God was especially significant. According to Surah 9, "Repentance," "Those who believe, and suffer exile and strive with might and main, in Allah's cause, with their goods and their persons, have the highest rank in the sight of Allah: they are the people who will achieve [salvation]" (20).

Alongside *hijra* in importance for Islam is *al-hajj*, or pilgrimage. As noted above, according to the Qur'an, Abraham instituted the Great Pilgrimage to Mecca, which is one of the five pillars of Islam.[19] Muslims through the centuries have been and continue to be expected at least once in their lifetime to make this pilgrimage, which takes place during the last month of the year, known appropriately as *Dhū al-Hijjah* in Arabic. While undertaking such a journey today is relatively easily, in centuries past, it often entailed the expenditures of enormous amounts of money and considerable time for those traveling great distances, to say nothing of the dangers of such a journey. Once one arrives in Mecca, there are a series of proscribed rites and prayers that take place in and around the Kaaba in Mecca. Other pilgrimages have emerged in Islamic tradition over the centuries, many of them with local or regional meaning. But none compares in spiritual importance to the Great Pilgrimage to Mecca, signified in the manner in which Muslims through the centuries have often added *hajj* to their names after completing it.

While still in Mecca, the Prophet Muhammad undertook a different kind of pilgrimage that has also been important to Islam. The episode is known as the "Night Journey." According to Islamic teaching, one night the Angel Gabriel appeared to the Prophet and took him on a steed, first to Jerusalem and then to paradise, where the Prophet was addressed directly by God. The journey is the basis for Surah 17, in which the instruction from Allah to the Prophet that established the centrality of prayer in Islam is found.[20] Pilgrimage and prayer have thereby remained closely connected in Islam.

The first round of Muslim migrations following the death of the Prophet in 632 CE took the form of military excursions by his immediate associates. Under the leadership of the first Caliphs ("Successors"), Arab armies quickly defeated the armies of the East Roman or Byzantine Empire in Syria, Palestine, and Egypt to the east, and of the Persian Empire to the west. At first the Arabs did not migrate to the regions that they conquered. The first generation of Muslim rulers lived in camps outside the cities they had taken. Eventually, however, they began the process of migration. The Umayyad rulers established their capital in Damascus. The Abbasids, who came to power in 750 CE, built a new capital at Baghdad, which became the center of their growing empire. Islam continued to expand not so much through military conquest as through mercantile activities. The patterns of migration were similar to those that characterized other economic powers through the centuries.

The spiritual meaning of migration that was found among Christians quickly appeared in Islam as well. As with Christianity, migration and pilgrimage were connected in Islam with the development of a transregional identity and an expression of its universal faith.[21] Wandering came to characterize a group of Muslim holy women and men known as Sufis, who were in many ways the counterparts to the nuns and monks of Christian tradition. Sufis emerged in Islam in the eight century CE. Like monks and nuns, they linked self-denial or asceticism with holiness and spiritual advancement. They were also often wanderers. One of the earliest Sufi mystics was a woman named Rabi'a, who came from Persia. Rabi'a practiced a limited form of itinerancy, and like many of her Christian counterparts from earlier centuries, she eventually migrated to live in the desert, to be able to practice holiness and asceticism without the distractions of human society.[22]

One of the most important Sufi mystics was Mansur al-Hallaj, who lived in the tenth century CE. Hallaj made the *hajj* to Mecca three times in his life, staying for extended times in the holy city. He also wandered widely from Persia throughout Central Asia and into India for spiritual reasons. His mysticism eventually brought him into conflict with the ruling authorities, however, and in 922 CE, he was executed in Baghdad for having claimed to be one with Allah.[23]

The tropes of wandering and exile are connected with pilgrimage in Christianity and Islam in the way that scattering and gathering, of going out and coming back, are connected in Judaism. All of these Abrahamic traditions have forms of migration that are part of a larger narrative of salvation, and in all, salvation has connotations of connectedness, of being joined to others and to the divine in ways that are both transcendent and enduring (or using the more common religious terms, "eternal" or "everlasting"). There is also in all three a link between migration and salvation that calls for deeper reflection.

Toward a Theology of Migration: Migration as Homecoming

As noted earlier, human beings migrate across boundaries and move into new terrains (geographical, political, social or cultural) for a variety of reasons. Sometimes they are forced to migrate against their will, as when they are taken captive, or expelled from a particular political region or nation, or forced by circumstances to give up the place that they call home. More often in recent history, they have moved willingly. In cases of voluntary or willing migration, the reasons are almost always associated with the perception or hope of improved living conditions, or for a better life. Sometimes people migrate because they seek increased financial security or opportunity. Sometimes it is to gain access to what appear to be greater educational opportunities, or greater freedom of political expression and participation. Sometimes it is to join family members or close associates who have migrated earlier, with the perceived good of maintaining community or keeping family together. Sometimes it can even be for the simple sake of adventure. In any case, the majority of migration that has taken place over the past century or so has been driven by hopes for a more positive life, a better future, a greater degree of freedom, or a more interesting life. People leave the land that they consider home for the most part because they are in search of a better home. Migration is not so much driven by rejection of home as it is in search for home, or a new home. Exile, which is so closely connected with the condition of homelessness, is not necessarily an abandonment of home as it is a search for (a new) home.[24]

Thomas Tweed has argued that making homes and crossing boundaries are part of the very definition of religion.[25] He identifies the kinetics of homemaking with dwelling and the kinetics of itinerancy with crossing. Religions seek to constrain some kinds of crossings and to facilitate others, which is to say, they seek both to establish boundaries and limits, and to transcend or transgress them. The boundaries and borders that religions seek to construct and to cross can be terrestrial,[26] corporeal[27] or cosmic.[28] The "teleographies" that religions offer, those "representations of the ultimate horizon and the means of crossing it" can furthermore be either transporting or transforming, Tweed argues.[29] They call for crossings in location or in condition, be they terrestrial, corporeal, or cosmic.

Tweed's identification of dwelling with homemaking, and situating this as a fundamental characteristic of or practice achieved by religion, is compelling. I would argue further, however, that Tweed does not make it clear that the crossing in both the transporting and transforming dimensions is also driven by a desire for home. Religion is not just about homemaking; it is also about homecoming. These teleographies are inevitable representations of a better home.

In the remaining part of this chapter, I want to look at homecoming as a trope for salvation, focusing particularly, although not exclusively, on Christianity, and offer it as a contribution to the larger task of constructing a theology of migration. From the earliest days of the Christian movement, beginning with the pages of the Second Testament, salvation has been identified as an experience of ultimate homecoming. "In my Father's household (*oikia*) there are many dwelling places (*monai pollai*)," Jesus is remembered as saying to his followers in John 14:2. "I go to prepare a place (*topon*) for you," he continues. Whether the *oikos* or household of God is thought of as a garden (*jannah* in Arabic, *parádeisos* or "paradise" in Greek) or as a city, it was a place where one could dwell in peace. The journeying of life, both through time and across geographical space, was configured religiously as a migration toward home. This experience of more ultimate homecoming thus entails an experience of departure from what one currently knows to be home. Homecoming in theological terms is the same as *homegoing*. The trope has the effect of calling one to embrace a certain kind of homelessness spiritually (and sometimes even materially) precisely because it calls one to come home. It invites one to embrace the identity of a stranger or an alien in the present world, whether this world was conceived of temporally as an era, or spatially as the cosmos.

Homi K. Bhabha notes the critical role that the cultural memory of a home that is not here can play in negating the present, especially among those who are subordinated or subjugated in the modern world. He calls this experience the "unhomely," or being "unhomed":

> The negating activity is, indeed, the intervention of the "beyond" that establishes a boundary: a bridge, where "presencing" begins because it captures something of the estranging sense of the relocation of the home and the world – the unhomeliness – that is the condition of extra-territorial and cross-cultural initiations.[30]

For Bhabha, the experience of being simultaneously at home and not at home is an experience of being on a boundary, or in the interstices: those spaces that are "in-between." The boundary between home and world is crossed, as is the boundary between public and private, or the social and the psychological.[31] In the post-colonial context, it points toward the manner in which the home of the subjugated "other" becomes an uncanny place of interstitial dwelling, or a way of living in the eerie interstices of existence. One is left wandering at home,[32] remembering unfamiliar things and forgetting familiar things. One's homeland becomes a foreign land, even as foreign lands become homelands.

Bhabha borrows the term "unhomely" from Sigmund Freud. Freud's term, *das Unheimlich*, is most often translated into English as "the uncanny," meaning that which is strange or unsettling.[33] Freud meant more than this in his use of the term, however. *Das Unheimlich* is something that is both strange and familiar at the same time. It is simultaneously home and not-home. It is both eerie and comforting, both deceitful and revealing. Freud conceptualized it as something that was repressed in the psyche and thus unsuccessfully hidden or inadvertently revealed. The term is close in meaning to what Rudolf Otto called the "numinous" or the "holy," which brought together the experience of *mysterium tremendum*, the mystery that is terrorizing, and the *fascinans*, that which is fascinating. For Otto, the holy is a source of both dread and attraction.[34] Freud understood the manner in which this experience of the holy is also one of being both at home and not at home at the same time.

I want to suggest that this understanding of the "unhomely" and of "unhoming" is more than descriptive of religious life. It is prescriptive for theology in the traditions of Abrahamic faith. One is called or lured to undertake a migration of the psyche, of the soul, that renders one exilic precisely in the hope of going home. The call is experienced as a doubling: both the call to go forth and the call to come home. In Tweed's terms, it is both transporting and transforming.

This call for the homecoming begins with a disruption, an unsettling moment, a moment of unhoming, that is also uncanny. Christians are to be pilgrims in this world, the tradition says. As the Lutheran theologian Johann Arndt wrote in *True Christianity* in 1610, "Since the Lord says that we are guests and strangers, it is necessary that our fatherland must be elsewhere.... For true Christians...this is an exile, a veil of tears, indeed, a dark grave and a deep prison."[35] The eighteenth-century German Pietist theologian Johann Heinrich Jung-Stilling followed in this tradition. Jung-Stilling published a four-volume novel between 1794 and 1796 that was titled *Das Heimweh* (*Homesickness*). The novel opens with a traditional German proverb: "Blessed are the homesick for they shall reach home."[36]

The general purpose of Jung-Stilling's work, like that of the better known English author of the previous century, John Bunyan, after whose *The Pilgrim's Progress* Jung-Stilling's work was modeled, was to inculcate in the reader a spiritual longing for—in the words of the subtitle of *Pilgrim's Progress*—"that which is to come." One is not turned *from* the present home so much as one is turned *toward* the home that is to come as a means of forming and encouraging the will to move. The full title of Bunyan's original work conveys well the migratory impulse that its author sought to inculcate in his readers: *The Pilgrim's Progress from this World to that which is to Come, Delivered under the Similitude of a Dream, Wherein Is Discovered the Manner of his Setting Out, His Dangerous Journey, and Safe Arrival at the Desired Country.*

The Abrahamic traditions of faith have long identified this desired country with the future. As Arnold Eisen notes, for Judaism, "home remains an affair of the imagination, located in the future perfect tense."[37] Eisen argues that after the destruction of the Temple in 70 CE, "homelessness, comprehended through the inherited categories, had to be resisted; homecoming, initiated by God's Messiah, could only be awaited."[38] For many Jewish thinkers, homelessness, wandering, and exile became a trope for present existence. Homecoming would only be realized in the messianic future.

The same could be said for many Christian and Muslim thinkers. Heaven, be it *jannah* or paradise, lies beyond the current horizon of one's journey as the ultimate destiny that one cannot see. One knows of this home, but not because one has been there. One only has hints and intimations of it. Despite the best efforts of numerous theologians within the long Christian tradition to offer a picture of the heavenly home or a description of that desired country, it continues to escape the fullness of imagination. Nevertheless, the foreshadowings that the tradition offers are enough. They lure one to go forth. They encourage one to embrace exile. They "unhome" one even as one is still at present at one's home.

The images, memories, hopes, and promises of a better home and a more desirable country have a functional purpose within the tradition. Often they have been intended to serve ethical ends, by encouraging people to lead a better life, or devotional purposes, by encouraging the worship of God. Heaven was often offered as an incentive in sharp contrast to another eternal option, hell, which was depicted in such horrific terms precisely to scare pilgrims into going in the opposite direction. One need only recall Dante Alighieri's *Divina Commedia*, with its vivid portrayals of the inferno, purgatory, and paradise, to see the tradition here at work. But these images had more than a functional purpose, as can be seen in Dante's work in an exceptional way. They had a theological purpose insofar as they intended to say something about God. The homeland is characterized not so much as a place as it is a person. God is the homeland.[39] Theology of migration is about more than a homecoming. It is about God, who is our home.

I offer this last image for constructive purposes concerning any theology of migration. God is not just any homeland. God is a desirable homeland. The divine habitation is a place filled with joy. The homecoming will be a festival, even a carnival, as Mikhail Bakhtin would say.[40] As Elaine Padilla argues in her work, *Divine Enjoyment*, we migrate towards a festive welcoming within the divine self. God is revealed as the desire and the fulfillment of our enjoyment, as much as the one who *in*timately enjoys us.[41]

The divine homecoming that is our end is ultimately about joy. Such joy, moreover, accompanies not just humanity but the full creation on its journey toward the divine. As Padilla points out, God truly enjoys the universe that God has created, and embraces it within the divine self, offering it a home. God is with the world in its exile but is also the one to whom the exiles finally come home.[42] This means the divine is found in exile as well as at home (i.e., the divine uncanny or the divine "unhoming"). Joy characterizes not just the coming home, but the journeying there, even as it is mixed with suffering. The festivities of the homecoming are not confined to its conclusion. They characterize the journey toward it as well. Indeed, theology of migration is also about this joy and celebration that attend the journeying. As the Irish hymn writer John Monsell penned in 1863,

> On our way rejoicing
> As we homeward move,
> Such for us Thy purpose
> O Thou God of love…
> On our way rejoicing,
> Ever, evermore![43]

Notes

1. United Nations, *International Migration Report 2009: A Global Assessment* (New York: United Nations Publications, 2010), xviii.
2. See Steven Vertovec, *Transnationalism* (London and New York: Routledge, 2009), and Ludgar Pries, ed., *New Transnational Social Spaces: International Migration and Transnational Companies in the Early Twenty-First Century* (London and New York: Routledge, 2001).
3. See, for example, Michael W. Foley and Dean R. Hoge, *Religion and the New Immigrants: How Faith Communities Form Our Newest Citizens* (New York: Oxford University Press, 2007); and Organisation internationale pour les migrations, *Migrations et faits religieux à l'ère de la mondialisation: Rapport final de la Conference / Migration and Religion in a Globalized World: Final Report of the Conference*, 5–6 December 2005, Rabat, Morocco (Geneva: OIM, 2006).
4. See, for example, Glenda Tibe Bonifacio and Vivienne S. M. Angeles, eds., *Gender, Religion, and Migration: Pathways of Integration* (Lanham, MD: Lexington Books, 2011). See also Lionel Cantú, "A Place Called Home: A Queer Political Economy of Mexican Immigrant Men's Family Experiences," in Matthew C. Gutmann et al, eds., *Perspectives on Las Americas: A Reader in Culture, History, and Representation* (Malden: Blackwell Publishing, 2003), 259–273.
5. Thomas A. Tweed, *Crossing and Dwelling: A Theory of Religion* (Cambridge: Harvard University Press, 2006).
6. All biblical quotations are taken from the New Revised Standard Version.

7. Archie C. C. Lee, "Exile and Return in the Perspective of 1997," in Fernando F. Segovia and Mary Ann Tolbert, eds., *Reading from this Place: Social Location and Biblical Interpretation in Global Perspective*, (Minneapolis: Fortress Press, 1995), 97–108; and Nāsili Vaka'uta, *Reading Ezra 9–10 Tu'A-Wise: Rethinking Biblical Interpretation in Oceania* (Atlanta: Society of Biblical Literature, 2011) have both noted that the "resettlement" was also a colonization project that met with resistance from those who were already inhabiting the region and who also had descended from the house of Israel.
8. Arnold Eisen, "Exile," in Arthur A. Cohen and Paul Mendes-Flohr, eds. *20th Century Jewish Religious Thought: Original Essays on Critical Concepts, Movements, and Beliefs* (New York: Charles Scribner's Sons, 1987 [reprinted Philadelphia: Jewish Publication Society, 2009]), 222, writes: "It is clear from the Mishnah—redacted several generations after the Destruction in 70 CE and reformulated in part amidst the chaos that preceded and attended it—that exile for the rabbis was coextensive with the earth. No place in the world lay outside its domain, the land of Israel included."
9. See Robert Chazan, *The Jews of Medieval Western Christendom, 1000–1500* (Cambridge: Cambridge University Press, 2007), 209–242.
10. George K. Anderson, *The Legend of the Wandering Jew* (Providence: Brown University Press, 1965).
11. See Tudor Parfitt, *The Lost Tribes of Israel: The History of a Myth* (London: Phoenix Books, 2003).
12. See Michael Barkun, *Religion and the Racist Right: The Origins of the Christian Identity Movement*, rev. ed. (Chapel Hill and London: University of North Carolina Press, 1997), 3–46.
13. The close relationship between scattering and gathering can be seen in the traditional *Haggadah* that is read or recited at Passover. Early in the *Haggadah*, Deuteronomy 26:5 is quoted: "A wandering Aramean was my father and he went down into Egypt and sojourned there." Yet the *Haggadah* ends with "next year in Jerusalem."
14. Ramban, *The Disputation at Barcelona*, Charles B. Chavel, trans. (New York: Shilo Publishing House, 1983); and Robert Chazan, *Barcelona and Beyond: The Disputation of 1263 and Its Aftermath* (Berkeley: University of California Press, 1992).
15. See Nina Caputo, *Nahmanides in Medieval Catalonia: History, Community, and Messianism* (Notre Dame, IN: University of Notre Dame Press, 2007). It should be noted that while Maimonides was forced into exile from Muslim-ruled Spain in 1168, he journeyed first to Morocco and then Israel before settling in Cairo, Egypt, where he became head of the Jewish community. Maimonides also was a migrant.
16. See John Wilkinson, *Egeria's Travels* (Oxford: Aris and Phillips, 2006). An earlier standard text of her work in English can be found

in M. L. McClure and E. L. Feltoe, eds. and trans., *The Pilgrimage of Etheria* (London: Society for Promoting Christian Knowledge, 1919).
17. See William R. Cook and Ronald B. Herzman, *The Medieval World View: An Introduction* (New York: Oxford University Press, 2003), 106–108; a more general history of Western Christian pilgrimage practices that developed from these early *peregrini* is found in Diana Webb, *Medieval European Pilgrimage, C.700—C.1500* (New York: Palgrave MacMillan, 2002).
18. See Ineke Van Kessel, ed., *Merchants, Missionaries & Migrants: 300 Years of Dutch-Ghanaian Relations* (Amsterdam: KIT Publishers, 2002), 79–100.
19. M. E. McMillan, *The Meaning of Mecca: The Politics of Pilgrimage in Early Islam* (London: Saqi Books, 2001), 19–21.
20. Verses 78–78 read: "Establish regular prayers—at the sun's decline till the darkness of the night, and the morning prayer and reading: for the prayer and reading in the morning carry their testimony. And pray in the small watches of the morning: (it would be) an additional prayer (or spiritual profit) for thee: soon will thy Lord raise thee to a Station of Praise and Glory!" All quotations from the Qur'an are from Abdullah Yusuf Ali, *The Meaning of the Holy Qur'an* (Beltsville, MD: Amana), 1983.
21. See Dale F. Eickelman and James Piscatori, eds., *Muslim Travellers: Pilgrimage, Migration, and the Religious Imagination* (Berkeley: University of California Press, 1990).
22. See Margaret Smith, *Muslim Women Mystics: The Life and Work of Rābiʿa and Other Women Mystics in Islam* (Oxford: Oneworld Publications, 2001, original publication 1928).
23. Nile Green, *Sufism: A Global History* (Oxford: Wiley-Blackwell, 2012), 39.
24. See Elaine Padilla, "Border-Crossing and Exile: A Latina's Theological Encounter with Shekhinah," *Cross Currents* 60, no. 4 (2010): 526–548.
25. Tweed, *Crossing and Dwelling*, 54.
26. Ibid., 124–136.
27. Ibid., 136–150.
28. Ibid., 150–163.
29. Ibid., 151.
30. Homi K. Bhabha, *The Location of Culture* (London and New York: Routledge, 1994), 13.
31. Ibid., 13, writes: "To be unhomed is not to be homeless, nor can the 'unhomely' be easily accommodated in that familiar division of social life into private and public spheres."
32. See Leila Baradaran Jamili and Sara Faryam Rad, "Unhomeliness: Deconstructing Western Master Narratives in Toni Morrison's *A*

Mercy," *International Proceedings of Economics Development and Research* 26 (2011): 309–313.
33. Sigmund Freud, *Das Unheimliche; Aufsätze zur Literatur,* Klaus Wagenbach, ed. (Frankfurt am Maine: Fischer, 1963; original 1919); translated into English as *The Uncanny,* David McLintock, trans. (London and New York: Penguin Books, 2003).
34. Rudolf Otto, *The Idea of the Holy,* John W. Harvey, trans. (Oxford: Oxford University Press, 1923).
35. Johann Arndt, *True Christianity* (New York: Paulist Press, 1978), 92.
36. Johann Heinrich Jung-Stilling, *Das Heimweh* (Dornach: Verlag am Goetheanum, 1994).
37. Eisen, "Exile," 221.
38. Ibid., 222.
39. As James Kirwan writes in *Beauty* (Manchester: Manchester University Press, 1999), 64, "'there,' our true homeland, is God, and 'here' only exists as a separation from this homeland."
40. Mikhail M. Bakhtin, *Speech Genres and Other Late Essays,* Vern W. McGee, trans. (Austin: University of Texas Press, 1986), 170, writes of the dialogical encounter in literature: "Nothing is absolutely dead: every meaning will have its homecoming festival."
41. Elaine Padilla, *Divine Enjoyment: A Theology of Passion and Exuberance* (New York: Fordham University Press), 2014.
42. See also Padilla, "Border-Crossing and Exile."
43. John S. B. Monsell, *Hymns of Love and Praise for the Church's Year* (London: Bell and Daldy, 1863), 124–125.

Chapter 2

"You Will Seek From There": The Cycle of Exile and Return in Classical Jewish Theology

Devorah Schoenfeld

And the Lord will scatter you among the peoples, and you will be left few in number among the nations where the Lord will lead you... But you will seek from there the Lord your God and you will find Him, if you search for Him with all your heart and soul. (Deuteronomy 4: 27–29)[1]

The cycle of exile and return is built into many classical Jewish texts. From the Bible through the Middle Ages, these texts show a tension between longing for the land of Israel and accepting the possibilities for finding God in places of exile. Exile is fundamentally a tragedy, yet these texts suggest, it is one that can be overcome in order to both strive for return and build a thriving diaspora existence.

Judaism is not a religion that grounds itself in doctrine. The biblical text is full of contradictions and ambiguities that, for the Jewish exegete, provide many opportunities to come up with varied and contradictory interpretations. The Talmud, the most widely read and influential post-biblical Jewish text, ends many of its discussions by stating a disagreement. Although some Jewish theologians, such as Maimonides, have attempted to set out a list of Jewish beliefs, there is always another Jewish theologian who refuses to accept them.[2] There is, therefore, no set Jewish theology of migration. It is, however, central to the experience of Jewish life, and thus a major preoccupation of classical Jewish thought.

In Jewish experience, migration can be positive, a way of seeking a new and better life. It can also be a tragedy, a way of being forced away from a homeland. In this essay, instead of the term "migration," I will be using the term "exile," a translation of the biblical and rabbinic term *galut*, as a way of expressing the tragedy of Jewish forced migration. I will also be using the term "diaspora," which in the classical Jewish context indicates an involuntary movement of people away from their homeland to multiple locations. The homeland, in the exilic reality, is always the place you are coming from, never the place you are going to. The messianic hope, in these terms, is the hope of return from exile, a final migration back to a homeland.

In order to give a broad overview of Jewish thinking on exile and diaspora, I have restricted my discussion to a few of the most theologically influential Jewish texts of the classical and early medieval periods. I have only briefly mentioned the innovative reinterpretation of exile in kabbalistic texts, since some of the most creative kabbalistic theologies of exile are addressed in Melissa Raphael's article in this volume.

Locations

The biblical narrative is centered around the land of Israel, although not all of its important events take place there. In the post-biblical period, many Jews continued to live in the land of Israel, primarily in the Galilee, a poor rural area approximately 100 miles north of Jerusalem. Galilean Jews wrote the earliest rabbinic texts: the second- and third-century Mishnah and Tosefta, which were represented as the written versions of traditions that had previously been transmitted orally. These texts formed the theological basis for post-exilic Jewish life, replacing a land-centered spirituality with one that focused primarily on texts and their study.

Galilean Jews also wrote the first of the two Talmuds: the Jerusalem or Palestinian Talmud. Although it was written in the Galilee, it was called the Talmud Yerushalmi, the Jerusalem Talmud, by medieval Jewish scholars who wanted to give honor to Jerusalem.[3] In English, it is typically called the Palestinian Talmud because it was written in the Galilee while the area was part of the Roman province of Palestine. The Galilean rabbis also wrote "midrash," or works of creative biblical interpretation. These collections brought together homilies and interpretations by rabbis who tried to creatively answer and solve questions in the biblical text. These questions included those about how to relate the biblical text to the reality of their own day. One of the questions they had to deal with was how to come to terms with the biblical passages on exile and return in a situation in which, although they were living in their own land, they were nevertheless exiled from the holy city and kept in conditions of subjugation.

As the centuries passed, the center of Jewish life shifted from the Galilee to the ancient Jewish community of Babylon. Jews had lived in Babylon since the destruction of the First Temple in 586 BCE, but the community only became the center of Jewish life in the third century. There is little record of the Jewish community of Babylon between the rebuilding of the Second Temple and its destruction. It seems that a large part of the Jewish community remained and thrived there, with some communal autonomy.[4]

Babylonian rabbis wrote the Babylonian Talmud, which developed over hundreds of years from the third through the eighth centuries and became the most important source of Jewish law and philosophy. The Babylonian Talmud, often called simply the Talmud, is written as a transcript of discussions that may have happened between rabbis in the study hall. In the course of these widely ranging debates, which are often left unresolved, they touch on virtually every aspect of Jewish life.

Babylonian rabbis struggled a great deal with the reality of creating a Jewish existence that was, for the first time, centered firmly in the diaspora. They did not see their situation as entirely negative. One model they saw in the biblical text was Abraham, who was Babylonian before he lived in the land of Israel. This allowed them to imagine the place in which they were living as a different kind of homeland, although a temporary one. At the same time, they grappled with the legacy of the biblical longing for the land of Israel, and the messianic longing for return.

In the Middle Ages, the center of Jewish life shifted to Europe, predominantly Moorish Spain, France and Germany. Although Jews often migrated within the medieval world for economic reasons, a major driver of migrations was the frequent expulsion of Jews from the countries in which they lived. This was sometimes followed by invitations to return and then subsequent expulsions. Jews were expelled from various parts of France four times between 1182 and 1394, from England in 1290, and from various places in Germany in the twelfth century. The expulsion of the Jews from what had since become fully Christian Spain in 1492 was the last, most famous, and possibly the most traumatic, of the medieval Jewish expulsions.

Biblical Backgrounds: The Centrality of the Land, Exile as Punishment and Inevitability

In the Torah, the land is the means and end of Jewish life. The land, in biblical terms, gave the Israelites the opportunity to fulfill the agricultural commandments. These included the right of poor people to harvest the corners of everyone's fields and to take fallen sheaves that were left behind by reapers, as well as the commandment to let the land rest every seven years (Deuteronomy 24:19–20, Leviticus 19:9 and 23:22).

In the biblical economic system, land was inalienable. It could never be sold but only leased for a period of up to 50 years until it was returned in the jubilee (see Leviticus 25:10). Even during the 50 years when land could be sold, it was considered a positive commandment to 'redeem' the land by returning it to its original owners (Leviticus 10:25–28). Ideally, land was not to be sold, but if it were, it had to be redeemed immediately by the next of kin. If that person was not able to redeem it, then the sellers might do so when able, even years later. But in any case, the buyer (or, more accurately, the lessee) could not keep it past the jubilee year. These commandments about agricultural law and property rights are at the core of the biblical conception of economic justice, but they could only be practiced in pre-exilic conditions.

The laws of sacrifices are also central to biblical Judaism and take up much of the book of Leviticus as well as substantial parts of the books of Exodus, Numbers and Deuteronomy. The book of Deuteronomy emphasizes that sacrifices can only be offered in one particular place (Deuteronomy 12:12–14): the temple in Jerusalem. In biblical Judaism, then, two of its most central preoccupations—societal justice and proper worship—are only most fully possible in the land of Israel.

The land is not only the means of Jewish observance, but also its goal. There is no afterlife reward in the Torah. The reward is to return to the land, and the punishment is expulsion from it. As stated in Leviticus 20:22, "You shall therefore keep all my statutes and all my laws, and do them, so that the land will not vomit you out." The only hope is repentance, which in Hebrew is exactly the same word as "return":

> When all these things happen to you, the blessings and the curses that I have set before you, if you remember them while among all the nations where the Lord your God has sent you, and if you return to the Lord your God, and listen to His voice as I am commanding you today, you and your children obey him with all your heart and with all your soul, then the Lord your God will return you from captivity and have mercy on you, and will return and gather you from all the peoples where the Lord has sent you. Even if you are exiled to the

ends of the world, from there the Lord your God will gather you, and from there he will bring you back. The Lord your God will bring you into the land that your ancestors possessed, and you will possess it, he will make you more prosperous and numerous than your ancestors (Deuteronomy 30: 1–5).

Even in biblical terms, despite the centrality of the land, there is still a sense that the cycle of exile and return is inevitable. This is the case from the very beginnings of the Jewish relationship with God. In Genesis 15:3, in the covenant in which God promises the land to Abraham, God also tells Abraham that his children will be strangers in a land which is not theirs. When the land was promised, so was exile. In these texts, exile is not the end but the *middle* of the process, and has been part of Jewish theology from its earliest beginnings. Exile leads to suffering, suffering leads to calling out to God, and calling out to God begins the return of the Jewish people to their God and to their land.

Exile as Sin in Rabbinic Literature

The rabbinic world is one in which exile is a disturbingly new, yet oddly persistent, reality. The destruction of the Second Temple, as it is referred to in rabbinic and Jewish exegetical literature, is a synecdoche for the Roman conquest of the kingdom of Judea, and in particular the destruction of Jerusalem, in which Romans, according to the contemporary witness and historian Josephus, killed over one million Jews and enslaved another 97,000,[5] and in the process demolished the Jewish political leadership.

In coming to terms with this destruction, some rabbinic texts saw the exile resulting from the destruction of the temple as punishment for sin. Two early midrashic texts, the *Sifra* on Leviticus and the *Sifre* on Deuteronomy, both dating from the late third century, referred to exile primarily in the context of identifying the specific sinful acts that caused Israel to be exiled. In particular, sexual sins and judicial injustice were invoked and referenced as the sins for which Leviticus promises, "The land will spit you out".[6] Tractate *Avot* (Chapters of the Fathers) of the Mishnah, which gives a variety of ethical teachings from Mishnaic rabbis, has a list of punishments that come on the world for specific crimes; for example, "Exile comes upon the world because of idolatry and incest and the shedding of blood; and because of neglect to give release to the soil during the sabbatical year" (*Avot* 5:9). Idolatry, incest and murder are traditionally the three worst sins in Judaism, and also those that one may not even commit to save a life.[7] The commandment to rest the soil on the seventh year is one of the commandments that can only be observed in the land of Israel. So this interpretation sees the sin of the Israelites that led to the exile as a combination of general depravity and, in particular, not appreciating the land while they had it.

The *Sifra* on Leviticus also raises the possibility that neglect of the sabbatical and jubilee years were the sins that caused the exile. Therefore, the exile was necessary to the land so that it could finally have the rest that it was not allowed to have while the Israelites were living on it. This is an oddly positive interpretation of the idea of exile for sin, seeing it as a way of saving the land from overuse and exhaustion.[8]

The sin most commonly blamed for destruction and exile in rabbinic literature is *sinatchinam*, "causeless hatred":

> But why was the second Sanctuary destroyed, seeing that in its time they were studying Torah, observing commandments, and practicing charity? Because there was among them hatred without cause. That teaches you that groundless hatred is considered as severe as the three sins of idolatry, immorality, and bloodshed together (Babylonian Talmud, Yoma 9b).[9]

Some texts make this more specific, preferring to give concrete examples of causeless hatred. The Babylonian Talmud (Gittin 55–56) tells a story of two men, Kamtza and Bar Kamtza, whose senseless conflict over a dinner party invitation led one to slander the Jews to the Roman government, which in turn led to the destruction of Judea. *Tosefta*Kippurim 1:12 describes one priest killing another in a fight over the right to serve at the altar. Another story, from the Babylonian Talmud Gittin 58a, tells of a student who manipulated his teacher into divorcing his wife so the student could marry her, then manipulating the teacher again, this time to impoverish himself and become the student's servant. As a result, the teacher had to wait at the table for his former wife and student while they cavorted. All these stories of interpersonal horror are examples of the kinds of destruction that result from the sin of causeless hatred.

Seeing exile as a punishment for sin can be a way of exhorting the community to repent. It returns to the biblical idea that exile allows for and requires repentance, and that after repentance, return will come. Seeing exile as caused by causeless hatred is another way of asking the community to behave lovingly towards each other as a redemptive act.

Exile as punishment can also be seen positively, as a way of avoiding something worse. The fifth-century Midrash Genesis Rabbah has a positive take on suffering as punishment. Here, God asks Abraham if he would rather send his children to *Gehenna*(hell) or be exiled into foreign kingdoms (Genesis Rabbah 44). The implication here is that exile is an alternative to other, worse punishments. Genesis Rabbah gives two possibilities: one in which Abraham chose exile over *Gehenna*,and God approved his choice, and the other in which Abraham chose *Gehenna*, but God overruled him. In either case, exile was God's merciful choice to save the Jewish people from *Gehenna*. A theology like this maintains the structure of exile as punishment, but at the same time, imagines it as something merciful.

Mourning for Zion and the Shekhinah in Exile

The psalmist who wrote "How can I sing a song of the Lord in a strange land"(Psalm 137:4) was in fact singing a song to God while lamenting the impossibility of doing so. That paradox is at the center of the classical and medieval Jewish longing for Zion. Classical and medieval Jewish poets and liturgists wrote songs of longing and lament for Zion that became an integral part of Jewish liturgy.

TishaB'Av, the Ninth of Av, was set in the Talmud as the day for mourning over the ongoing reality of exile, traditionally the day on which the First and Second Temple were both destroyed.[10] A tradition developed to read the book of Lamentations on that day, and medieval liturgists added their own laments to those of Jeremiah.

During the rest of the year, mourning needed to have limits:

> Our rabbis taught: When the Temple was destroyed for the second time, there were many ascetics in Israel who refrained from eating meat and wine. Rabbi Joshua went to deal with then and asked, "My children, why are you not eating meat or drinking wine?"They answered, "Can we eat meat that used to be used for sacrifices when they are no longer happening? Can we drink wine that used to be used for sacrifices when they are no longer happening?"He said to them, "If that is so, we should not eat bread either, because the offerings of flour have ceased."They said, "Then we can manage with fruit."He said, "We should not eat fruit either, then, since the offering of first fruits has ceased.""Then we can manage with other fruits,"they said. "But,"he said, "we should not drink water, because there is no longer any ceremony of the pouring of water."They were silent. He said to them, "My children, come and listen to me. It is impossible for us not to mourn, since the awful decree has been carried out. But it is also impossible to mourn too much, because it is wrong to decree on the

community a decree that it is not able to endure. (Babylonian Talmud, BavaBatra 60b)

Setting a place and time for mourning helped limit mourning during the rest of the year. *TishaB'Av* was the time to fast, but at other times it was permitted to eat and rejoice. During the rest of the year, other customs developed, such as leaving an empty space whenever plastering a building to remember the imperfection of life in exile, or reducing the music at weddings.[11] The pain of exile was given its due, but was not allowed to consume Jewish life.

Not all commemorations involved sadness. On Passover, the absence of the biblically required Passover sacrifice, that could not be offered anywhere outside of the Temple Mount in Jerusalem, itself became part of the ritual performance of the Passover seder. During the seder (the ritual Passover meal), the seder leader was instructed to explain the Passover offering, which was no longer consumed, along with the matzah and bitter herbs, which are still part of the Passover ritual. The sacrifice itself could no longer be part of the seder, but its explanation still could be, and still was.

Remembrance of exile did not always feel like distance from God. Sometimes God was also involved in the process of exile and suffering through prayer or mourning. In the Babylonian Talmud, *Berachot* 3a, God is said to exclaim, "Woe to the father who had to banish his children, and woe to the children who are banished from their father." In *Berachot* 7a God is said to pray, "May it be My will that My mercy may suppress My anger, and that My mercy may prevail over all My other attributes, so that I may deal with My children in the attribute of mercy and, on their behalf, stop short of the limit of strict justice." God also mourns, in a way, for having to exile Israel, and prays to himself to have mercy.

One rabbinic way of articulating the presence of God in exile was the idea of the exiled *Shekhinah*. In the Bible, the root *skn* (dwelling) is most often used in the context of God's presence in the *mishkan*, the tabernacle, and then in the temple in Jerusalem.[12] A way of imagining God in diaspora was through the idea of the *Shekhinah*, or Divine Presence, which goes with the Jews wherever they are. This term is used to describe the most immanent experience of God, the aspect of God that feels closest to humanity, and is one of the names of God that takes a feminine pronoun in Hebrew.[13] The idea of *Shekhinah* in exile is a different way of thinking about the post-exilic reality; rather than being expelled from God's presence, it follows the Jewish people wherever they are.

The *Mechilta de Rabbi Ishmael* on the Song of the Sea, an early midrash,[14] juxtaposes the idea of the exiled *Shekhinah* with the story of the Exodus to construct a myth of recurring exile and return in which God is also a participant:

> "And it came to pass on that day, that all the hosts of the Lord went out from the land of Egypt"(Exodus 12:41). These are the ministering angels. And so you find that whenever Israel is subjugated the *Shekhinah*, as if it were, is subjugated alongside them...When they went into exile in Egypt, the *Shekhinah* went into exile with them, as it is said, "I exiled myself to the house of your fathers when they were in Egypt"(1 Samuel 2:27). When they went into exile to Babylon, the *Shekhinah* went with them, as it is said, "For your sake I sent myself to Babylon"(Isaiah 43:14). When they went into exile into Elam, the *Shekhinah* went with them, as it is said, "I shall set my throne in Elam"(Jeremiah 9:38). When they went into exile to Edom, the *Shekhinah* went into exile with them, as it is said, "Who is this that comes from Edom?"(Isaiah 63:1). And when they return in the future the *Shekhinah*, as if it were, will return with them, as it is said, "Then the Lord your God will return with your captivity."(Deuteronomy 30:3)[15]

The *Mechilta* here draws connections between the present and the biblical past. The expulsion of the Jewish people to the lands of Edom is code for the current diasporic reality, since Edom represents Rome in rabbinic literature. So just as God was with the Israelites in Egypt, so God is with them in every place at every time in every present or future exile.[16] Although the Jews are distant from their land, they are not distant from God. This can be comforting—knowing that God is always present—but it is also tragic—imagining that the Jewish people and even God suffer from the pain of exile.

The *Shekhinah* took on particular significance in later medieval kabbalistic writings. The Zohar, a central kabbalistic text composed in thirteenth-century Spain, developed an elaborate system of metaphors for understanding different aspects of God as *sefirot* (spheres or emanations). Ten *sefirot* flow from each other and interact with each other in complex ways. The most distant and incomprehensible of the ten is the *EinSof*, or the infinite, representing the way in which God is beyond all human understanding. The *Shekhinah*, or the Divine Presence, is the lowest or nearest of these ten *sefirot*, representing the deep intimacy between God and humanity; it is the way God interacts with the created world.

The original exile of the *Shekhinah*, according to the Zohar, occurred not with the destruction of the temple but with the beginnings of human sin. In its interpretation of Genesis 3, the *Shekhinah* Herself goes into exile along with Adam when he is expelled from the garden. Human sin, as if it were, creates disruption even in God, causing aspects of God as if it were, to break apart from one another. This interpretation takes the idea of the *Shekhinah* in exile out of the realm of history into the realm of myth. Instead of a response to the particular historical circumstance of a particular exile, the *Shekhinah's* exile is part of the nature of an unredeemed world.[17]

In the Zohar, the *Shekhinah* actively longs for reunion with the other aspects of God:

> R. Eleazar began (with the verse): "By night on my bed I sought (him whom my soul loves, I sought him but did not find him)"(Song of Songs 3:1). "On my bed": it should have been "in my bed." What is the meaning of "on my bed"? The Assembly of Israel (= the *Shekhinah*) spoke to the Holy One, Blessed be He, and petitioned him concerning the exile, since she dwells among the other nations with her children and lies in the dust... R. Isaac said, "By night on my bed." The Assembly of Israel said: "Concerning my bed." I pleaded with Him, that he might cohabit with me and give me pleasure, and give me complete joy, for we have learned that through the King's cohabitation with the Assembly of Israel, numerous righteous come into their sacred inheritance, and numerous blessings are brought into the world (Zohar III, 42 a/b).[18]

The Zohar presents two alternative understandings of the *Shekhinah's* longing for return, both based on the same verse of Song of Songs. In the first, she is longing for rescue, while in the second, the return is explicitly erotic and a plea for union. There is a sense in which the exile makes even God broken and incomplete.

Accommodation to Exile: The Story of Yavneh and the Four Cubits of the Halakhah

As tragic as exile was, rabbinic thought also considered the possibility that it was chosen, and a way of keeping Jewish teachings alive, rather than allowing them to be destroyed along with the nation. The Babylonian Talmud (Gittin 56a-b) tells of the siege of Jerusalem. The defenders (called zealots in the Talmud) fight for the city long after there is no hope. Rabbi Yohanan ben Zakkai escapes the city in a coffin, pretending to be dead, and makes his way to their commander, Vespasian, whom he greets as an emperor, even though he is not. Vespasian is stunned at the rabbi's disrespect in calling him Emperor, but immediately a messenger arrives with news that the notables of Rome have declared Vespasian the new emperor. As a reward for the rabbi's wisdom, Vespasian offers him one wish. He chooses to be given the town of Yavneh, its sages, the family line of RabbanGamaliel, and physicians to heal Rabbi Zadok.

Yavneh was, at this point, a prison colony on the coast and a place that had never been important in Jewish life, so Rabbi Yohanan was asking for permission to continue Jewish learning as his first priority. His wishes for RabbanGamliel and Rabbi Zadok each point to hope for the future in different ways. RabbanGamliel was a descendant of David, so preserving his family meant preserving the Davidic line. Rabbi Zadok, as well as being an influential sage, was also a priest who had served in the temple,[19] so he could preserve the priestly lineage and knowledge about the temple rituals.

This story, like many in the Talmud, was composed much later than the events it describes. The rabbis who wrote it lived in Babylon, and Yavneh was as distant from them as Jerusalem. Still, it was a way of coming to terms with the reality of diaspora by seeing it as something chosen, or even heroic. Rabbi Yohanan here is a hero. He shows wisdom and foreknowledge, and he passes through (symbolic) death to the new rebirth as a diaspora Jew.

And yet, the Babylonian Talmud is known for ending every discussion with a disagreement, and does so here as well. One rabbi raises the possibility that Rabbi Yohanan had acted foolishly by not taking the opportunity to simply ask Vespasian to call off the attack on Judea, and another counters that perhaps the rabbi had asked for as much as he had any chance of being granted.[20]

The Talmud leaves it as an undecided question. Was Rabbi Yohanan correct to accept the realistic option of exile, knowing that it might be the best he could ask for? Would it not have been better for him to fight in his way, using his cleverness to induce the Roman army to retreat and leave Judea? Was he foolish to ask for so little, or wise to save what could be saved?

For many rabbis, what happened at Yavneh changed the location of Jewish sacrality from a place—the land of Israel, or the temple—to the Torah and its process of study.

> Rabbi Hisda said: What is the meaning of the verse: "The Lord loves the gates of Zion more than all the dwellings of Jacob"(Psalms 87:2)?

The Lord loves the gates that are distinguished[21] through *Halakhah* more than the Synagogues and Houses of study. And this conforms with the following saying of Rabbi Hiyya son of Ammi in the name of 'Ulla: Since the day that the Temple was destroyed, the Holy One, blessed be He, has nothing in this world but the four cubits of *Halakhah* alone. So said also Abaye: At first I used to study in my house and pray in the Synagogue. Since I heard the saying of Rabbi Hiyya son of Ammi in the name of 'Ulla: "Since the day that the Temple was destroyed, the Holy One, blessed be He, has nothing in His world but the four cubits of Halachah alone," I pray only in the place where I study. Rabbi Ammi and Rabbi Assi, though they lived in Tiberias, which had thirteen synagogues, prayed only between the pillars where they used to study (Babylonian Talmud, Tractate Berachot, 8a).

The fourth-century Babylonian Rabbi Hisda here reinterprets a verse that in its most obvious reading seems to be saying that God loves the land of Israel, whether or not Jews dwell there. In Hisda's creative reinterpretation, Zion refers not to a place but to a process—the process of the interpretation of *Halakhah*. The Hebrew word *Halakhah* comes from the root "to walk" and can be translated as "the path" or "the way." It is usually translated as Jewish law or practice, but in rabbinic thought it is often more encompassing and can include discussions about everything related to Jewish life. Although the biblical verse might seem to say that God dwells only in Zion, from a Babylonian exilic perspective, it is equally true that God dwells in every house of study, which is made sacred by the human action of study, and can be found in any geographical location.[22]

A Medieval Question: Should Jews Settle in the land of Israel in Pre-Messianic Times?

As Jews accommodated to life in the diaspora, a different way of thinking about exile developed, as something that was inevitable until the coming of the messiah. The messiah, in rabbinic and early medieval Jewish theology, was primarily a leader of this-world, a human being descended from King David whose role would be to establish Jewish political sovereignty in the land of Israel.[23] This leader would not perform miracles, or rather the only miracle he would perform is the reestablishment of Jewish sovereignty and the rebuilding of the Temple.

As Maimonides writes, "in the times of the messiah the laws of nature will continue as they are. The difference is that there will be peace, as is implied by Isaiah's prophecy of the lion lying down with the lamb." (Laws of Kings 12.1) This is consistent with Talmudic discussions of the messiah, in which the goal is political establishment of Jewish sovereignty in the land of Israel in this-world.[24] But if the role of the messiah is to take Jews out of exile, perhaps it is not appropriate to leave exile in pre-messianic times. Jews who thought this way looked back to the story of "the Three Oaths" in the Babylonian Talmud *Ketubot* 111a:

> *Swear to me, O daughters of Jerusalem, by the gazelles, and by the hinds of the field, not to awaken or stir love until it desires* (Song of Songs 2:7)...Rabbi Yosi son of Rabbi Hanina...said: "What was the purpose of those three oaths? One, that Israel shall not go up as a wall, the second, that whereby the Holy One, blessed be He, asked Israel to swear not to rebel against the nations of the world, and the third is that the Holy One, blessed be He, asked the nations to swear that they would not oppress Israel too much."

In this story, Jews take an oath to God not to "go up as a wall," which later thinkers saw as meaning not to take back the land of Israel by military strength but rather to wait for Divine intervention. This story is read into verses of erotic longing from the Song of Songs, comparing Jewish consent to their exile to the willing separation of a bride anticipating her wedding. There are still separation and waiting, but they come with love, with joy, and with the promise of greater happiness in the future. It is a startlingly positive take on exile that both allows for Jewish existence outside the land of Israel and even sacralizes it without negating in any way the importance of the land to Jewish existence.

This text of the Three Oaths formed part of the basis of a theology of acceptance of exile. Remaining in exile became a fulfillment of the oath, and thus obedience to God. Maimonides drew on this Talmudic passage to comfort and reassure Yemenite Jews who were struggling to resist forced conversion on the one hand and a false messiah on the other. He admonished them to heed the injunction of Song of Songs and "not stir up love until it please," that is, not to follow a false messiah who would induce them to end exile before God wants it to be over (Maimonides Epistle to Yemen, Chapter 20).

Not all Jewish theologians accepted exile as a necessary pre-messianic reality. Nahmanides never did. In his commentary on Maimonides' Book of Commandments, he critiques Maimonides' omission of the commandment to live in the land of Israel, arguing that it t applies even in post-biblical and pre-messianic times.[25]

For Nahmanides, living in the land of Israel was not only a commandment, it was the basis upon which all other commandments rested. He explains in his commentary on Leviticus 18:25 that observing the commandments outside of the land of Israel is like a separated wife who continues to wear her jewels, so that when she is reunited with her husband, they will not be new to her. The implication is that the only reason to fulfill the commandments was as practice, so that "when you return they will not be as a new thing upon you." The true fulfillment of any commandment is only possible in the land.

This question of whether pre-messianic settling in the land of Israel is forbidden, permitted, required, or essential remained unsettled through the Middle Ages and into the modern period.[26] Medieval Jewish theologians who thought that moving to the land of Israel was required did not always do so themselves. One notable exception was Judah HaLevi, a Spanish-Jewish eleventh and twelfth–century poet and philosopher, who wrote poetry of longing for Zion. One classic example is his poem *Libi Ba-Mizrach*, "My Heart is in the East":

> My heart is in the east and I am in the end of the west
> How can I taste what I eat, how can I feel delight
> How can I fulfill my vows and obligations, while
> Zion is in Edom's chains, and I am bound by Arab nations?
> It would be a light thing for me to leave all the good of Spain, like
> It is precious for me to see the remains of the destroyed Temple."

Halevi lived most of his life in relatively tolerant Spain, but his poems of longing for the land of Israel and his conclusion in his book, *The Kuzari* (a fictional dialogue between a rabbi and a Khazar king) convinced him at the end of his life to make the journey to the land of Israel. Nahmanides ended his life in Israel as well.

Seek the Welfare of the Land Where You Live: Homelands in Exile

Lands of exile could have religious significance in their own right. Babylon was the first place of exile for the Jewish people, during the biblical period, after the destruction of the First Temple, and life as a diaspora Jew in Babylon is a major theme of the biblical books of Esther and Daniel. But Babylon also had a different significance in Jewish thought: the place where Abraham was born (in Genesis 11). To rabbis who saw Babylon developing as a center of Jewish life, this gave it a particular, positive significance.[27] Exile there, then, was a return to a different kind of homeland.

Those who lived in Babylon were able to see themselves as fulfilling a divine command:

> Thus says the Lord of Hosts, the God of Israel, to all the diaspora that I have exiled from Jerusalem to Babylon: Build houses and settle there, build gardens and eat their fruit...and seek the peace of the land to which I have exiled you, and pray for it, for in its peace you will have peace (Jeremiah 29:5–7).

For some rabbis, in the Babylonian Talmud (e.g., 110b), life in Babylon was even preferable to life in the land of Israel:

> One who goes up from Babylonia to the land of Israel violates a positive command, as it says: "They shall be brought to Babylon, and there they shall remain, until I take note of them, declares the Lord"(Jeremiah 27:22). One who lives in Babylonia, it is as if he lives in the land of Israel, as it says: "Away, escape, O Zion, you who dwell in Fair Babylon!"(Zechariah 2:11).

Medieval texts raise the possibility that diaspora life is preferable because Jews have a particular mission among the nations. Judah Halevi describes the Jewish people among the nations like the heart in a body, having a role that justifies the exile for the good that it makes possible for other nations. The fourteenth-century Spanish Jewish Bible commentator, Bahya ben Asher, makes the point most clearly:

> And in my opinion the reason for the Dispersion...[is] in order that Israel should spread to all the ends [of the earth] among the nations, who lack understanding. And they will teach them concerning belief in the existence of God, may He be blessed, and in the matter of divine Providence which influences individual men.[28]

Conclusion

Migration and exile are among the paradoxes of classical Jewish theology. Exile is both tragic and inevitable. Jews in diaspora mourned over Zion but also could appreciate the return to their ancestral land of Babylon. This paradox persists from the biblical through the medieval periods. The Torah records the promise to Abraham that his descendants would inherit the land but also be exiled from it. It prophesied exile as a tragic outcome of sin but also as necessary to bring about the possibility of repentance and return. Rabbinic and medieval texts considered return as necessary, but also forbidden.

There are a wide variety of approaches to migration, exile and the meaning of diaspora in classical Jewish literature. All of them, though, combine mourning and hope, by combining the memory of loss with the possibility of return or by attributing sacrality in the lands of exile, and even imagining God as participating in the process of exile and return.

Although I have ended this discussion in the Middle Ages, these texts continue to be theologically influential in Jewish life today, since they are still widely read by contemporary Jews, who need to come to terms with classical thinking about exile and diaspora in a very different reality. Is the current State of Israel a continuation of diaspora or an end to it? For many Jews, the state begins fulfillment of a this-worldly messianism, in which the role of the messiah is not to do anything supernatural but simply to bring about the return to a homeland and the end of exile. For some, there is the hope that it could be the beginning of a broader messianic vision, while others believe it is simply the continuation of diaspora reality in a different location.

The unprecedented integration of Jews in North American and European societies has also led Jews to question the traditional tragic understanding of diaspora. Could New York be a contemporary Babylon, a center of Jewish life with its own sacred history? The idea of multiple homelands can be useful for thinking about contemporary Jewish reality as well.

Acknowledgments

This essay developed out of conversations at the AAR/Luce Summer Seminar on Comparative Theology and Theologies of Religious Pluralism, and I am very grateful to all the participants, Elaine Padilla and John Thatamanil in particular. I would also like to thank Amanda Kunder for her research assistance and Bret Lewis for his thoughtful comments on earlier drafts of this essay.

Notes

1. All Bible translations are the author's own and based on the Masoretic text.
2. The most famous attempt at outlining a set of Jewish doctrines is Maimonides'thirteen principles of faith. For a discussion of these principles and their relevance to Jewish life, see Marc B. Shapiro, *The Limits of Orthodox Theology: Maimonides'Thirteen Principles Reappraised* (Oxford: Littman Library of Jewish Civilization, 2011). For a strong critique of any attempt to establish Jewish doctrine, see Menachem Marc Kellner, *Must a Jew Believe Anything?* (Oxford: Littman Library of Jewish Civilization, 2006).
3. For a history of the naming of the Palestinian/Jerusalem Talmud, see H.L.Strack and Gunter Stemberger, *Introduction to the Talmud and Midrash* (Minneapolis: Augsburg Fortress Press, 1996), 165.
4. For an overview of what we do know, see Isaiah Gafni, "Babylonian Rabbinic Culture,"*Cultures of the Jews: A New History 1*, ed. David Biale (New York: Random House, 2002), 224–228.
5. Josephus, *The Wars of the Jews*, VI.9.3
6. For a full discussion of the theology of sin and exile in early (Tanaitic) midrash, see Gary Porton, "The Idea of Exile in Early Rabbinic Midrash"in *Exile: Old Testament, Jewish and Christian Conceptions*, ed. James M. Scott, 251–256 (Leiden: Brill, 1997).
7. All other sins may be committed if a life is at stake, for example to obtain urgent medical care or in situations of persecution. The source for this is Leviticus 18:5, "You shall keep my decrees and my laws that a person will do and live by them, I am God." This idea is developed in the Babylonian Talmud, Sanhedrin 84a.
8. Porton, "The Idea of Exile,"256.Sifra Behukotai 7:2.
9. This idea also appears in the Jerusalem Talmud Yoma 1:1 and Tosefta Menachot 13:4.
10. It was also the date for commemorating other tragedies, such as the expulsion of the Jews from Spain in 1492.
11. For a comprehensive discussion of customs of mourning over exile from Jerusalem and their origins, see David Golinkin, "Jerusalem in Law and Custom: A Preliminary Typology,"*Insight Israel* 5, no. 9 (May 2005).
12. See, for example, Exodus 29:45.
13. In Hebrew, there is no neutral gender, so all nouns are either masculine or feminine. Most names of God are grammatically masculine.
14. The Mechilta as a collection seems to be from the second half of the third century, but individual sermons might go back substantially earlier. See Hermann Leberecht Strack and Günter Stemberger, *Introduction to the Talmud and Midrash* (Edinburgh, Scotland: T & T Clark, 1991), 254–5.

15. Translation from Michael Fishbane, *Biblical Myth and Rabbinic Mythmaking* (Oxford: Oxford University Press, 2003), 134–135. See also his discussion of the text on pages 135–136.
16. The idea of the *Shekhinah* in exile is also found in the *Sifre* on Numbers, see Porton 257–259, and in the Babylonian Talmud 29a.
17. For a discussion of the theological implications of the *Shekhinah* in exile and its relationship to Christian theologies of the Spirit, see Michael Lodhal, *Shekhinah/Spirit: Divine Presence in Jewish and Christian Religion* (Mahwah, NJ: Paulist Press, 1992).
18. This translation is from Michael Fishbane, *Biblical Myth and Rabbinic Mythmaking* (Oxford: Oxford University Press, 2003), 296. See also his discussion on pages 296–300.
19. Babylonian Talmud Yoma 23a, Tosefta Yoma, i. 12; Jerusalem Talmud Yoma ii. 39d.
20. Babylonian Talmud Gittin 56b.
21. In Hebrew, the word is Mezuyanim, hence the pun with Zion.
22. For a discussion of this text and its contemporary theological implications, see Aryeh Cohen, "Reading Exile and Redemption: A Meditation on the Talmudic Project," *The Reconstructionist* 61, no. 2 (Fall 1996): 34–35.
23. The classic statement of the "this-worldly" redemptive role of the messiah is from Maimonides' Laws of Kings 11.1, in which he writes: "The King Messiah will arise in the future and reinstate the Davidic dynasty, rebuild the Temple and gather in the exiles of Israel. Then, in his days, all the statutes will be reinstituted as in former times. We will offer sacrifices and observe the Sabbatical and Jubilee years and all related commandments as written in the Torah."
24. Philip Alexander, "The King Messiah in Rabbinic Judaism," in *King and Messiah in Israel and the Ancient Near East*, ed. John Day, 456–473 (Sheffield: Sheffield Academic Press, 1998).
25. *Mitzvah* 4. For more discussion of the theological implications of this position, see Aryeh Cohen, "Land and Messianism," *Journal of Textual Reasoning* 10, no. 1 (August 2011) and Aryeh Newman, "The Centrality of EretzYisrael in Nachmanides," *Tradition* 10, no. 1 (1968): 21–30.
26. The contemporary ultra-orthodox group Neturei Karta still uses the Three Oaths as the basis for their anti-Israel position. For a translation and discussion of Neturei Karta's charter, see Daniel Boyarin and Jonathan Boyarin, "Diaspora: Generation and the Ground of Jewish Identity," *Critical Inquiry* 19, no. 4 (Summer, 1993): 693–725.
27. Tosefta Bava Kamma 7:3 compares the exile in Babylon to a divorced wife who returns to her father's house: Just as this wife returns to where she was when her husband met her, so the Jewish people returns to where Abraham was when God met him.

28. Kad haKemach, Ge'ula, f. 25b. See Shalom Rosenberg, "Exile and Redemption in Jewish Thought in the Sixteenth Century: Contending Conceptions"in *Jewish Thought in the Sixteenth Century*, ed. Bernard Dov Cooperman (Cambridge: Harvard, 1983), 409. Parallels to this idea can be found in the works of Hasdai Crescas and others. See Rosenberg, 409–417.

Chapter 3

Divine Glory Danced: Jewish Migration as God's Self-Revelation in and as Art

Melissa Raphael

When Cain cries out in despair that God has made him a "restless wanderer on earth" and that anyone who meets him may kill him (Gen. 4: 14), he is not referring to his fate as that of merely needing to move from one place to another in search of improved living conditions. He knows his wandering to be a divine punishment for his disobedience. Although the Bible records migration in times of famine or conquest, and economic migration is far from unknown in Jewish history, "migration" is a rather pallid term for the movement of people that has more often than not been perceived by Jews as the condition of exile (*galut*): a misfortune that idolatry and other sins have brought upon them. Jewish exile is to be rectified by a return—both historical and metaphysical—to the longed-for place where not only the people, but also God-self, will once more be at home.[1] Exile may have a role to play in the dissemination of God's word as an exemplary light to the nations, but most Jews, at least liturgically, have lamented it as a condition to be brought to as speedy a close as possible.

Generally, but not invariably, diasporic journeying is not regarded as an instrument or medium of redemption. On the contrary, from Adam and Eve's banishment from the Garden onwards, exile maps history as a cosmic, existential, historical, and geographical wilderness of loss, homelessness, and above all, estrangement from God—even, in mysticism, God's estrangement from God's-self. For the Jew to be in exile is to have been sent to a place where one is a stranger and thereby condemned to otherness. Each successive expulsion leaves the Jew a stranger to the place she has left and a stranger to the place where she will resettle. And even the Jewish God is a God of departure: a God whose glory is glimpsed only as God passes by (Ex. 33: 22); as God's figure disappears into the distance.

The history of the Jewish people is one of migratory movement from one country to another, seeing the creation of multiple diasporas within the diaspora. Jews have been on the move since Abraham left his family and native country for another God would show him: the biblical journeys of settlement and conquest, the two exiles from the Land after the destruction of the First and Second Temples, the late fifteenth-century expulsion of the Jews from the Iberian Peninsula, the mass migration from Eastern Europe after 1880, the flight of European Jews from the Nazis, and the Nazis" deportation of Jews to ghettos and death and concentration camps across Europe, and the migration of Jews to the newly formed State of Israel from Europe and the Middle East before and after 1948.

And yet, without ignoring the fact that what drives any family's or people's migration is not the search for mere economic and existential adventure but the will to survive—to avoid famine, war or persecution—it is also possible to interpret Jewish diasporic movement more positively as a mapping of revelation. Revelation can be figured as an expressive process—a pathmaking or *halakhah* of sorts—where the migratory movement of the collective body of Israel across space patterns itself into an image of redemption as it carries the revealed word, Torah, from place to place.

Rather than offer a history of Jewish migration, or a survey of the concept and experience of exile in Jewish religious thought, this essay interprets Jewish movement across the world as a (paradigmatic) form of Jewish art. In other words, art need not only be the *locus theologicus* that aesthetic theologians know it can be, but the very form of revelation whose lineaments are traced by the moving body of Israel. In my recent Jewish theology of art, I suggested that Jewish art is *itself* the figure traced by the diasporic movement of Jewish bodies across space: a figure that might finally, kinetically, as in a dance, reveal the approach of God's presence in history.[2] The passage of Israel through the world constitutes the redemptive inscription of Torah onto the world—an image of how to live well, in accordance with God's will to justice and peace. This renders migration no mere historical contingency but part of the very mode and process of God's self-revelation to the world—a different sense of scripture: that of the drawing of God's self-revelation as an image of advent that is at once textual and figurative onto and within the material world. Migration, primordially, incarnationally, is the making of Jewish art.

In this essay, I also make use of particular paintings by modern Jewish artists to illustrate my suggestion that the tracing of the migratory path—as much the form of revelation as the literary text—defines what is Jewish about Jewish art. This goes somewhat against the contemporary academic grain. Aaron Rosen has recently argued that definitions of Jewish art are doomed to failure or overqualification. Jewish art is a part of the general history of Western art, engaging and utilizing it with few genuinely exclusive claims to ethnically or spiritually particular characteristics. Rather, using Margaret Olin's phrase, Rosen says that art cannot be Jewish in any ontological sense, but narratively can 'speak Jewish" in certain contexts and to certain interpreters, including theological ones.[3]

It would be hard not to agree with Rosen, yet from the perspective of a theologian, rather than a historian of art, I wonder whether the icon presented by Jews as a collective body has an interpretable narrativity that does, in fact, offer a kind of definition of Jewish art as the art of being a Jew in a historical relationship with God—one that configures into a disclosive image or revelation.[4] I want to ask if the visual appearance (and disappearance) of the people of Israel as a moving body is not itself an image that is perfectly faithful to its own proscription of idolatrous images. It may indeed be the ultimate anti-idolatrous Jewish image because it is that of a body or assembly that inhabits, impossibly, the caesura between eternity and the historical moment—at once an appearing and disappearing image —a broken image that anticipates its own mending.

Too often, modern Jewish thought has given an essentially ethical account of the nature of Israel in terms of the expression of a collective moral will. But the notion of Israel as a collective body that mediates divine self-revelation or presence is not entirely alien to modern and contemporary Judaism. Toward the end of the twentieth century, Michael Wyschogrod's book *The Body of Faith* proposed that God enters the world "through a people whom he chose as his habitation. Thus there came about a visible presence of God in the universe, first in the person of Abraham and later his descendants, as the people of Israel."[5] Wyschogrod follows Rosenzweig in refusing the anti-Semitic caricature of the Jew as grossly carnal by recasting that very carnality as the locus of God's presence. For Wyschogrod, it is the Jewish people who constitute Judaism and are the dwelling place of God, not a text, not an idea or a land.[6]

Elliot Wolfson has more recently given us further grounds to think about the possibility of a fully Jewish incarnational theology.[7] Wolfson notes that in biblical, rabbinic, and mystical texts, the divine glory appears or is invested in perceptible corporeal form. Prayer and study, and not only these, can offer a physical context wherein God appears imaginally to the Jewish people. Here, God's incarnation—whose

Hebrew equivalent would be *hitgashmut*—is not ontologically "reducible to linguistic anthropomorphization." Rather, it is that "mental images of God are somatic while having as their "objective correlative a spiritual entity." It is the "imaginal body of God" that enables human consciousness to grasp or access the transcendent as an incarnate form: the "incarnation of the divine body in Judaism" produces "theophanic images that are localised in the imagination."[8] This does not mean that God *is* a body, or that anthropomorphic hypostases of God can be represented in ordinary pictures. Indeed, Wolfson notes that the "paradoxical notion of the visible manifestation of the God who is hidden provides us with a different notion of embodiment."[9]

Holding Wolfson's point, and Michael Wyschogrod's conception of Israel as the "carnal" indwelling place of God in mind, that "body of faith" can be set in motion to see how its movement, as a form of dance, embodies and traces a dynamic figure of the glory that is a sign and medium of God's self-revelation to the world. And moved by the spirit, *ruach,* our movement is in the image of God's. As Gerhardus van der Leeuw reminds us, the biblical God is one who moves: his creative spirit moves over the waters of chaos, his pillar of fire leads the Israelites through the desert. Dance reminds us that God's movement is the expression of his creative love: "God moved, and he set us upon this earth in motion. That is sublime and impressive. It is the beginning of his work in creation and salvation. It is also the beginning of the dance."[10] If all of Jewish history—its ritual, familial, and political spectacle—is itself a devotional work of religious art, then its history becomes a processive dance or theatre of redemption, toward the reconciled, transformed state that one might call the messianic age.

Isaiah promises "Requital is coming" (35: 4). Redemption will come by road; "the Lord is marching before you" (52: 12). When Isaiah urges that God's path be made straight and clear, he means that a path must be cleared and made traversable, allowing God to find God's way by a meta-image of passage—a work of beauty laboured for on this earth, though visible, as it were, only from the air. As such, Jewish art is *itself* the figure traced by the diasporic movement of Jewish bodies across space: a figure that might finally reveal the form and approach of God's presence in history. Much has been written about the despised figure of the Jew in anti-Semitic representation and discourse, and about the damaging internalisation of anti-Semitism in Jewish consciousness.[11] But Jewry has also surely created its *own* figure. As a bodily assembly before God, Israel is itself an incarnational figure. Its dance, like cloud or fire, is a metonymic representation of God's coming glory; just as the body, Israel, dancing, is a metonymic representation of the presence of God.

Granted, in a contemporary age of ever-heavier human traffic—on roads, through the skies, on the Internet—movement cannot be regarded as a self-evident good. Ours is an age that follows hard on the heels of the twentieth century's crowds of refugees on the move the world over, from advancing hostile or revolutionary armies and in fear of genocidal persecution. Although it was possible for Paul Tillich, in a theology inflected by Marxism, to see images of mass movement as celebrating the power of the people, where the crowd itself is the vanguard expressive of the outworking of a new idea,[12] mass migration, rather differently, is too often an experience of traumatic displacement. It should not be forgotten that the displaced of the contemporary world, as much as the ancient one, long for place and stillness, settlement and roots.[13] From the beginning, Jews have had a strong sense that it is the *end* of movement that is promised to them by God. Since 1948, settlement has been an immediate material possibility to those who make *aliyah* (literally, "ascent") by returning to the Promised Land, but to many others, home also remains an eschatological or messianic possibility yet to come.

Construing the migrations of the diaspora theologically as a dance or series of rhythmic movements through space by whose progression Israel makes straight the path of the Lord (Is. 35:4–10; 40:3–5) develops Halevi, Rosenzweig and others' notion that Jewish diasporic movement is purposive or necessary agent of sanctification and redemption. This representation of Israel as a dancing figure—a dynamic figure drawn in movement across the earth—therefore challenges recent declarations that because a part of the Jewish people has returned to the promised land, and the rest no longer see the United States (in particular) as the diaspora but as their home, the terminology of exile is now defunct. A theology of diasporic movement as dance also challenges postmodernist denials that the Jewish people and its destiny can be referred to in the singular as a historical and spiritual unity.[14]

For it is precisely the notion of the assembly and history of Israel as a collective dance rather than, as Wyschogrod would have it, a habitation for God, which affirms Jewish unity in diversity. To conceive of the assembly of Israel in terms of motion rather than habitation suggests a more mutual, embodied, affective possession in love. Rosenzweig sees dance as a moment of self-recognition—a people recognizes itself in festive processions and parades—and a moment of praise offered with the whole body that signals entry into the sphere of redemption.[15] His notion of dance is implicit in his conception of Israel as a constellatory figure of revelation, but not developed. Nonetheless, of modern Jewish thinkers, Rosenzweig has come closest to imagining Israel as a figure of revelation in envisioning the transcendental figure of the star as a dynamic constellation, embodying the relationship between God, world, and humanity as each intersects with the other in the great moments of creation, revelation, and redemption. Rosenzweig makes the aesthetic spectacle of Jewish worldlessness an instrument of revelation and redemption. The meta- or extra-historical positioning of Israel as within-but-without to history presents an uncanny spectacle to the world. Homeless, the Jewish people are neither here nor in the world to come. And where, for Rosenzweig, the Christian mission follows a centrifugal historical and geographical course, using conquest and preaching to extend its evangelical reach to the very ends of the earth, Judaism concentrates and intensifies revelation centripetally by closing in on itself through its own set-apartness or holiness.[16]

But, in the end, Rosenzweig's constellatory figure may be too contracted and abstracted or unimaginable an image of Jewish presence and absence, arrival and departure. Instead, as a dancing figure, revelation is patterned into a dynamic image: a representation of and to God in the world as a fully embodied, vital, and finally beautiful narrative spectacle whose very unity of form leaves no one's experience uncomprehended. The historic rifts between Left-wing secular Zionists who have understood exile and return as a purely political struggle, religious Jews who have spiritualized exile as a metaphysical process, and those who have found Jerusalem not in any ingathering of the people but everywhere and anywhere that God's word is heard,[17] are overcome. Home is not endlessly deferred; rather, its possibility may be created on the way home. This in all senses moving spectacle is offered back to God as a continuous gift of praise. As the Psalmist wrote, "Let them praise His name in dance; with timbrel and lyre let them chant His praises. For the Lord delights in His people" (Ps. 149.3–4).

Emmanuel Levinas, predictably, regards the sub-personal elation of collective dance as essentially pagan, turning the ethical drama of salvation into theatre.[18] Similarly, Lional Kochan has presented another uncompromising Jewish attack on visual images. For Kochan, like Levinas, Jewish holiness cannot be assimilated into a general hierophany.[19] Torah cannot be reduced to the dimension of the aesthetic, so that, finally, it "calls for nothing more than admiration and lacks all power to address any capacity for volition."[20] Like Levinas, Kochan casts the appeal of the aesthetic as passive, disarming: an emasculation of the ethical imperative by feeling alone.[21] For the visual to become preeminent is, he says, eventually to degrade Torah to a spectacle and thus mute its ethical summons.[22]

But the different historical and geographical forms of Jewish dance belong to a single transcendent dance that, in its process, is hardly a delirious bacchanal; in fact, it is hardly a spectacle alone. For history is appointed in the light of God's glory as it breaks through the rushing clouds. The interplay of light and darkness, where those who seek the shelter of God are also cast in the shadow of God's hand (Ps. 91:1; Is. 51: 16), is such that the revelation is as much constituted by concealment as illumination. Contra Levinas, a theology of migration affirms Levinas's biblical reminder that Jews see only the back of God. Ours is a God in retreat, a departure, an absence in the making. This is a God of "pure passage," a God that "shows itself as past."[23] Put more positively, this is the God who is, as Arthur Cohen used to say, "the God of our futurity": the God who is always going on before.

Paul Tillich has observed that the individual is the bearer of history only in relation to what he calls "a history-bearing group." A man or woman's individual life story is not history, but it accrues significance as the story of someone who both actively and symbolically represents that of a history-bearing group.[24] The Jewish people are just such a history-bearing group, but its internal power is virtually a function of the external powerlessness of its members when suffering repeated exile through expulsion. Therefore, the theologically inflected "going on before" has none of the sure linearity of an arrow fired toward its target. It is the multiple and repeated dislocations of a history-bearing group such as the Jews that produce the encounters between persons, communities, and cultures that map the history of the divine-human encounter.[25]

Biblical and rabbinic theodicy commonly construes diaspora as a punishment for Israel's various defections from its covenant that might be summarised under the heading "idolatry." Secular economic historians have shown that Jews have not only migrated at the time of persecution but also in legitimate pursuit of economic advantage in other centers of the Jewish diaspora. Postmodern cultural critics have deconstructed Israel as a collective noun for a unitary people with a unitary history that transcends its diasporic difference. Yet there remains a stubborn tradition in which Jewish theologians construe diaspora within a larger, unifying redemptive scheme. (Thus Psalms 44:23, "It is for Your sake that we are slain all day long.")[26]

Rosenzweig, early in the twentieth century, drew upon the Jewish philosophers Philo in Roman Alexandria and Yehuda Halevi in tenth-century Spain, both of whom had argued that Jews *had to be* dispersed in order to spread the word of God to the nations. Halevi in particular had portrayed the Jews as individually carrying the seeds of the divine logos among the nations. Rosenzweig, largely indifferent to the Zionist cause, is further indebted to the medieval rabbinic commentator, Rashi, who, echoing Christian theologies of Christ's suffering for the sins of the world, understood the Servant of Isaiah 53 to refer to the people of Israel who suffered vicariously for the world.[27] This para-Christian scheme helped Rosenzweig to justify Jewish wandering and its afflictions theologically. God afflicts Israel so that the nations will be healed.[28] For Rosenzweig, parting company with German-Jewish rationalism, Jewish suffering is not something that can be reasoned away through the enlightened progress of culture. Rather, anti-Semitism is part and parcel of the prophetic sign that is the Jewish people. The Jew, carrying God's presence within his own, is an aesthetic disturbance. He is uncanny or *Unheimlich*; he is not at home in this world. For Rosenzweig, this homelessness, as Leora Batnitsky notes, is the aesthetic dimension of Jewish revelation to the world.[29]

Taking one's cue from Rosenzweig's aestheticization of redemption, it becomes possible to see the Jewish people as a tableau or positioning of bodies, the choreography of whose movement through the world is an image of the pathos and the triumph of a God in exile and return. If, for most of Jewish history, revelation is not centralized in Jerusalem but given on the way, what we see and understand of God may be carried not only as words in books but also on the carts laden with furniture rumbling through the mud and dust, and in the suitcases of pots, pans, and clothing that are also necessary to the daily fulfilment of the commandment. An aesthetic of Jewish movement can be found in Jewish art, but for obvious reasons, Jewish art has also been deeply troubled by it. The ideational image of Jewish history as passional movement on an epic scale is a very old one. The iconography of the refugee dates back at least as far as Assyrian reliefs depicting refugee-prisoners leaving Lachish holding their few belongings. In the modern Jewish imagination, the painting of the Polish Jewish artist Samuel Hirszenberg (1865–1908), *Exile* (c. 1904, whereabouts now unknown) is perhaps the most striking of all depictions of the mass movement of Jewry. Painted in response to the Kishniev pogrom of 1903, this large, sombre canvas depicts destitute Russian Jews of all ages and types walking onward as one body across an empty steppe shrouded in snow, carrying nothing but a few religious and domestic necessities. After Hirszenberg, paintings of large huddled groups of Jewish refugees carrying meager bundles of possessions and trudging across empty landscapes on foot became the visual epitome of *Judenschmerz* (Jewish trauma) in an age of pogroms.[30]

I have suggested that the transmissive continuity of revelation can be visualised as a sacral procession—"I will make all my goodness pass before thee" (Ex. 33: 18–19). Revelation is a "showing" of God's purpose to those assembled, not in congregational rows, but a people lining history's route and joining the procession as its standard passes by. But that *levayah* (or funeral procession) has too often been caricatured, even by Jews themselves (quoting Jeremiah and Isaiah), as that of docile lambs to the slaughter: a passive shuffle of the herd through the slaughterhouses of history (cf. Jer. 11.19; Is. 53. 7). As in Jan Burka's *Deportees*, an undated chalk drawing made in Terezín, Jewry forms a long line; its congregational shadow moving as one along the walls of the building anticipates Jewry's transformation into ghosts. Depicted as a death march, the line passes between two long buildings along a cobbled street whose abyssal perspective funnels the procession into darkness. The street narrows, and the Jews and their possessions disappear into an opening onto nothingness: into what we now know to be the line for the gas chambers.[31]

Understandably, after the holocaustic death marches such as those recorded in photographs of Budapest Jews assembled for the forced marches between November and December 1944 that would kill many of them along the way, post-Holocaust art remains preoccupied by Jewish movement toward the abyss. In Yosl Bergner's painting, *Flying Spice Box* (1966), dented pots, pans, and spice boxes fly through the air on the winds of holocaustic dispersion, and land where they fall. In his *Destination X* (1974), all sense of a cultivationary dispersion is lost, and it is now no more than a long processive line of furniture—tables, mirrors, and chairs that represent the deported crowd forming a long, slow, congested line for death.

A post-Holocaust theological geography cannot but be an anguished one. But a messianic dance is not only a joyous one—if the path must be made straight, it is now a crooked, muddy and overgrown path. And sometimes the great pathos of the dance overwhelms its beauty. The dancing Jew can seem abjected by his dance when that dance becomes the kitsch entertainment of his persecutors—as in Poland before the Holocaust, when Jewish tenant farmers were sometimes forced by the squire or *poritz* and his jeering, drunken party to sing and dance before them to the traditional Sabbath hymn, or during the Holocaust, when rabbis were forced to dance on desecrated Torah scrolls. And yet, even at the time, Jews knew this dance to have a sacrificial pathos akin to that of male Hasidim like the Dombrover Rebbe, who is known to have led 20 Jews in ecstatic dance toward *devekuth*: a state of communion with God by which to rejoice at their sacrificial sanctification of his name before they were shot into the graves they had dug themselves.[32] This is a sacral movement manifest in the long, slow dance toward *devekuth* (cleaving), Hasidim would have used for *kavannah* (focus) to prepare for hearing a master's teaching, or that sometimes a rebbe would do no more than dance as the non-verbal answer to his followers' questions.

A sacrificial theology of redemption makes it more than possible to represent the procession of Jewish history as if it were something of a funeral cortege, as if the railway lines of Jewish history all lead with no return into the death camp of Auschwitz-Birkenau. Jewish diasporic art has often, and understandably, reinforced what Salo Baron has called "the lachrymose account" of Jewish history, belonging with that countertradition of the Messiah who is eternally on his way, but will never arrive.

Messianic movement assumes turmoil even as it anticipates peace. But something of a more positive missiological image of Jewish diasporic movement can also be inferred from the visual spectacle of modern Eastern European Jewish piety. In Leviticus 25:23, God says, "you are but strangers resident with Me," and before the Holocaust, Ashkenazic folk culture was densely populated by God's sojourners: the poor and the simple of no fixed abode with whom God says go; the Thirty-Six Just Men of Jewish legend who, to save God's heart from breaking, would slip, weary and unnoticed, from shtetl to shtetl, carrying the burden of the world's sin on their back;[33] the Luftmenschen—the peddlers who once showed us how to live on air; and the Purimspielers—the itinerant groups of actors, acrobats, and clowns who, from the sixteenth century, carried the Purim story of redemption from death, from one remote rural community to another.

Consider, also, how the great Hasidic rabbis are identified with and by the names of towns and regions in a Jewish Europe that once was and is no longer. Their names remember real places that their disciples would journey for days to reach, and where their piety invited and welcomed God's presence. The recitation of these men's names—Rabbi Shmelke of Nikolsburg, Rabbi Moshe of Kobryn, Rabbi Shelmo of Karlin, Rabbi Mordecai of Lekhovitz, Rabbi Yehudah Zevi of

Stretyn, Rabbi Mendel of Kotzk, Rabbi Yitzhak of Vorki—calls part of a long register of devotion to HaShem—the Name of all names, and one of whose other names is Ha Makhom, "the place." As it says in the Midrash (Gen. R. 68), "The Holy One blessed be He is the place of the world but the world is not His place." Unsettled, God's Shekhinah, or presence, also in exile, moves with the people, not aimlessly but missiologically, from place to place. While the Hasidic *kfitzas haderech*—the miraculous journey in which vast distances were covered with a giant stride in the wink of an eye—may now be undertaken by Hasidic emissaries in aircraft, still, today, Chabad Houses are often run by lone Lubavitch Hasidim bringing Torah to other Jews living or staying in parts of the world that are either geographically remote or lacking in Jewish facilities. In them, and in all Jews who seek to be a light to the nations, the beacon of divine presence can be tracked as when, on a clear night, bonfires or torches are lit in succession across the land; as one light is seen, another is lit.

So just as Chabad's *schluchim*, or emissaries, establish outposts of renewed Jewish observance wherever they are sent, something of a more positive missiological image of Jewish diasporic movement— God's passing with Israel over the land—might be imagined as a messianic dance or series of rhythmic movements and trajectories through space by whose progression Israel makes straight God's path into the world and thereby draws a renewed future onto the world.

The experience of expulsion makes stasis—the maintenance of the interminable same—impossible. Its catastrophe brings one into the realm of new possibilities. Just as arrival in new places necessarily marks the beginning of new histories, migration can be a messianic entry into the realm of the radically unprecedented. Modern Jewish theologians writing after the trauma of the First World War knew that only an interrupted history is a messianic one. It was not the progressive evolution of moral and scientific consciousness that would bring the new world that the Enlightenment had signally failed to deliver. With modern humanity laboring under an ever heavier burden of suffering, Franz Rosenzweig, Walter Benjamin, and Gershom Scholem all, in different ways, understood that the messianic could only consist in the unpredictable irruption of the new from the ruins of the old: from out of the experience of rupture and dislocation.[34]

However, modern Jewish art, which can be read as a theological text like any other, may also help us locate hope in the maintenance of the ordinary and in spite of death. Many modern Jewish artists have celebrated the carnivalesque festivity of a Jewish life that was not always "back-shadowed" by knowledge of what catastrophe was to come. This more festive mood is evident in Marc Chagall's idiomatic theatrical set designs painted on the walls of the Kamerni Yiddish Theatre, Moscow, incorporating the rhythms and burlesque of the circus. Or again, Yefim Ladizhinski's recent panoramic canvases of Jewish life in Odessa depict brightly colored parades of sailors, men gathered for prayer in synagogues, weddings, funerals, children playing, and mothers hanging out the washing.

Festive movement in anticipation of the coming of the messiah can be traced through to the Zionist art of the first 40 years or so of the twentieth century. Zionist art depicted *aliyah* not merely as a renewal of nationhood but as a return: a resurrective "getting up" from the pit of persecution that was Eastern Europe. Where Reuven Rubin had once painted weary, destitute, hunched, and huddled Jews, often seated on the ground with their heads held in their hands, after his emigration to Palestine in 1923, Rubin ceased to paint images of diasporic Jewish suffering and instead created joyous images such as *The Dancers of Meron* (1926), which conveys a messianic vision of Jewish unity through the dynamic embrace of dance: the customarily divided communities of Sephardic and Ashkenazi Jews dance as one people in their ecstatic celebration of Lag b'Omer in Safed.[35]

Recall how God says in Isaiah 43. 19, "I am about to do something new; even now it shall come to pass, suddenly you shall perceive it." As part of a process of rhythmic movement, the process(ion) of Israel will finally configure into an ordered, graceful whole, and by virtue of its process, the dance, like any dance, is always open to the re-formations of the future. This could even be so in the Warsaw ghetto, a place of ends that had no past because it had no future. On October 11, 1942, Zelig Kalmanovitsh wrote in his diary that his first *hakafa* (danced circuit of the synagogue) on Simchat Torah moved him to address the congregation with the affirmation, "I know that the Jewish people will live" (*Am Yisrael Chai*). This moment is an image of spiritual resistance to genocide in anticipation of the messianic renewal of life, for in Jewish dance, especially in the circular form, all arms are linked in an image of the eternity, equality, and solidarity of the Jewish people. Ashkenazic dance includes the worldwide custom of "dancing" the young and the weak on the shoulders of the other dancers. Even as Jewish history's individual subjects stumble with thirst, hunger, and exhaustion; they, too, are carried high on the shoulders of others in the long dance toward Jerusalem.

Notes

All scriptural references are taken from *Tanakh: The Holy Scriptures* (Philadelphia, Jerusalem: The Jewish Publication Society, 1985).

1. To some extent, since modernity, everyone has been on the move: mass migration has been a defining feature of modernity and is seen by historians as normal rather than catastrophic. Jews are not the only people to have suffered expulsions, and not all Jewish movement has been catastrophic or the result of expulsion. Jews have also migrated to enjoy the benefits of modernization, emancipation, and greater economic prosperity. In the seventeenth century, Manasseh Ben Israel, for example, commended the entry of Jews from Amsterdam into London to Oliver Cromwell as conducive to economic profit. See further, Simon Kuznets, E. Glen Weyl, and Stephenie H. Lo, eds., *Jewish Economies: Development and Migration in America and Beyond: The Economic Life of American Jewry*, vol. 1 (Piscataway, NJ: Transaction Publishers, 2011). Moreover, referring to the reinforcement of stereotypes such as the eternally "wandering Jew," social historians have warned of the dangers of rendering migration the specific habitus of Jews alone. See also Tobias Brinkmann, *Jewish Migration*, accessed December 3, 2010, http://www.ieg-ego.eu/en/threads/europe-on-the-road/jewish-migration/tobias-brinkmann-jewish-migration.
2. This argument can be found in chapter 6, "The Dancing Figure of Jewish History" of my book *Judaism and the Visual Image: A Jewish Theology of Art* (London and New York, Continuum, 2009), 150–179. The present chapter is a shorter version of this chapter and updates some of its thinking.
3. Aaron Rosen, *Imagining Jewish Art: Encounters with the Masters in Chagall, Guston, and Kitaj* (Oxford: Legenda, 2009).
4. This question, and the present chapter as a whole, is underpinned by insights from Zachary Braiterman, *The Shape of Revelation: Aesthetics and Modern Jewish Thought* (Stanford University Press: Stanford CA, 2007), esp. xxi, where, arguing that religion is "the sensate shape of revelation," Braiterman writes, "As a composition, religion is neither static nor dynamic. The graphic and verbal images at play across its system grow more or less stable at any one geographical place and historical moment. Continually disfigured and reconfigured by collective and individual actors in response to local conditions, they form an overlap between intersecting planes, between visible and invisible bodies."
5. Michael Wyschogrod, *The Body of Faith: Judaism as Corporeal Election* (New York, Seabury Press, 1983), 36, 103, 174. See also page 57.
6. Marc A. Krell, *Intersecting Pathways: Modern Jewish Theologians in Conversation with Christianity* (New York: Oxford University Press, 2003), 141. Leora Batnitzky, *Idolatry and Representation: The Philosophy of Franz Rosenzweig Reconsidered* (Princeton NJ:

Princeton University Press, 2000), 200–205, notes certain affinities between Rosenzweig and Wyschogrod's conception of Israel, though Wyschogrod does not appear to acknowledge them.
7. See, for example, "Judaism and Incarnation: the Imaginal Body of God," in *Christianity in Jewish Terms*, eds. Tikva Frymer-Kensky, et al, 239–261 (Boulder CA: Westview Press, 2000).
8. Ibid., 240–1.
9. Ibid., 242–3.
10. Gerhardus van der Leeuw, *Sacred and Profane Beauty: The Holy in Art*, trans. David E. Green (London, Weidenfeld and Nicolson, 1963), 74. See also, W.O. E. Oesterly, *Sacred Dance* (New York: Cambridge University Press, 1923).
11. See, for example, Sander Gilman, *Jewish Self-Hatred* (Baltimore, John Hopkins University Press, 1986).
12. Paul Tillich, "Mass and Personality," (1922), in *On Art and Architecture*, eds. J. and J. Dillinger, 58–66 (New York: Crossroad, 1987).
13. See George Pattison, *Crucifixions and Resurrections of the Image: Christian Reflections on Art and Modernity* (London, SCM, 2009), 129–30.
14. See, for example, Caryn Aviv and David Shneer, *New Jews: The End of the Jewish Diaspora* (New York: New York University Press, 2005). Note that this resistance to the terminology of exile is not only contemporary. Many modern Jews (in post-Emancipation, pre-Holocaust Germany especially) had relatively few reasons to be particularly enthusiastic Zionists.
15. Franz Rosenzweig, *The Star of Redemption*, trans. William W. Hallo (Notre Dame, IN: Notre Dame Press, 1985), 372–3.
16. Rosenzweig, *The Star of Redemption*, 328–331, 336, 405–409, and 420; Gregory Kaplan, "'In the End Shall Christians Become Jews?': Franz Rosenzweig's Apocalyptic Eshatology," *Cross Currents* 53 (Winter 2004), 511–529.
17. See Arnold Eisen, "Exile," in *Contemporary Jewish Religious Thought*, eds. Arthur A. Cohen and Paul Mendes-Flohr, 219–225 (New York: Simon and Schuster, 1987).
18. Emmanuel Levinas, "Reality and its Shadow," reprinted in *Emmanuel Levinas, Collected Philosophical Papers*, ed. Alphonso Lingis, 1–13 (Dordrecht: Martinus Nijhoff, 1987), and in *The Levinas Reader*, ed. and trans. Seán Hand, 130–143 (Oxford and Cambridge MA: Blackwell, 1989).
19. Lional Kochan, *Beyond the Graven Image: A Jewish View* (Basingstoke, Hampshire and London: Macmillan, 1997), 31.
20. Ibid., 110.
21. Ibid., 111.
22. Ibid., 101.

23. Emmanuel Levinas, "Enigma and Phenomenon," in *Emmanuel Levinas, Collected Philosophical Papers*, trans. Alphonso Lingis (Dordrecht: Martinus Nijhoff, 1987), 69.
24. Paul Tilllich, *Systematic Theology*, vol. 3 (Chicago: University of Chicago Press, 1963), 308–313. Tillich notes that this relation of the individual to the group is especially obvious in persons who have left the community to go into seclusion in the "desert" or into "exile."
25. For a non-theological account of the visual dimension of diasporic movement, see Nicholas Mirzoeff, "Introduction: The Multiple Viewpoint: Diasporic Visual Cultures," in *Diaspora and Visual Culture: Representing Africans and Jews*, ed. Nicholas Mirzoeff (London, Routledge, 2000), 3, 6–7.
26. Cited in Moshe Idel, "The Land of Israel in Medieval Kabbalah," in *The Land of Israel: Jewish Perspectives*, ed. Lawrence A. Hoffman (Indiana: University of Notre Dame Press, 1986), 177.
27. See Krell, *Intersecting Pathways*, 38.
28. See Rosenzweig, *The Star of Redemption*, 306–7, 314; Krell, *Intersecting Pathways*, 38–9, 64–5.
29. Leora Batnitzky, *Idolatry and Representation*, 91–94.
30. Ziva Amishai-Maisels, *Depiction and Interpretation: The Influence of the Holocaust on Visual Arts* (Oxford: Pergamon Press, 1993), 19.
31. Glenn Sujo, *Legacies of Silence: The Visual Arts and Holocaust Memory* (London: Philip Wilson Publishers, 2001), 58.
32. See, for example, Eliezer Berkovits, *With God in Hell: Judaism in the Ghettos and Deathcamps* (New York and London, Sanhedrin, 1979), 75, 112; Pesach Schindler, *Hasidic Responses to the Holocaust in the Light of Hasidic Thought* (Hoboken, NJ: Ktav, 1990), 60–65.
33. See further, Melissa Raphael, "The Face of God in Every Generation: Jewish Feminist Spirituality and the Legend of the Thirty-Six Hidden Saints" in *Spirituality and Society in the New Millennium*, ed. Ursula King, 234-46 (Brighton: Sussex Academic Press, 2001).
34. Stéphane Moses, *The Angel of History: Rosenzweig, Benjamin, Scholem*, trans. Barbara Harshav (Stanford: Stanford University Press, 2009), 4–16 and *passim*.
35. See Dalia Manor, "The Dancing Jew and Other Characters: Art in the Jewish Settlement in Palestine in the 1920s," *Journal of Modern Jewish Studies* 1 (2002): 73–89, 82; Gabrielle Sed-Rajna, *Jewish Art*, trans. Sara Friedman and Mira Reich (New York: Harry N. Abrams, 1995), 337, 498.

Chapter 4

Theology of Migration in the Orthodox Tradition

Kondothra M. George

Properly speaking, the Orthodox theological tradition has no specific "Theology of Migration," though migration has always been a reality in the life of the faithful in all Orthodox churches, both Eastern and Oriental,[1] particularly since the latter part of the nineteenth century until present times. A word needs to be said about this apparent incongruity.

An overview of classical and contemporary Orthodox theological writings would reveal that the Orthodox tradition seldom produces any "genitive" or "adjectival" theologies, for instance, "a theology of hope," "a theology of the Cross," or "a subaltern theology." In fact, Orthodox theology is rather reluctant to subdivide itself into different specialized domains. The so-called subdivisions like christology, pneumatology, and ecclesiology are rather modern and scholastic and are modeled on Western academic distinctions. According to St. Gregory of Mazianzus, a well-known fourth century theologian, and architect of the Trinitarian doctrine, theology (*theologia*) in its primary sense refers to the inexpressible mystery of the Holy Trinity.[2] In this sense, the mystery of God can only be worshipped and loved, not examined with our rational tools of analysis, cognition, and comprehension. At this level, theology is simply doxology, worshipping the triune God. Since there is no attempt here to know God with the human intellect, theology in its simple and pure form in the Orthodox tradition is not what we call "theology" today in academic circles.

In Orthodox views, only in a secondary and derivative sense can one speak of theology as a human rational reflection on God and the created reality. For example, a systematic exercise of the human intellect on any topic in relation to the scriptural and traditional understanding of God, world, and humanity, will be based on the revelation in Jesus Christ, the incarnate Son of God. Maintaining the integral connection between human reason and faith is essential for a sound Christian life and reflection. The proper balance between the apophatic and the cataphatic theologies—or the negative and positive approaches to human knowledge of both the transcendent reality and our earthly existence—is deemed pivotal.[3]

The customary reluctance of Orthodox theology to adopt exclusive specialization and fragmentation does not, however, prevent theologians from recognizing the need for theological reflection on current and contextual issues that affect the lives of people in church and society. Yet again, reflection and contextualization are done mostly out of a deep pastoral concern rather than merely academic interests.

Furthermore, the Orthodox churches in general are not in the habit of making public statements in immediate response to ethical or socio-political issues that emerge from time to time. Individual leaders, teachers, and theologians of the church may speak or write and make their opinions public. These theological opinions carry some weight, depending on the personalities that make them, but they tend not to be binding on the church. They can serve as guidelines for the faithful to exercise their freedom and discretion in ethical, social, and political domains.

The Local and the Universal

The traditional distinction between the East and the West in Christianity is no longer justifiable in a geographical sense due to the Western colonial and missionary movements, migration, and the interpenetration of populations. In the old geopolitical and cultural contexts, the Roman Catholic and Protestant streams of Christianity are typically from the West, and Orthodox Christianity is from the East. In pre-colonial times, this territorial division had some legitimacy. With the European colonial movement and the stupendous Western missionary enterprise that accompanied the political-cultural expansion of Europe into Asia, Africa, and Latin America, the scenario has changed. On the one hand, the Roman Catholic Church, which was once the local church of the West centered in Rome, and the provincial European Protestant churches became global entities through missionary expansion. The Roman Church also claimed to be universal, interpreting Catholicity in a geographical dimension of global expansion. On the other hand, political, economic, and religious reasons pushed many Orthodox Christians from Eastern Europe, Greece, the Middle East, Africa, and Asia to emigrate to richer countries in Western Europe and North America where they found a relatively higher degree of individual freedom. So these traditional local churches have also become practically global churches by virtue of their extensive diaspora.

Although traditionally there was very little popular knowledge of Orthodoxy in the West, the living presence of the diaspora Christians from Orthodox countries, particularly in the twentieth century, brought some substantial knowledge of Orthodox Christianity to the West. The Bolshevik Revolution in Russia in 1917 and the subsequent emergence of Communist regimes, and the suppression of religion in Eastern Europe were major reasons for Orthodox Christians to flee to the West.[4] The newly created axes of ecclesiastical life and pastoral and teaching centers were located in cities like Paris, London, Oxford, New York and other places. These diaspora communities largely maintained their ethnic and linguistic identity as well as faithfulness to their mother churches in their countries of origin. As a result, in Western Europe, North America, and Australia, Orthodox church communities emerged mostly in urban centers with parallel hierarchies and jurisdictions. Canonically, this created a problem for Orthodox theology since the principle of "one bishop in one locality" was not maintained. The younger generation of the émigré Christians was more and more distanced from the mother church, its language, and other cultural assumptions. Particular ethnic allegiance of the immigrants from different countries raised canonical and theological questions for the Orthodox Church. The formation of the Orthodox Church of America, for example, was an attempt to go beyond the rivalry of ethnic, linguistic, and cultural identities to become "one church in Christ."

The Middle East and its political instability in the second half of the twentieth century— and the continuing conflicts in countries like Syria and Egypt—have provoked massive emigration from Middle Eastern countries to the West. Beyond Eastern Europe and the Middle East, Oriental Orthodox churches in Ethiopia, Eretria, and India have also experienced the phenomenon of their faithful emigrating to more affluent countries. Even a small, though ancient, Oriental Orthodox church like the Malankara Orthodox Church in India has a substantial diaspora in the Persian Gulf countries and in North America. Migration in this case happened purely because of economic and educational reasons.

The Biblical Saga of Migration

The Orthodox Christian spiritual and theological heritage, as shaped particularly by the monastic tradition, understands the whole earthly existence as a life in exile. The book of Genesis tells the story, couched in mythological garb, of the expulsion of the first parents, Adam and Eve, from the Garden of Eden. Coming to the earth and living in the pain of labor and child-rearing, humanity was confronted with the existential realities of conflict, death, and dissolution. But humanity always retained nostalgia for its original home: the Paradise in the East. The Orthodox liturgical practice of turning to the East during public prayer expresses this homesickness and deep craving for the lost home. The story of the fall of Adam and Eve viewed from a historical perspective, and within a linear temporal scheme, made humanity aware of the beginning and the end of their journey as exiles. The story of the peregrinations of the people of Israel as recounted in the Pentateuch, as well as in the historical and prophetic literature of the Hebrew Scripture, further buttressed the Christian sense of being aliens and sojourners on earth.

The legendary journey of Abraham from the civilized land of the Chaldeans toward the totally unknown territory of the promised land as recounted in the Bible, set the prime model for the Christian sojourners as well. The stories of the slavery of Israel in Pharaonic Egypt, the Exodus out of Egypt led by Moses, the long years of wandering in the desert, and the final entry to the promised land have been employed to symbolize a form of pilgrimage and have been used to refer to the movement of the People of Israel toward the New Israel, the Christian Church. There are differing interpretations of the Hebrews' conquest of Canaan, whether it happened gradually by intermarriages between the Israelites and the local people, or by wars and mass killings, presumably under Yahweh's order. It is clear however that . according to the biblical texts, possessing the land was God's command. Early Christians followed this scriptural view in a spiritual and metaphorical sense, without raising questions about the political nature of the entry of the people of Israel into the promised land. The Christian understandings of salvation history having been fulfilled in the past, of the journey that they had to complete in their present time, and of their future and final destination, were mutually shaped by the metaphorical interpretation of the migration story of the people of Israel as narrated in the Hebrew Scriptures.

Christ himself was a wandering teacher, moving from village to village and town to town, with no permanent residence. He described his own situation when he said, "Foxes have holes and the birds of the air have nests; but the Son of man has nowhere to lay his head" (Matt 8:20).[5] Most likely, the disciples and the early community of believers interpreted this self-understanding of Jesus in a messianic manner, and thus as followers of Jesus understood themselves to be "aliens and exiles" on earth, having "no lasting city" here and travelling home to the "Jerusalem above...our mother" (1 Pet. 2:11; Heb. 13:14; Gal. 4:26).

Christian existence thus was considered a pilgrimage. This image has gone deep into the psyche of the early Church. The traveller does not carry any heavy baggage of material possessions, and passes through strange and hostile lands. In focusing her or his attention on the final destination, there is no tarrying on the way with any excessive concern for food, clothing and shelter.

Evidence of how ingrained this notion of pilgrimage became in early Christian imaginary can be found in the writings of Clement, bishop of the church of Rome early in the second century. When writing to the church in Corinth, as was typical of many of his letters, Clement describes the Christian Church as: "The pilgrim Church of God in Rome writing to the Church of God in Corinth which is in pilgrimage."[5] Obviously these were genuine churches, locally organized and administered with their own respective bishops and clergy or leadership, independent of each other in administrative and organizational structure, but deeply interdependent in one faith in Jesus Christ and the one communion in the Eucharist with all the love and sharing it implied. These local churches were en route to the final destination, their common goal being the kingdom of God where God will be all in all.

In another celebrated document, the anonymous second century Letter to Diognetus, the earthly existence of the Church is beautifully expressed:

> For the Christians are distinguished from other men neither by country, nor language nor the customs which they observe. For they neither inhabit cities of their own, nor employ a peculiar form of speech, nor lead a life which is marked out by any singularity.... But, inhabiting Greek as well as barbarian cities, according as the lot of each of them has determined, and following the customs of the natives in respect to clothing, food, and the rest of their ordinary conduct they display to us their wonderful and confessedly striking method of life. They dwell in their own countries, but simply as sojourners. As citizens, they share in all things with others, and yet endure all things as if foreigners. Every foreign land is to them as their native country, and every land of their birth as a land of strangers. They marry, as do all others; they

beget children; but they do not destroy their offspring. They have a common table, but not a common bed. They are in the flesh, but they do not live after the flesh. They pass their days on earth, but as the citizens of heaven.[6]

Migration and Eschatology

Eschatology plays a key role in Orthodox theology and spirituality. The eschaton is not simply the endpoint of a linear, progressive scheme of time, as it is generally assumed in many theological textbooks and popular teachings. The eschaton is the final goal that reinterprets the past in a refreshingly new way and shapes the present order and agenda of Christian life. In the ascetic-monastic spiritual understanding of the Orthodox tradition, the whole Christian life is a dedicated journey undertaken with the purpose of realizing the kingdom of God. This is essentially a pilgrim's final goal . The ethical and social involvement of the church and its historical configuration are shaped by this ultimate goal. Therefore, there is a hierarchy of values in the life of the church community that subordinates material possessions and worldly power and authority to the overwhelming ideal of the kingdom of God. The reign or kingdom of God in the Orthodox understanding is a radically new and transfigured order of reality that is totally transcendent and "in our midst" at the same time. It is the final fulfilment of the Christian aspiration for love, justice, and salvation, but it can be experienced here and now as well. History and life on earth viewed from the lens of an Orthodox faith can and must manifest signs of the kingdom of God, as did the life and actions of Jesus Christ. All Christian ethics arise from this vision of the kingdom of God (God being all in all).

In many instances of the life of the institutional Church, there is conflict between history and eschatology. Underlying such conflicts is the erroneous assumption that the notion of the eschaton as end or the last things is otherworldly and takes us away from our social and ethical responsibility for the world..

This dichotomy—between this earthly existence and the eternal, between the secular and sacred, between history and salvation—continues to theologically and spiritually deadlock the Church. Orthodox theology, however, considers the eschaton to be the driving force for our commitment in history. The ethics we practice with the understanding of the integral and positive connection between all dimensions of reality is a form of consequential ethics in the sense that our human conduct at sociopolitical and economic levels is judged on the basis of their long-term implications and meaning for human well-being and salvation. It is not a short-sighted attitude out of arising out of vested interest or the desire for immediate gains.,. v

The future dimension provided by the eschaton is normative for our understanding of the temporal aspect of present existence without fragmenting time into past, present, and future. This concept of time helps us to overcome that superficial psychological division and see the temporal order as drawing light and inspiration from the eternal.

In the Eucharistic liturgical tradition, anamnesis (recollection or remembrance) represents the whole human history in its totality and catholicity. Here is memory or remembrance in its total sense, not simply confined to the historical past. So we remember the future, which is psychologically inadmissible since memory is associated with the past. Doxologically, the Church celebrates the whole of history as redeemed by the death and resurrection of Jesus Christ. Hence, anamnesis, furthermore, enkindles our expectation for our future which includes all created reality. with the whole of created reality.

One of the ancient prayers in Syriac of St. James' liturgy for anamnesis is, "Lord we remember your death, we confess and proclaim your resurrection and we look forward to your second coming." The centrality of eschatology in the liturgy entails its centrality for Orthodox theology. As John Meyendorff, the well-known Orthodox theologian and historian, puts it, "Without Eschatology, traditionalism is turned only to the past: it is nothing but archaeological antiquarianism, conservatism, reaction, refusal of history, escapism. Authentic Christian traditionalism remembers and maintains the past not because it is past, but because it is the only way to meet the future, to become ready for it."[7] In this, eschatology is no supplement to the study of Christian thought, rather the method needed in guiding each and every Christian teaching towards its aim: the kingdom of God. Likewise, the Metropolitan of Pergamon, John Zizioulas would hold that eschatology is not just an aspect of theology but "an approach, a methodological issue for theology."[8]

Orthodox theology, from its beginning, has taken on an eschatological orientation, and continues to view and judge history from the aim of Christian faith. Putting "remembering the future" at the center of doxology, as Pantelis Kalaitzidis suggests, means that only in the eschatological light can one:

> ...understand why the Divine Eucharist, in its authentic form, represents a foretaste of the eschaton and a proleptic manifestation of the

coming kingdom of God, the Kingdom of love, justice and freedom, since it entails 'the unity of all' and reconciliation, victory over the demonic and divisive spirit of authoritarianism, the overcoming of the law and power, and the decisive destruction of the power and tyranny of death.[9]

Historically, the contrary to this principle of doxological anamnesis became evident in how the church, particularly in the imperial setting of the Byzantine Empire, became an institutional entity that enjoyed all the political and economic privileges, and remained close to the imperial structure and authority in the spirit of what was called the "Byzantine symphonia," or the concept of the church and state as complementary to each other and working in close collaboration. A major risk of this sort of alliance was the attempt by the hierarchy of the church to imitate the order of the worldly government and its temptation to enjoy worldly power and privileges, forgetting the church's eschatological destiny.

Nevertheless, the authentic theological tradition of the church would direct its attention to transform politics and economics as well as the secular culture in light of its eschatological orientation and ultimate calling. Nicholas Berdyaev, prominent Russian émigré thinker and theologian, believes that the secular culture ultimately comes to a blind alley, and it is the responsibility of the church to bring hope to human civilization. True creativity arises from the Church's understanding of its spiritual vision and sense of transcendental destiny. Berdyaev writes:

> In a godless civilization the image of the human being and the freedom of the spirit will perish and creativity will dry up; already a barbarization is beginning. The church must once again save the spiritual culture and spiritual freedom of humanity." It is about the transfiguration of the world, receiving inspiration from the conviction that, "the kingdom of God is realized in eternity and in each moment of life, and its realization does not depend on the extent to which the power of evil outwardly prevails.[10]

Migration and Diaspora

In the twentieth century, Orthodox churches from different nations of Eastern Europe, Middle East, Africa, and Asia became the hosts of a large diaspora spreading into Western Europe, North America, Latin America, Persian Gulf Countries, North East Asia, Australia, and New Zealand. Outside of its home countries, Orthodoxy began to be known mainly through this diaspora. Orthodox Christians emigrated either by compulsion or voluntarily for various political, economic, educational, or commercial reasons. The emigration of the Orthodox from Russia and other East European countries in the former Soviet block to Western Europe was of great theological and historical significance.[11] While there were always Orthodox emigrants from the Ottoman Empire after the fall of Constantinople, the migration that occurred with the Bolshevik Revolution in Russia in 1917 made an important mark on the Roman Catholic and Protestant churches and the general population in the countries that received the immigrants.

Some highly educated theologians, thinkers, and teachers from Russia came to cities like Paris, Berlin, London, Belgrade, and Prague. The new immigrants brought with them the rich theological and liturgical tradition of Orthodoxy to the host countries. Institutes like St. Serge, St. Denys in Paris, as well as theological-spiritual initiatives like St. Alban and St. Sergius in England, created a new wave of theological reflection and sensitivity in Western Christianity and its Roman Catholic, Anglican, and Lutheran mainstreams. It also contributed enormously to the new ecumenical movement, particularly in the framework of the World Council Churches in Geneva. Orthodox theology played a decisive role in the Faith and Order movement and other areas of ecumenical theological reflection.

Great names like Bulgakov, Florovsky, Lossky, Berdyaev, Ouspensky, Afanassieff, Schmemann, and Meyendorff brilliantly interpreted Orthodox theological tradition to the Western world. These eminent teachers and a host of their disciples and converts to Orthodoxy witnessed what they generally called "the undivided Christian tradition" represented by the Orthodox Church. The emphasis was on the return to patristic sources, to the liturgy and its transcendental experience, to the eschatological orientation, and to the vision of beauty through the arts, especially its iconography. Orthodox believers made significant inroads into the monocultural West, in which religion and spiritual practice were swinging mainly between Roman Catholicism and Protestantism. Despite the fragile exilic condition of these immigrant communities, they brought a refreshingly holistic theology and a liturgical spirituality centered on the indomitable hope in the Risen Christ.

Although the Orthodox churches, particularly in the diaspora situation, had no missionary movement similar to the Western missionary initiatives, the witness of Orthodoxy was gently brought home to theological circles in the Western world, which had already entered a ruthless course of secularization. The distinguished converts to Orthodoxy, like lay theologian Olivier Clement and Timothy Ware (later Bishop Kallistos Ware), and Lev Gillet, inspired by the eminent émigré teachers, demonstrated the power of the spiritual, theological, and liturgical tradition of Eastern Christianity in their highly acclaimed writings and lectures.

The early immigrants brought with them a deep sense of loss and nostalgia for their home countries, cultures, and traditions. In these diaspora communities, the liturgical gathering for the celebration of the Eucharist and the major feasts of the church to a great extent compensated for their losses by fulfilling their deep desire to be rooted in the spiritual and cultural heritage of their home churches. As Ivana and Tim Noble describe it, and as Mother Skobtsova has argued, God's act of "kenosis" or self-emptying of God in Christ, brings about the "theosis" (divinization) of the human person. This theological understanding helps the immigrants look at their own condition in a new way. Their deprivation and alienation can be viewed from the perspective of God's self-emptying and compassionate love in Jesus Christ, and of Jesus' restoration of humanity and ultimate state of glory.[12] Consequently, today, many believers living in the diaspora think that their experience of migration is like a scattering of seeds. Quite likely, they hoped for some of these seeds to sprout, flourish, and bring forth fruit in unimaginable ways, for the glory of God and in witness to Jesus Christ, crucified and risen.

I remember the well-known Dominican theologian, M. D Chenu, leading a seminar at the Institut Catholique in Paris in the early 1970s and joyfully telling us students that the Russian Orthodox émigré theologians brought to Catholic France the joy of the resurrection of Christ as the pinnacle of Christian theology and experience rather than the sadness of suffering, pain, and crucifixion. This awareness has certainly contributed also to the Second Vatican Council and its theological reflection. In this regard, the Orthodox diaspora was reminiscent of the exile and captivity of Israel in alien empires, and how the exilic condition of the people fostered a great and creative prophetic dimension to the Jewish religion.

Migration and Hospitality

The apostolic tradition maintained that hospitality was one of the vital Christian virtues (Heb. 13:2; 1 Pet. 4:9; 1 Tim. 3:2). There is, however, nothing exclusively Christian about the place of hospitality in human society. An example of the appreciation of this virtue in the traditions of the "Abrahamic faith" is found in the book of Genesis 18. Abraham received into his tent three strangers who were passing by. He washed their feet, as was usual in ancient Middle Eastern practice of hosting visitors, and prepared them a sumptuous feast. He did it purely out of compassion to those travelers who were making the journey in the heat of the desert. It so happened that the three strangers whom Abraham received were angels of God. They were so pleased with the lavished welcome, and promised that the elderly couple, Abraham and Sarah, who had no children, would soon be raising their own child. The whole story of the Jewish nation is thus traced to the hospitality of this barren couple who became parents of a great nation.

In Orthodox theology, this biblical reference became particularly significant through the celebrated icon by Andrei Rublev, a Russian Orthodox iconographer of 15th century, who was canonized in the twentieth century as a saint. Reimagined beyond the biblical text, the philoxenia (hospitality) of Abraham, according to the patristic interpretation, prefigured the Holy Trinity. According to Rublev's icon, this passage symbolizes both "Three" and "One" in the figure of the three visitors. Since Orthodox iconography cannot represent any human form of God outside of the frame of incarnation, the three angels in the story are icons of the Father, Son and Holy Spirit, or of the three persons (*hypostases*) in one substance (*ousia*).

Rublev's Trinitarian icon is reminiscent of the migrant communities for whom hospitality is a central concern: how they were received and treated by the inhabitants of the host countries, and how they themselves responded as guests in unfamiliar circumstances. Obviously, the immigrants arriving in a country are not always unequivocally welcomed. They have to pass through barriers in language, culture, climate, health and education of children, finding a means for livelihood, and the general integration in the new environment. So hospitality assumes a broad meaning for the immigrants. Also the deplorable conditions of refugees and immigrants who are being driven out from their home countries are a sign of the increased scarcity of resources plaguing our world. Continuing wars, conflicts, and political and economic instability in different parts of the world turn hospitality, in addition to being a moral virtue, into a great international necessity. The mass exodus of refugees fleeing violence, oppression, and discrimination assumes gigantic proportions in today's world.

International political and economic relations as well as internal relations within various communities and national interest groups can fruitfully be reviewed in the light of a hospitality paradigm in which the guest and host respect and care for each other. Such has been the sentiment of perceptive individuals in several Orthodox migrant communities who seem to appreciate cultural hospitality as a new value. For them, the give and take of spiritual and material resources is key to the emergence of a new civilization based on justice, peace and love.

Diaspora, Mission and Witness

As noted by Bishop Kallistos Ware, there are today far more Orthodox Christians in major Western cities than in the historic centers of Eastern Christianity like Constantinople or Jerusalem.[13] He deems the twentieth-century Orthodox diaspora, not as an accident, rather as the moving force of God's providence and love. In fact, this gives to the Eastern Orthodox a great opportunity to live side by side with Westerners and other Christians for the first time, who can witness the catholicity of Orthodoxy. It also gives Orthodox believers an occasion to share the vision of truth with people of other faiths, thus opening a missionary dimension of the Orthodox faith.[13]

As we have seen, several Orthodox diaspora communities have deliberately taken upon themselves the task of witnessing to their faith in Christ in the new contexts in which they are placed. The United States seems to be the major host country for Orthodox immigrants of all ethnicities. Actually, the mission in America started in the eighteenth century, not through immigrants, but through the active evangelization of the Russian Orthodox Church in Iaska. Although many Orthodox communities retain their ethnic, liturgical, and cultural patrimony in present day America, there also emerged the autocephalous and local Orthodox Church of America (OCA) from different ethnic and cultural traditions of Eastern Orthodox immigrants to America as well. The self-awareness of this Church is that of a genuinely local Church, taking into serious account the language and context of contemporary America rather than those of an immigrant minority community.

Conclusion

The reality of migration in the present life of Orthodox churches is a powerful reminder to them, and to Christians at large, that their life can be compared to a pilgrimage and that they live like exiles and aliens. Therefore, many wise teachers in these Churches advocate the need to constantly review and reorder the Christian priorities in society. According to them, the church can exercise a prophetic vocation in discerning and redirecting the agenda of the secular world, in view of the values of the Kingdom of God. In its pilgrimage, the church needs to be particularly sensitive to the poor, the marginalized, and the vulnerable in every country. The Church can interpret the ancient virtues of hospitality, mutual respect, and care in relation to people of other faiths and of no faith. For the Christian church—as people of God, journeying with Christ in faith, hope, and love—the ultimate meaning of its migrant status on earth is to be revealed.

Taking into account the demographic situation of our contemporary world and the great injustice that globally reigns in matters of basic needs like food, clothing, shelter, education, human rights, and dignity, we may positively say, with due sensitivity to the great pain and suffering of all uprooted people, that migration, forced or willed, can lead to God renewing the face of the earth in our time.

Notes

1. It is conventional in ecumenical circles to distinguish the two families of Orthodox churches as Eastern and Oriental, the former referring to the churches in the Byzantine liturgical tradition, such as Greek, Russian, Rumanian and others, and the latter to the different Oriental churches like the Armenian, Coptic, Syrian, Ethiopian, Eritrean and Indian (Malankara). In spite of the Christological disputes around the Council of Chalcedon in AD 451, both families have now come to formal agreements regarding their common apostolic tradition and unity in Orthodox faith, though Eucharistic communion is yet to be restored. See K. M. George, "Oriental Orthodox—Orthodox Dialogue," in *Dictionary of the Ecumenical Movement*, eds. N. Lossky, et al., 757–759 (Geneva: WCC, 1991).
2. Gregory of Nazianzus, *On God and Christ: The Five Theological Orations and Two Letters to Cledonius* (New York: St.. Vladimir Seminary Press, 2002). See particularly Orations 27 and 28, in which Gregory outlines the method of theology typical of the Cappadocian Fathers. See also Kallistos Ware, *The Orthodox Way*, rev. ed. (New York: SVS Press, revised edition 1995), esp. 11–25.
3. Ware, *The Orthodox Way*, 121–122. See also K. M. George, *The Silent Roots: Orthodox Perspectives on Spirituality* (Geneva: WCC Publications 1994), 8–13.
4. See Ivana Noble and Timothy Noble, "Orthodox Theology in Western Europe in the Twentieth Century," in *European History Online* (2013), accessed March 10, 2014, http://ieg-ego.eu/en/threads/crossroads/religious-and-confessional-spaces/ivana-noble-tim-noble-orthodox-theology-in-Western-europe-in-the-twentieth-century.

5. The Revised Standard Version of the Bible is used throughout in this essay.
6. Clement of Rome, *Letter to the Corinthians*, in *The Faith of the Early Fathers Vol. 1*, sel. and trans. W. A. Jurgens (Bangalore: Theological Publications in India, 1992), 6–13.
7. *Letter to Diognetus*, in *The Faith of the Early Fathers Vol. 1, op.cit.* 40–42.
8. John Meyendorff, "Does Christian Tradition have a Future?" *St. Vladimir's Theological Quarterly* 26 (1982); quoted in P. Kalaitzidis, *Orthodoxy and Political Theology* (Geneva: WCC Publications, 2012), 89.
9. Quoted in *Orthodoxy and Political Theology, op.cit.* 105.
10. Kalaitzidis, *Orthodoxy and Political Theology*, 104.
11. Nicolas Berdyaev, "Salvation and Creativity: Two Understandings of Christianity," in *Western Spirituality: Historical Roots and Ecumenical Routes*, ed. M. Fox (Santa Fe Bear & Company, 1981), 133.
12. See Noble and Noble, *art. cit.* See also, Kallistos of Diokleia, "The Witness of the Orthodox Church in the Twentieth Century," *Sourozh—A Journal of Orthodox Life and Thought*, no. 80 (May 2000): 1–14.
13. See Noble and Noble, *art. cit.*
14. Kallistos of Diokleia, "The Witness of the Orthodox Church," 1–14.

Chapter 5

Embracing, Protecting, and Loving the Stranger: A Roman Catholic Theology of Migration

Peter C. Phan

From its very beginnings, observing the Jewish injunction of hospitality for the stranger (Deut 10:17–19; 24:17–18)[1] and remembering Jesus' foreign ancestors (Tamar, Rahab, Ruth, and Beersheba), his birth far from home (Lk 2:1–7), his and his family's escape to Egypt as refugees (Mt 2:13–14), his ministry as a homeless and itinerant preacher with nowhere to lay his head (Lk 9:58), his fate as an unwelcome stranger in his own country (Jn 1:11), and his self-identification with the stranger (Mt 25:35), Christianity has consistently inculcated *philoxenia*, that is, love of and hospitality to aliens, strangers, and migrants.

The author of First Peter, who directs his letter to "the exiles of the Dispersion" (1:1), reminds the Christians of northern and central Asia Minor that they are " aliens and exiles" (*paroikous kai parepiderous*), referring not only to their spiritual other-worldly condition but also to their social and economic status as migrant workers socially and ethnically marginalized in these regions (1 Pt 2:11). The Letter to the Hebrews speaks of Christians, like Abraham and Sarah, as "strangers and foreigners" (*xenoi kai parepidemoi*) on earth and seeking a better, that is, heavenly homeland (Heb 11:13–15). James addresses his letter to the "twelve tribes in the Dispersion"—an apt metaphor for Christians. Tellingly, the new religion is called *ho hodos* (the "Way" or the "Journey"), highlighting its character as a constant movement/migration (Acts 18: 25–26; 19:23; 22:4; 24:14, 22). Because Christians are themselves strangers, aliens, and *paroikoi* (literally "not-at-home"), the New Testament insistently and repeatedly urges Christians to practice that which all strangers need, that is, *xenophilia*—love of or hospitality to the stranger. (Mt 25:35, 38, 43, 44; 1Pt 4:9; Heb 13:2).[2]

In the patristic period (roughly from the second to the seventh century AD), Christians continued the migratory movement of the apostolic church, especially as they engaged in the task of announcing the "good news" to the ends of the earth. Five geographical areas were the main destinations of Christian migrations, where eventually Christians built a great number of vibrant and mission-oriented communities: Mesopotamia and the Roman province of Syria, Greece and Asia Minor, the Mediterranean countries, Egypt, and East Asia. In this missionary context, Christians' identity as "strangers and sojourners" was deeply and vividly ingrained in their consciousness. It was further intensified by martyrdom during the persecutions by the Roman Empire; later it is nurtured by the practice of monasticism. Even when Christianity was codified under Theodosius as the sole *religio licita* of the Roman Empire, Christians still maintained a profound sense of being migrants, powerfully and eloquently expressed by the anonymous *Letter to Diognetus*: "Christians live in their own countries, but only as aliens (*paroikoi*). They have a share in everything as citizens (*politai*), and endure everything as foreigners (*xenoi*). Every foreign land is their fatherland, and yet for them every fatherland is a foreign land."[3] Matching this consciousness of being-in-exile and being-in-migration with deeds, the early church spent much of its material resources to care for the strangers and the poor by means of charitable institutions such as *hospitia* and *xenodochia* (guest house) designed for social assistance and hospitality.

Ironically, in spite of the ancient roots of these reflections on the nature of Christianity as a migratory movement and its longstanding practices of hospitality for foreigners, a Christian, and more specifically, Catholic *theology of migration* is only of recent vintage—its beginnings since the middle of the nineteenth century—and is in fact still in its infancy. Like a migrant, it is very much an alien and a stranger in the citadel of Christian theology. As we will see, it took seismic world events that severely threatened the Catholic faith of migrants and jeopardized their physical and economic well-being for the leaders of the Catholic Church to pay heed to their plight as migrants and take steps to improve their lot.

This essay begins by tracing the roots of Catholic theology of migration in the papal *magisterium* [teaching authority], from Pope Pius IX (pope 1846–78) to Pope Benedict XVI (pope 2005–13). Next it examines some of the key official documents and highlights their most salient teachings on migration and the pastoral care for migrants. It ends by outlining the major themes and features of a contemporary Catholic theology of migration.[4]

Recent Popes and Migration, 1846–2013

The immediate context and stimulus for the popes' action in favor of migrants and papal teachings on migration is the great waves of continental and transoceanic migrations since the nineteenth century.[5] From 1800 to 1850, Europe experienced a dramatic demographic increase—from 150 to 220 million—which created enormous economic problems. The Industrial Revolution caused a massive migration within Europe, as people in search of work migrated from the country to the city, the new hub of commercial and industrial activities. As Europe was unable to meet all the demands for land and labor, migration to the other continents beckoned as an attractive albeit profoundly unsettling option. The United States' declaration of independence in 1776 opened the door for other countries in Latin America to claim independence as well, such as Argentina, Chile, Colombia, Venezuela, Peru, Brazil, and Mexico, all of which achieved national autonomy between 1816 and 1822. The reorganization and development of all these newly independent countries, in both North and South America, required a massive labor force, both free and slave, and therefore liberal policies of immigration were adopted to welcome migrant workers from all parts of the world.

In the nineteenth century, migration occurred in three distinct phases. In the first (1814–46), migrants came mostly from northern Europe (England and Scotland), and the main destinations were the United States and Canada and countries with warmer climates (Algeria, Australia, and New Zealand). In the second wave (1846–80), the migratory flows were more regular and steadier (about 400 thousand annually). Because of agricultural problems and famine, the Irish were the most numerous among migrants, followed by the English and the Scots (a total of 21 million from the British Isles), the Germans (5.6 million), the Scandinavians (2.5 million), and the French (2 million). The countries of destination included the United States, Venezuela, Mexico, Brazil, Argentina, Morocco, and Algeria. The third phase (1880–14) represents the climax of migration (800 thousand annually and 2 million in 1910). To the United States came not only the Anglo-Saxons but also people from eastern Europe (Ukrainians, Poles, Czechoslovaks, Russian Jews, and Austro-Hungarians), southern Europe (especially Italians, with 6 million within Europe and 8 million to the United States), China, and Japan. During this period, the United States took in 15 million Europeans, Argentina 3 million, and Brazil 2 million.[6]

Though the migration of Italians in the nineteenth century, especially to the United States, was not the largest among various national groups, it caught the attention of the popes, who sought to protect their Catholic faith against the dangers of Protestantism and secularism. Whereas the spiritual and material welfare of German Catholics was well looked after by their voluntary association, St. Raphaelsverein, established in 1871, both at their departure ports and in the destination countries, especially through "national parishes," Italian Catholics were largely left to their own devices.

Pius IX (pope 1846–1878)

At the invitation of Pius IX, several religious orders undertook missions to assist Italian migrants: the Pallottini in London, the Salesians in Argentina, and the Barnabites in Brazil. After his visit to Brazil in 1845, Bishop Gaetano Bedini recommended the erection of an apostolic vicariate for the Germans in Petropolis, and after his visit to the United States and Canada in 1853–54, the bishop did the same thing for the Italians, also proposing the founding of an institute in Rome to train the clergy to minister to migrants in their own languages.

Leo XIII (pope 1878–1903)

Leo XIII, much more socially and politically progressive than his predecessor, was deeply engaged in responding to the challenges of the modern world, especially in international and social matters, among which migration featured prominently. In his *Orientalium Dignitas* (1894) Leo insists on the respect due to the culture and religious traditions of the migrants, in this case Catholics of Eastern Rites, who were pressured into accepting the Latin rite, especially in the United States. The pope's concern led to the establishment of parishes and eparchies (dioceses) for Catholics of the Eastern Rites with their own priests and bishop in Canada, the United States, Brazil, and later, in Australia. In 1882, on the occasion of the Congress of Catholics in Naples, Leo XIII urged the founding of a philanthropic association in the model of the German St. Raphaelsverein for Italian migrants.

As the result of the pope's solicitude for the Italian migrants in the United States, and after the American bishops acknowledged at their plenary council in Baltimore in 1884 their inability to care for the Italians without a clergy who could speak their language, the Sacred Congregation for the Propagation of the Faith (now renamed as Congregation for the Evangelization of Peoples) appealed to the Italian bishops for help. Notable among those who responded positively is Bishop Giovanni Battista Scalabrini (1839–1905) of Piacenza, who founded the Congregation of Missionaries of Saint Charles (in 1887 for men and in 1895 for women) to work among the Italian emigrants in the United States and Brazil. In his 1888 apostolic letter, *Quam Aerumnosa*, Leo XII denounces migration as an evil, not only because it causes untold sufferings to the emigrants and their families, but also because it exposes them to the danger of the loss of faith, in countries such as the United States, due to the dominance of Protestantism and Freemasonry, and in Europe due to anarchy and atheistic socialism.

Pius X (pope 1903–14)

To promote spiritual assistance to migrants, in 1912, Pius X created within the Sacred Consistorial Congregation (now renamed as Congregation for Bishops) an office dedicated to the care of Roman Catholic migrants. He also envisaged the founding of a Pontifical College for the Formation of Priests for Italian emigrants, which was opened only in 1920, due to the First World War. Pius X, though aware of the potential conflicts between the native and migrant Catholics, especially in the United States, favored the erection of national parishes for migrants. Like Leo XIII's, the pope's major concerns were the threats of Protestantism, socialism, and Masonry to the Italian migrants' Catholic faith.

The First World War at first disrupted the transoceanic migration, but at its end there erupted a veritable flood of fugitives, refugees, and prisoners of war on the heels of the Russian Revolution, the breaking up of the Ottoman Empire, the persecutions of ethnic, political, and religious minorities (e.g., the Armenian genocide), and the redrawing of national boundaries. The war caused three million migrants in Europe alone. Furthermore, in 1919–1939, a million Turks, Greeks, Bulgarians, Romanians, Germans, and Poles migrated to the United States. In the post-war period, the birth of dictatorial regimes such as Russian bolshevism, Italian fascism, German nazism, Spanish francoism, and Portuguese salazarism, with their ruthless elimination of ideological and political opponents, caused fresh waves of migrants and refugees. On the other hand, during the Great Depression, there was a drastic contraction of the migratory flow to the United States, which in 1924 enacted the Immigration Act, introducing highly restrictive quotas for immigrants.

Benedict XV (pope 1914–21)

Benedict XV assumed the papacy on the eve of the First World War, which he attempted in vain to prevent through mediation among the warring countries. The pope had to deal with a huge migration problem. In 1918, he appointed a bishop for refugees in Italy, urged the European, especially German, bishops to undertake social activities like those of the *St. Rapahelsverein*, and entreated the American bishops to welcome and assist refugees who fled to the United States. Benedict XVI appointed a bishop for Italian migrants and opened the above-mentioned college for training Italian migrants as priests.

Pius XI (pope 1922–39)

The papacy of Pius XI coincided with the period between the two World Wars, during which there was a significant slowing down of migration. As a result of the restrictive 1929 Immigration Act in the United States (which allowed only 6,000 Italian entrants per year) and the anti-emigration policy of the Italian fascist government, the number of Italian migrants fell dramatically, from 250,000 annually in 1921–1930 to 50,000 annually between 1936 and 1940. Nevertheless, as migration persisted, the pope asked the bishops of eastern Europe, especially Poland, and the American bishops to intensify their care for refugees and migrants, especially Catholics of Eastern Rites. Furthermore, as Mexicans began to migrate to the United States, the pope also urged the bishops of both Mexico and the United States to provide them with assistance.

The lull in migration was dramatically broken by the Second World War, which was a truly global conflict, involving the Axis powers of Italy, Germany and Japan. The number of refugees, migrants, and forced laborers reached apocalyptic proportions worldwide, not counting the victims of the Nazi concentration camps and the bombings of Hiroshima and Nagasaki. Europe was divided into two blocs—the NATO and the Warsaw Pact—together with the redrawing of national boundaries, which forced huge migrations. Eight million people were displaced in the Federal Republic of Germany (West Germany), and 3 million in the German Democratic Republic (East Germany). The demand for workers in countries in northwestern Europe attracted migrants from countries in southern Europe (Italy,

Spain, Portugal, Greece, and later Yugoslavia and Turkey) as well as those of north Africa (Morocco, Algeria, and Tunisia). During the two decades after the Second World War, Italy lost 3.5 million of its citizens to migration during their flight from country to city and from south to north. Finally, the process of decolonization in Africa and Asia took place during the Cold War between the two superpowers, the United States and the Soviet Union, and added a huge multitude of migrants, both within and outside these two continents. It is in the context of these complex and tragic international events that the leaders of the Catholic Church formulated their doctrine on migration.

Pius XII (pope 1939–58)

Pius XII guided the Catholic Church during the Second World War and the Cold War. With regard to migration, he was the first pope to grasp all of the demographic, social, political, economic, moral, and spiritual dimensions of migration as a global phenomenon. His 1952 apostolic constitution *Exul Familia,* which we will discuss in the second part of this essay, has been rightly billed as the Magna Carta of the Catholic theology of migration and the Catholic Church's pastoral care of migrants. In his many radio messages, Pius XII affirms the right to emigrate, the right of migrants' to be reunited with their families, the universal destination of earthly goods, as well as the necessity of international organizations to protect the rights and well-being of migrants. While noting that emigration is an evil, the pope also acknowledges its benefits, such as acquisition of a better life, dialogue among cultures, and contributions to a common progress of humanity. Against restrictive immigration policies and xenophobic tendencies, the pope urges the creation of a public opinion favorable to migration and notes that migration is an international problem that can be resolved only by collective agreements.

The world of the 1960s rapidly underwent profound changes. The decolonization movement was in full swing; the opposition between the Global North and the Global South was growing; the first rumblings of the breaking up of the Soviet bloc were discernible; and the process of European unification had begun with the birth of the European economic community in the 1957 Treaty of Rome. Within the Catholic Church, despite the massive centralizing efforts by the popes and the Roman Curia since the First Vatican Council (1870), which defined papal infallibility and primacy as dogma, there were insistent voices demanding church reforms to meet the challenges of the times.

John XXIII (pope 1958-63)

The greatest contribution of Pope John XXIII to the Church is his convocation of the Second Vatican Council (1962–65), though he did not live to see its completion. Concerning migration, in his 1963 encyclical *Pacem in Terris* (Peace on Earth), which he published two years after the erection of the Berlin Wall and a few months after the Cuban Missile Crisis, John XXIII, like his immediate predecessor, places migration in the global geopolitical context, urging the circulation of capital and promoting actions by international organizations to achieve a better coordination among demographic growth, equitable distribution of material goods, and availability of work so as to avoid profound imbalances that are detrimental to human dignity and to moral and religious life. On the other hand, John XXIII also insists that the migrants have the duty to overcome the tendency to isolate in cultural ghettos, to learn about the history, culture, and religions of their host countries, and to contribute to the development of these countries from the resources of their own cultural and religious heritages.

Vatican II (1962-65)

Vatican II, the twenty-first and most important ecumenical council of the Catholic Church, enacted a process of *aggiornamento* (updating) of the Church. While it says little explicit about migration as such in its 16 documents, it had a profound impact on how migration and the migrants should be viewed through its teaching on the Church as "the people of God," the nature of the Church as "communion" of churches, and the collegial relationship among all the bishops as heads of particular churches and the pope as the head of the universal Church. In such an ecclesiology (theology of the church), the migrants, no matter where they are settled, are full members of the Church with rights to participate in the life of the local church.

In the 1970s several new features marked migration. First, there was the repatriation of European expatriates from the decolonized countries. In 1960–1970, 1.4 million French, 800,000 Portuguese, 330,000 English, 300,000 Dutch, 200,000 Italians and 100,000 Belgians returned home. Second, over 2 million people from formerly colonized countries in Africa and Asia emigrated to Europe.

Third, some Western countries of emigration now became countries of immigration, especially Italy, Spain, Portugal, and Greece. Fourth, migrants to the West brought with them their cultures and religions (in particular Islam, Buddhism, Hinduism, and Sikhism) and for the most part tended to preserve them, thus introducing cultural and religious pluralism into their countries of destination. This happened especially in the United States, where in 1965 the ethnic quota system was abolished (the Immigration and Nationality Act), enabling the dramatic influx of Asians who emigrated, mostly due to political instability in their home countries (the Chinese, Japanese, Koreans, Vietnamese, Cambodians, Pakistanis, and Indians). Fifth, restrictive immigration policies produced irregular migration, especially in the United States, where in the 1970s there were more than 10 million undocumented migrants, mostly from Mexico. Sixth, while European countries were closing their doors to migrants, in Asia, countries that were economically advanced or oil-rich but with small or declining demography (Brunei, Malaysia, Singapore, Japan, Saudi Arabia, and the Arab Emirates), imported the work force from poorer Asian countries such as the Philippines, Indonesia, China, India, and Vietnam. Finally, the African continent was in full transformation. The wars of anti-colonial liberation, the establishment of dictatorial regimes, the exploitation of mineral riches, the apartheid system in South Africa, and regional, interregional and tribal conflicts produced a steady stream of refugees and migrants.[7]

Paul VI (pope 1963–78)

It was in this turbulent context that Paul VI, who brought Vatican II to an end, developed his theology of migration in his many encyclicals on social matters and instituted policies of the pastoral care of migrants. The pope founded new ecclesial organizations to defend human dignity, and more specifically that of migrants, such as the Pontifical Council for Justice and Peace, the Pontifical Council *Cor Unum* for Human and Christian Development, and the Pontifical Commission for the Pastoral Care of Migrants and Tourism (later renamed as Pontifical Council for the Pastoral Care of Migrants and Itinerant People). On the doctrinal level, on August 15, 1969 Paul VI issued a *motu proprio* (personal rescript) entitled *Pastoralis migratorum cura* (The Care of Migrants) and charged the Congregation of Bishops to undertake an updating of Pius XII's above-mentioned constitution *Exul Familia*. On August 22, 1969, the congregation issued the instruction *De Pastorali migratorum cura* (On the Pastoral

Care of Migrants). This document, which will be discussed below, constituted, at the time of its publication, the most comprehensive teaching and practice of the Catholic Church on migration. In addition, in 1971 Paul VI issued the apostolic letter *Octogesima Adveniens* in commemoration of the eightieth anniversary of Pope Leo XIII's influential encyclical *Rerum Novarum*, in which he asserts the right to emigrate and the necessity to work toward integrating the migrants into the host society, promoting their professional development, and ensuring their access to a decent life.

The 1990s saw the emergence of a "new world order," and as a result, migration took on a new contour. Thanks to globalization, practically *all* countries became countries of emigration, transition, and immigration at one time or another. Migrants came from all parts of the world and moved in all directions. From sub-Saharan Africa, where tribal, ethnic, and racial violence repeatedly broke out, came streams of refugees. From Central America, due to political upheavals and economic poverty, a steady flow of refugees poured out either toward the north or to other South American regions. In Southeast Asia, countries that enjoyed an economic boom, such as China, India, and the so-called Asian Tigers, imported unskilled, often exploited, workers. The collapse of Communism in 1989 injected into the global labor market the populations of the countries of the former Soviet Union and Eastern Europe. The internecine war in the former Jugoslavia produced a huge number of refugees and exiles in the very heart of Europe. The Iran-Iraq War (1980–88) and the first Gulf War (1990–91) wrought untold devastation in the Middle East. The oil-producing Arab countries imported workers from nearby countries (Palestine, Yemen, Jordan, and Egypt) as well as from Asian countries (3.2 million Indians, 1.8 million Pakistanis, 800,000 Bangladeshis, 700,000 Filipinos and Sri Lankans). In this New World Order, dominated by the capitalist economy and aided by the World Bank and the International Monetary Fund, migration, forced and voluntary, permanent and temporary, national and international, is a global fact of life and contributes not a little to the creation of the disorder in the New World Order.

John Paul II (pope 1978–2005)

John Paul II, the first non-Italian to be elected to the papacy since the death of Adrian VI in 1523, was dedicated to the transformation of the globalization of economic competition into the globalization of solidarity and to the defense of human dignity and human rights.

It is in this context that his concern for migration and migrants must be viewed. In his speech to the United Nations in 1979, John Paul II strenuously defends the right of everyone to free movement and to migration, both internal and external, to residence and nationality, to political participation, and to cultural development. These rights apply in a special way to migrants and refugees as migration constitutes, according to the pope, perhaps the greatest tragedy of our time. Forced migration is, in the pope's arresting phrase, equivalent to "civil death." In addition to refugees, the pope is also concerned about migrant workers, both regular and irregular, and urges the State and the Church to find means, legal and economic, to prevent all types of discrimination against them. John Paul II's speech also reminds the host countries of the contributions migrants make not only with their labor but also with their cultural traditions. In his 1981 encyclical, *Laborem Exercens* (On Human Work), the pope points out that migration not only constitutes a loss for the country of emigration but also is an evil for the migrants and their families, insofar that it exposes them to a series of moral evils associated with discrimination. Nevertheless, the pope acknowledges that migration may be a beneficial thing and argues that the right to emigrate belongs not only to individuals but also to their families. Furthermore, according to the pope, the total well-being of migrants requires that the state and the Church facilitate migrants' integration into both without forcing them to renounce their cultural and religious heritages.

Throughout his teaching on migration, John Paul II was deeply aware that it is a complex and accelerating phenomenon with global dimensions. In contrast to a purely economic perspective of globalization that sees the migrants simply as a useful tool of production, the pope insisted that there should be a "culture of interdependence in solidarity" calling for a politics of welcome and collaboration among states. It was under John Paul II's pontificate and with his approval that the Pontifical Council for the Pastoral Care of Migrants and Itinerant People issued on May 3, 2004 an instruction entitled *Erga Migrantes Caritas Christi* (The Love of Christ Towards Migrants), the Catholic Church's most comprehensive and landmark treatment of the problem of migration and the pastoral care of migrants to date. We will discuss this document at great length in the next part of this essay.

Benedict XVI (pope 2005–2013)

Having spent almost his entire life in academia and in the Roman Curia, Pope Benedict XVI did not have firsthand experience with migration. Furthermore, his papacy was consumed by internal church problems such as the clergy sex abuse scandals, financial irregularities at the Institute for the Works of Religion (also known as the Vatican Bank), church schisms (e.g., the Society of St. Pius X), and various unfortunate incidents (e.g., the Vatileaks). Citing his health and age, Benedict resigned from the papacy effective February 28, 2013, paving the way for the election of the Jesuit Jorge Bergoglio, archbishop of Buenos Aires, Argentina, to the papacy on March 13, 2013, who chose the name Francis.

As a theologian, Benedict XVI is a prolific writer, but his pre-papacy writings on migration are minimal. As pope, however, he addressed the issue of migration, especially in his messages on the World Day of Migration. In the message for the 92nd World Day of Migration, Benedict XVI recognizes that migration is a "sign of the time." He notes the "feminilization" of migration and condemns sex trafficking by the sex industry. In his 2006 speech to the members of the Pontifical Council for the Pastoral Care of Migrants and Itinerant People, he singles out the migration of Muslims and calls for respect for their cultural and religious traditions. In his message on the 93rd Day of World Migration, the pope recalls the international convention for the protection of the rights of all the migrant workers and their families. In his message for the 94th Day, he refers to the migration of youth and their difficulty of double-belonging, that is, to their native culture and that of the host country. In the message on the 95th Day, he singles out the example of the apostle Paul the Migrant and emphasizes how the work of evangelization should lead to the unity of all peoples without distinction of nationality and culture. Finally, in his 2009 encyclical, *Caritas in Veritate* (Love in Truth), Benedict XVI urges that to the de facto interdependence among people of today there should correspond an ethical and spiritual interaction to ensure a truly human development. In this context, the pope affirms that the problem of migration in all its social, economic, political, cultural, and religious dimensions can be resolved only by means of a politics of international collaboration among the countries of emigration and those of immigration.

Major Documents of the Catholic Church on Migration

Part of the method of Catholic theology is *auditus fidei* (hearing of faith), that is, a listening-in-faith to the Bible and Tradition in which the Bible is interpreted and lived. Tradition includes the authoritative teaching of the episcopal or hierarchical *magisterium* (teaching authority), consisting of, but not limited to, the pope, the various offices of the Roman Curia, the national conferences of bishops, and individual bishops. There is also the *magisterium* of theologians whose specific task is to examine the Christian beliefs critically and systematically and to propose an *intellectus fidei* (understanding of faith), that is, an understanding of Christian beliefs that is both adequate to the faith and appropriate to the contemporary culture. There is finally a third *magisterium*, namely, the *sensus fidei* (the sense of faith) or the *sensus fidelium* (the sense of the faithful), that is, the understanding and living of faith exhibited by all the faithful, the overwhelming majority of whom are lay—especially the poor—in our case, the migrants themselves, who can teach the Church what migration means. Ideally, the three *magisteria* should function in collaboration, enriching and correcting each other, for the sake of an ever more adequate understanding and effective living of the faith. In this section, we will examine the three most important documents of the episcopal *magisterium* mentioned above, with greater attention given to the third. In the final section, we will rely on the teaching of theologians and migrants to elaborate a Catholic theology of migration.*Exul Familia* As mentioned above, Pius XII's apostolic constitution *Exul Familia* (the Migrant Family, 1952) is the first official document of the Catholic Church that treats migration in all its various dimensions: social, economic, cultural, demographic, political, anthropological, moral, and religious.[8] For this reason, it has been billed as the Magna Carta of Catholic theology of migration. The title of the constitution, *Exul Familia*, refers to the Holy Family of Joseph, Mary, and Jesus, which fled into Egypt to avoid the persecution by Herod, and is taken by Pius XII as the archetype and protector of every refugee family.

Exsul Familia

Exsul Familia came out at a highly opportune moment, as there were an estimated 12.6 million displaced persons and refugees in various West European countries as the result of World War II. It is composed of two parts, historical and normative. In the first part, the pope rehearses the various past interventions of the Catholic Church in favor of migrants up to the period of his pontificate. The normative part presents a canonical basis for new structures and forms of pastoral care to assist Catholic migrants of the Latin Rite. It affirms the principles that migrants have the right to appropriate pastoral care by clergy of their own language and country who are respectful of their culture and able to assist them in the process of incorporation into the country of destination.

The new policies and structures ushered in by *Exul Familia* include 1. establishment within the Sacred Consistorial Congregation of a Superior Council for Migration to be led by a Delegate for Works for Migration whose task is to coordinate the activities of the national episcopal commissions; 2. appointment of the Delegate for Works for Migration by the secretariat of state, whose job is to confer the certificate of "Missionary for Migrants" and "Chaplain on Board" and keep contact with the local bishops; 3. appointment of a national director by the Sacred Consistorial Congregation in each country or group of countries whose job is to promote and coordinate the activities of the missionaries for migrants but who however does not have juridical authority over the missionaries and the missions themselves.

The central figures in these new arrangements by *Exul Familia* are the missionary for migrants and the chaplain on board. The missionary for migrants is a diocesan or religious priest who has received from the Sacred Consistorial Congregation the certificate attesting to such a function and is permitted by the local bishop to act as "personal parish priest" or as "missionary with the care of souls." The chaplain on board functions as a parish priest within the territory of the ship for all Catholic passengers and throughout the trip.

In this connection, *Exul familia* proposes three specific pastoral structures:

1) "Parishes according to languages and nationalities," the establishment of which requires an indult of the Sacred Consistorial Congregation, similar to already existing "national parishes";
2) "Missions for the care of souls," which may be established according to the pastoral needs of the communities of migrants and for the establishment of which an indult of the Sacred Consistorial Congregation is not required;
3) Appointment of a missionary or chaplain for the migrants with such faculties granted by the local bishop as needed for their ministry.

Exul Familia

marks a significant step forward in the Catholic Church's understanding of the phenomenon of migration and its pastoral care of migrants. However, its perspective was still limited to the Italian migration, and the structures it set up were highly centralized. As a result, it was not able to deal with migration as an international phenomenon and the pastoral care for migrants was not regarded as involving the whole local church.

De Pastorale Migratorum Cura

This 1969 instruction of the Congregation of Bishops, as was mentioned above, was intended as an update on *Exul Familia*.[9] It goes beyond its predecessor in providing a wider, more international perspective on migration and employs an ecclesiology derived from Vatican II that places a greater role on the laity in pastoral care. It defends the human rights of the migrants and condemns every form of discrimination against them. It asserts the right of every person to emigrate and the duty of states to welcome them and integrate them into their societies, though the states have the right to regulate immigration. On the other hand, the instruction also emphasizes that the migrants have the duty to contribute to the common good of their new countries.

With regard to church structures, the instruction continues to endorse the establishment of "personal parishes" and "missions for the care of souls" according to the various needs of the migrants. On the international level, the care of migrants falls under the responsibility of the Congregation of Bishops (the new name of the Sacred Consistorial Congregation), and within it, under the Superior Council for Migration presided by the Delegate for Works for Migrants. At the level of national Conferences of Bishops, there should be an Episcopal Committee for Migration, and its executive secretary is the national director. In countries of emigration, the bishops are encouraged to institute diocesan offices of migration composed of clergy and laity to assist emigrants. In countries of destination, it is the responsibility of the local bishop to determine what needs to be done in the pastoral care for migrants and the means for it (personal parishes or missions for the care of souls, for instance). Religious societies, both male and female, are encouraged to engage in such pastoral work. In line with Vatican II's ecclesiology, the instruction devotes a chapter to the role of the laity, whose work is indispensable in welcoming and integrating the migrants into their communities, both ecclesial and civil, fostering legislation in defense of their human rights, and assuring that migrants are treated as human beings and not simply means of production.

The newness of *De Pastorale Migratorum Cura* consists precisely in this emphasis on the responsibility of *all* members of the

Church, especially that of the laity, in the pastoral care of migrants. Unfortunately, however, there is a residual clericalism, endemic to the Catholic Church, in the organization of the various structures for the care of migrants. Furthermore, its perspective remains that of pastoral caring for migrants emigrating from a Catholic country to a Catholic country. An ecumenical and interreligious breath is still missing.

Erga Migrantes Caritas Christi

The emergence of increasingly multicultural, multi-ethnic, and multireligious societies due to worldwide migrations at the end of the twentieth century produced new challenges and problems demanding effective policies and concerted action. For example, at the international level, many international organizations to protect the rights of workers were founded, such as the International Labour Organization (which received the Nobel Peace Prize in 1969), and several documents came out of the United Nations High Commissioner for Refugees, notably *Convention Relating to the Status of Refugees* (1951), *Protocol Relating to the Status of Refugees* (1967), and *International Convention on the Protection of the Rights of All Migrant Workers and Members of Their Families* (1990). It is in this context that the Pontifical Council for the Pastoral Care of Migrants and Itinerants issued in 2004 the instruction *Erga Migrantes Caritas Christi*.[10] The document, which is the lengthiest of the three examined here, has the richest and most mature reflections of the Catholic Church on migration and its pastoral care of migrants.

The document is composed of four parts. The first part recognizes the challenge of human mobility as expressed in international and domestic migration as a "sign of the times" and presents a theology of migration in the context of the history of salvation and that of the Catholic Church. The second part deals with the pastoral care of welcoming migrants in general and especially Catholic migrants of the Latin Rite, those of the Eastern Rites, and Christian migrants of other Churches and ecclesial communities. The third part discusses various kinds of church personnel engaged in pastoral care for migrants in the home as well as host churches. The fourth part discusses the church structures and organizations in the pastoral care of migrants and ends with a list of 22 juridical pastoral regulations.

Several salient features of this document deserve special notice. First, pastoral care for migrants is no longer understood as a special ministry for a few people in the Church but is inserted into the general pastoral ministry of the Church. This insertion is necessary not only to make the pastoral care for the migrants more effective but also to transform the Church as a whole into a welcoming home to them. In this way, the Church becomes truly a house for all, a place of communion, solidarity, reconciliation, mutual welcome, and a community for authentic human and Christian development.

Second, pastoral care for migrants is presented not as an optional act of charity but an obligatory fulfillment of the migrants' fundamental right, based on their baptism, to be full members of the Church and active participants in its life. In this way, the migrants offer the Church the opportunity to grow in the four marks of the true Church: "unity" not as uniformity but as communion in diversity, "holiness" in its practice of love toward the strangers, "catholicity" in its ethnic, ritual, and cultural pluralism, and "apostolicity" in its mission to all peoples.

Third, the instruction, while deeply aware of the negative impact of migration, also points out more clearly than the previous documents not only the benefits that migration brings to individual migrants and their families but also the opportunity to build a new global multiethnic, multilingual, multicultural, and multireligious community of mutual solidarity and enrichment through an intercultural dialogue.

Fourth, the instruction envisages new ecclesial structures in response to this globalized migration. These include intercultural, interethnic, and interritual parishes, local parishes with special services to members of diverse ethnicity and rites, youth centers, formation centers for pastoral workers with ministry to migrants, and study centers with special courses on the phenomenon of migration.

Fifth, in contrast to the previous two documents, *Erga Migrantes Caritas Christi* devotes much attention to Catholic migrants of the Eastern Rites coming from eastern Europe and Asia, to Christian but non-Catholic migrants, and to non-Christian migrants, especially Muslims. These three groups of migrants afford the Catholic Church the opportunity to preserve the cultural and religious heritage of Catholics of Eastern Rites, ecumenical dialogue with non-Catholic Christians, and interreligious dialogue with the followers of other religions.

There are, however, areas in which the instruction, despite its admirable achievements, needs correction and improvement. One such area is interreligious dialogue. No doubt the presence of non-Christian migrants, especially Muslims, in the midst of Christian communities presents serious challenges. In spite of its significant improvement over its predecessors, the instruction's attitude toward non-Christian migrants still remains defensive, given the Catholic

Church's conviction that it is the "ordinary means of salvation" and that it alone possesses the fullness of the means of salvation. The norms set by the instruction for the use of Catholic places of worship and Catholic schools by non-Christians and for interreligious marriage are unduly restrictive. Furthermore, the "principle of reciprocity," which the instruction advocates—that non-Christian governments should extend to Christians the same religious freedom that the Christian Church extends to non-Christians—fails to sufficiently recognize the precarious, marginalized, threatened, and endangered condition of non-Christian migrants in the West.[11]

Toward a Catholic Theology of Migration

On the basis of the teachings of the Bible and of the Catholic hierarchical *magisterium* on migration as well as of the insights of the *magisteria* of contemporary theologians and migrants, it is possible to offer a sketch of a Catholic theology of migration. "Theology of migration" means not simply a theology *about* migration or human mobility but a theological reflection using the history of migration and the experiences of migrants as its *locus theologicus* or source. As a consequence, the teachings of the Bible and the hierarchical *magisterium* on migration will be interpreted as well as enriched, and when necessary, corrected by the concrete experiences of migrants. As alluded to at the beginning of this essay, such a theology is still in its infancy due to the fact that the number of theologians who are themselves migrants or work with migrants, as well as the number of pastoral ministers who reflect theologically on their work in the field of migration, still remains small. In what follows, only a schematic outline—as was implied in the "Toward" in the title of this section—of a Catholic theology of migration can be offered, and it is to read in conjunction with the other essays in this book on the theologies of migration espoused by the other two Abrahamic religions.

A Multidisciplinary and Intercultural Approach

As migration has been recognized as a sign of the times, Catholic theology, following Vatican II's practice of "reading the signs of the times and of interpreting them in the light of the Gospel,"[12] has adopted a multidisciplinary approach as the most fruitful way to construct a theology of migration. This means that in addition to properly theological disciplines such as biblical study, church history, systematics, and practical theology, a theology of migration must first derive its data from such disciplines as sociology, geography, demography, anthropology, psychology, history, politics, and legislation of migration, and especially the life stories of the migrants themselves. In this way, theologians, especially if they themselves are not migrants or do not share their day-to-day lives with migrants, may have a deep appreciation of and empathy with the migrant's situation of displacement and suffering, of being betwixt-and-between worlds in their everyday life. The migrant's experiences are narrated not only in words, in private conversation or public witness, in novel or short story, in prose or poetry, but also in song, drama, ritual, symbolization, visual art, and folklore.

As a result, the theologian will develop a multi- and intercultural epistemology of seeing from the margins and the underside of reality. The first step of a theology of migration then is a sociopolitical and cultural analysis of migration, one that is not simply based on abstract numbers and grand theories of migration but is deeply rooted in the flesh and blood stories of migrants as human beings whose dignity and rights have often been trampled upon. This "socio-analytic mediation" is followed by the "hermeneutic mediation," by which life stories of migrants, sociological, historical, and cultural data, and theories of migration are given a properly theological meaning. This is done both by interpreting these data in the light of the teachings of the Bible and the episcopal *magisterium*, and by interpreting and evaluating these teachings in the light of what can be learned from the social sciences and the experiences of migrants. Thus, there must be a mutual illumination, complementation and, when necessary, correction between the sources of faith and secular knowledge.

The third step of the theology of migration is "practical mediation." In this mediation, the theological understanding of migration is brought to fruition by the theologian's "option for the poor," in this case, "option for the migrant." This option must not, of course, remain at the level of empty or romanticizing rhetoric but must be translated into the theologian's concrete actions with and for the migrants. Such an option for the migrant as such does not of course validate the truth of a particular theology of migration, nor, it must be added, does a particular theology of migration validate a specific action in the option for the migrant here and now. In other words, whether one practices what one holds does not make what one holds true or false, just as whether one holds what one practices does not make what one practices good or bad. The relationship between theory (orthodoxy) and practice (orthopraxis) is not one of reciprocal epistemological and axiological justification (true or false and good or bad) but rather one of mutual fecundation (dynamic theory or uninformed action): Does theory (orthodoxy) enable a good practice (orthopraxis), and does good practice (orthopraxis) produce a deeper understanding (orthodoxy)? There is therefore a dialectical tension between praxis and theory: praxis exerts pressure on theory to critically evaluate itself; theory, in turn, reacting, modifies praxis; next, theory and praxis are transcended in search of a more adequate understanding and more effective practice; and the spiraling never-ending circular movement goes on and on.[13]

Thus, a Catholic theology of migration must first begin with a scientifically informed and up-to-date understanding of the phenomenon of migration in all its dimensions, then engage in a hermeneutics of the contemporary data on migration in the light of the sources of the Christian faith and vice versa, and finally test the fecundity of this theology of migration in a practice with and for the migrants with an eye toward developing a richer theology of migration itself, which in turn leads to another more effective practice. With this method, a Catholic theology of migration does not simply formulate a theology *about* migration. Rather, with migration as the searching light and as a *locus theologicus*, it revisits the traditional *loci theologici* and raises the basic question: How do migration and the migrant's experiences challenge and enrich our traditional conceptions of the Christian faith? In light of migration as the existential characteristic of our human condition, a theology *of* migration asks: Who is God (Trinitarian theology)? Who is Jesus (Christology)? Who is the Holy Spirit (pneumatology)? Who is a human being (anthropology)? What makes a Christian (spirituality)? What is salvation (soteriology)? What do we hope for (eschatology)? What is the Church (ecclesiology)? How do we worship (liturgy and sacramentology)? How do we relate to non-Christians (interreligious dialogue)? How do we behave and act (theological ethics/moral theology)? How do we minister to others, in and outside the Church (pastoral theology and missiology)? How do we preach the Good News (homiletics)? How do we teach and transmit the faith (catechetics)? How do we theologize (theology)?

Answering these and other questions while keeping migration and migrants front and center entails a radical reformulation of Christian theology and most likely requires a collaborative effort, since rarely can a single theologian master all these different fields and disciplines. In what follows, I will not deal with all of these issues and can do no more than sketch the barest outline of a Catholic theology of migration.[14]

Deus Migrator, *God the Primordial Migrant*

Christian theology is speaking about God as God is manifested in God's intention and action for humanity and the world, as well as about realities insofar as they are related to God. From what God has done in the world—theologians call this God the "Economic Trinity" or "God for us"— we try to get a glimpse into who God is—in theological parlance, the "Immanent/Transcendent Trinity" or "God in Godself." Etymologically, theology is *logos* (word) about *theos*, a human discourse about God made possible and authorized by God's own speech to humanity, that is, God's self-revelation in history. In fact, we can only speak about God because God has spoken to us first. Our *theologia* is rooted in God's own theologia. Though God's Logos is spoken always and everywhere, especially in religions and their founders and prophets, God has spoken through God's Spirit, according to the Christian faith, in a special way to the people of Israel, and in a final and definitive way in Jesus of Nazareth, who is called God's incarnated Logos. God's words and deeds in history have been recorded in writings—the Bible—that Christians regard as inspired and containing all the truths necessary for their salvation.

Because God is Absolute Mystery, to use the German theologian Karl Rahner's expression, our speech about God, even the most learned, is nothing but a stammering, by means of analogies, to describe who God is, or to be more precise, what and who God is *not*. As mystics and proponents of negative theology do not tire of reminding us, all language about God is by way of affirmation, negation, and transcendence. For instance, we *affirm* that God is "father." At the very same moment, we *deny* that God is "father" in the way all the fathers we know in our experience are. Further, we *transcend* both our affirmation and negation by saying that God is "father" in the sense that God possesses all the good qualities of a "father," shorn of all imperfections, but to an infinite degree (God is infinitely "father"). If asked what we mean by that, we must confess we do not know. There is an inherent agnosticism (non-knowledge) in our *gnosis* (knowledge) of God. Thus, our knowledge about God is, to use Nicolas of Cusa's expression, *docta ignorantia* (learned ignorance), and all our talk about God ends in silence, and for believers, adoration.

Because of this intrinsic deficiency of human language about God, it is necessary to use a variety of metaphors, images, and analogies to speak of God. Some of these are "authorized"— that is, used and licensed by the Bible—and therefore should not be discarded without cause. Others are not, but they must be used either to counteract the abuses of biblically licensed images detrimental to human dignity (for example, the use of the "fatherhood" of God to bolster patriarchy and androcentrism) or to expand our understanding of God (for example, the use of feminine and motherly images in speaking of God).

It is in this context that a theology of migration can refer to God as *Deus Migrator* (God the Migrant) or "the Primordial Migrant." Of course, the threefold movement of affirmation-negation-transcendence in God-talk must also be applied here: God *is*, is *not*, and is *infinitely* a migrant. With this caution in mind, we can explore how the Christian God can be thought of as the "God the Migrant" or "Migratory God." Even though the term "migrant" is not explicitly used of God in the Bible, there are hints suggesting that God possesses the characteristics commonly associated with migration and migrants.

Migration means movement, and the Christian God is a "mover" par excellence. To explain the possibility of change in the world, Aristotle argues that in order for there to be movement at all, there must be *ho ou kinoumenon kinei* (the Unmoved Mover), *proton kinoun akineton* (the Prime Mover Unmoved), *protaitios* (the First Cause), that which moves everything in the universe but is itself not moved by any prior action. Subsequently, classical metaphysics of substance portrays God as immutable and impassible (the Unmoved). But it does not follow from the notion of "Unmoved" that God cannot be conceived as living and hence, "moving" since, as Aristotle himself puts it, "life also belongs to God; for the actuality of thought is life, and God is that actuality, and God's essential actuality is life most good and eternal. We say therefore that God is a living being, eternal, most good, so that life and duration continuous and eternal belong to God; for this *is* God."[15]

It is to be noted that in denying change and suffering in God, the intent is to affirm God's absolute perfection or God's eternal and perfect life. What is denied is the idea that there is within God change as increase from imperfection to perfection, from lack to fullness (or as Aristotle puts it, from potency to act), or loss of perfection and fullness. But this denial does not entail that God cannot and does not "move," "change," and "suffer," not out of necessity or chance but out of God's own free will and out of love. At any rate, whatever philosophical arguments can be mounted in defense of God's immutability and impassibility, from the point of view of the Christian faith in God's creation of the world, and especially in God's incarnation in Jesus of Nazareth, it is incontrovertible that there are "events" or "movements" in God. These events or movements, while not necessarily entailing increase or loss of divinity and temporality in the sense of successive moments of time in God, do affirm a real movement within God from a non-creative God to a creative God (whose creative act occurred with, and not before or after, the creation of time) and from an unincarnated God to an incarnated God (whose becoming-human occurred in the "fullness of time"). I submit that these two movements in God may be interpreted as God's migratory acts.

First, God's creative act can be interpreted as God's migration out of what is divine into what is not, a movement that bears all the marks of human migration. In creating that which is other than Godself, God crosses the border between Absolute Spirit and finite matter, migrating from eternity to temporality, from omnipotence into weakness, from self-sufficiency (aseity) to utter dependence, from secure omniscience to fearful ignorance, from the total domination of the divine will over all things to the utter subjection of the same will to the uncontrollability of human freedom, from life to death. In the creative act, God experiences for the first time the precarious, marginalized, threatened, and endangered condition of the migrant.

Thus, the migrant is not only the *imago Dei*, as any other human being equally is, created in the image and likeness of God, which is the ontological ground of the human rights. As such, the migrant possesses all the human rights which must be respected by all.[16] However, as imago Dei, the migrant does not enjoy any stronger claim to human dignity and human rights than the citizens of the host country, or anyone else for that matter.[17] What is distinctive and unique about the migrant is that he or she is the *imago Dei migratoris*: the privileged, visible, and public face of the God who chooses, freely and out of love, to migrate from the safety of God's eternal home to the strange and risky land of the human family, in which God is a foreigner needing embrace, protection, and love. Thus, when the migrant is embraced, protected, and loved, the migratory God—*Deus migrator*—is embraced, protected, and loved. By the same token, when the migrant as imago Dei migratoris is rejected, marginalized, declared "illegal," imprisoned, tortured, or killed, it is the original of that image, the Deus migrator, who is subjected to the same inhuman and sinful treatment.

Second, the Incarnation of God's Word in Jesus of Nazareth can equally be regarded as God's migratory movement.[18] Indeed, if Duns Scotus's, rather than Thomas Aquinas's, theology of the Incarnation is followed, the Incarnation is to be understood not as simply God's emergency plan after humanity's fall into sin, but rather as the *telos* and culmination of God's first migration into creation. In this migration into history as a Jew in the land of Palestine, God, like a human migrant, entered a far country where God, as part of a colonized nation, encounters people of different racial, ethnic, and national backgrounds, with strange languages, unfamiliar customs, and foreign cultures, among whom God, again like a migrant after a life-threatening journey, "pitched the tent" or "tabernacled" (*eskenosev*, John 1:14).

Furthermore, as truly divine and truly human, the incarnated Logos, like the migrant, dwelt betwixt-and-between two worlds, acting as a mediator between God and humans. Not unlike the migrant, the incarnated Logos is rooted both in his native country (divinity) and makes a new home as a stranger in the land of Israel (his Jewish humanity), acquiring thus a double identity and a double belonging (he is both divine and Jewish), so that he is no longer just divine and yet not just human. Consequently, the traditional doctrine of *unio hypostatica* in Jesus (the unity of the two "natures"—divine and human—in the one "person" of the Logos) should not be taken to mean a kind of static joining of two opposite ontological states but a dynamic movement back and forth between them, just as the migrant has to move and "mediate" constantly between the two existential conditions of being this-and-that.

Jesus the Paradigmatic Migrant

As the Logos/Son of God made flesh, Jesus of Nazareth is the perfect imago Dei Migratoris, and to paraphrase Hebrews 1:3, the "reflection of the glory" of God the Migrant and the "exact imprint of God's very being" as a migrant. At the beginning of this essay, I alluded to Jesus' status as a stranger and migrant in his own country: his foreign ancestors (Tamar, Rahab, Ruth, and Beersheba), his birth far from home (Lk 2:1–7), his and his family's escape to Egypt as refugees (Mt 2:13–14), his ministry as a homeless and itinerant preacher with nowhere to lay his head (Lk 9:58), his fate as an unwelcome stranger in his own country (Jn 1:11), and his self-identification with the stranger (Mt 25:35).

Suffice it to add here that Jesus carried out his ministry at the margins of his society. A migrant and border-crosser at the very roots of his being, Jesus performed his ministry of announcing and ushering in the kingdom of God always at the places where borders meet, and hence at the margins of the two worlds separated by their borders. A marginal Jew himself, he crossed these borders back and forth repeatedly and freely, whether they were geographical, racial, sexual, social, economic, political, cultural, or religious. What is new about his message about the kingdom of God, which is good news to some and scandal to others, is that for him it removes all borders, both natural and man-made, as barriers and is absolutely all-inclusive. Jews and non-Jews, men and women, the old and the young, the rich and the poor, the powerful and the weak, the healthy and the sick, the clean and the impure, the righteous and the sinners, and any other imaginable categories of peoples and groups: Jesus invited them all to enter into the house of his merciful and forgiving Father. Even in his "preferential option for the poor," Jesus did not abandon and exclude the rich and the powerful. These, too, are called to conversion and to live a just, all-inclusive life.

As a stranger and migrant, Jesus gratefully and gracefully accepted the hospitality others showed him. He was the guest at the homes of Lazarus, Martha, and Mary (Lk 10:38–42), of Andrew and Simon (Mk 1:29), and of Zacchaeus (Lk 19:1–10), and he did not hesitate to share table fellowship with sinners and tax collectors (Mk 2:15). Paradoxically, though a stranger and a guest, Jesus also played the host. In his many parables, he presents the kingdom of God as a banquet to which all are welcomed, especially "the poor, the crippled, the blind, and the lame" (Lk 14:21). In the same vein, once, when he was invited to dinner, he told his host: "When you give a banquet, invite the poor, the crippled, the lame, and the blind" (Lk 14:13). At the Last Supper, he put on a towel and washed his disciples' feet, though he was their "Master and Lord" (Jn 13:1–20). After his resurrection, he prepared a barbecued breakfast for his exhausted disciples after a night of unsuccessful fishing (Jn 21:4–13).

Standing between the two worlds, excluding neither but embracing both, Jesus was able to be fully inclusive of both. But this also means that he is the marginal person par excellence. People at the center of any society or group, as a rule, possess wealth, power, and influence. As the threefold temptation shows, Jesus, the border-crosser and the dweller at the margins, renounced precisely these three things. Because he was at the margins, in his teaching and miracle-working, Jesus creates a new and different center, one constituted by the meeting of the borders of the many and diverse worlds, often in conflict with one another, each with its own center which relegates the "other" to the margins. It is at this margin-center that marginal people meet one another. In Jesus, the margin where he lived became the center of a new society without borders and barriers, reconciling all peoples, "Jew or Greek, slave or free, male or female" (Ga 3: 28).

A marginal person throughout his life, Jesus also died as such. His violent death on the cross was a direct result of his border-crossing and ministry at the margins, which posed a serious threat to the interests of those occupying the economic, political, and religious centers. Even the form of his death—that is, by crucifixion—indicates that Jesus was an outcast, and he died, as the Letter to Hebrews says, "outside the city gate and outside the camp" (Hebrews 13:12–13). Symbolically, however, hung between heaven and earth, at the margins of both worlds, Jesus acted as the mediator and intercessor between God and humanity.

But even in death, Jesus did not remain within the boundaries of what death means: failure, defeat, destruction. By his resurrection, he crossed the borders of death into a new life, thus bringing hope where there was despair, victory where there was defeat, freedom where there was slavery, and life where there was death. In this way, the borders of death become frontiers to life in abundance.

As the paradigmatic migrant, Jesus holds up to migrants a way of life that is not exclusively centered on the well-being of oneself and one's family but is also committed to the promotion of the kingdom of God, marked by justice and love for all, and by solidarity with other migrants, especially those who are poorer and weaker than they are. As a gracious host, Jesus reminds migrants, though poor and marginalized, that they must be generous hosts to others, especially to their fellow migrants. Lastly, Jesus' final victory over his suffering and death in his resurrection is a source of patience and hope for the migrants on their own way of the cross as they struggle for their survival.

The Holy Spirit, The Push and Pull of Migration

In the Bible, the Holy Spirit is depicted with various images, such as fire, wind, breath, life, power, energy, spirit, gift, grace, and love. Subsequently, Christian theology of the Holy Spirit (pneumatology) highlights the Spirit's different activities within the Trinity, such as Holy Spirit "proceeding" from the Father and/through the Son, or as the bond of love uniting the Father and the Son, or as divine gift. Within the history of salvation, the Holy Spirit is presented as the loving and gracious God dwelling in human beings and as the divine power pushing history toward the fulfillment of the kingdom of God.

In this sense the Holy Spirit may be said to be the "push" and "pull" of the kingdom of God.

Among the many theories of migration, one traces its origin to the "push" and "pull" of the international labor market.[19] The low wages and the high rate of the unemployment in the sending countries "push" their people to migrate, while the countries—normally the developed ones—with decreasing work force, low birth rate, high labor demand, and better pay exert the "pull" on the migratory flow. From the Christian perspective, the Holy Spirit can be said on the one hand to "push" the migrants out of their poverty and inhuman living conditions, infusing them with courage, trust, and imagination to envision a different life for themselves and their families, one that is consonant with the promise of a world of justice given by the Deus Migrator, whose image and likeness they are. On the other hand, the Holy Spirit, as the *entelecheia* (goal) of history, can also be said to "pull" the migrants toward its final goal which, though inclusive of a minimum of material conditions required for a life with dignity for all, transcends all that humans can ever hope to achieve.

Eschatology and Migration

That the Holy Spirit is the final goal of the migrant's journey brings up another important aspect of the Catholic theology of migration: the impact of migration on eschatology.[20] To be a migrant is to be on the move, and one of the most fundamental virtues required of people on the move is hope. Movement and hope are precisely the two essential elements of Christian eschatology. A movement or journey entails a goal; otherwise, it is blind and directionless. For Christians, that goal is the kingdom of God, or Godself as the common destiny of all human beings and human history. Because the kingdom of God is God's reign of universal justice, perfect peace, total reconciliation, and unbounded happiness, by definition it cannot be achieved by human efforts. Essentially, a utopia—literally, a good place and no-place—it is the deepest desire of the human heart, yet it remains forever beyond human reach. It lurks behind all messianic ideologies, driving history forward. Yet this collective dream will never be fully realized in our midst or by our own doing.

This truth is driven home more vividly and bitterly to migrants than to anyone else, as their hopes for a better life are dashed again and again, and that is why, more than anyone else, migrants need to have hope. But hope is not simply a wish that may or may not come true, or a velleity for something ephemeral, or a desire for something without which one feels merely indifferent, or a passive waiting for some fateful future happening. In contrast, hope is vigilant, standing on tiptoe, a longing expectation, a leaning forward into the future, and above all, hope is embodied in actions to bring about, or at least prepare for and anticipate, the coming of the reality that is hoped for.

Because the object of eschatological hope is beyond human power, the person who hopes for it must renew her or his hope again and again by calling to mind the promises that God has fulfilled in history, and for Christians, what God has accomplished in creation and redemption, especially in Israel and Jesus Christ. Thus, eschatological hope is deeply rooted in the past. However, this remembering (*anamnesis*) is not just a private mental act, a nostalgic hankering after the good old days in the old country. Rather God's past deeds and faithfulness are celebrated here and now in the community of other migrants, by word and sacrament, so that together they can look forward (*prolepsis*) to the eschatological future that God promises. This future reality is, in Anselm Min's precise summary,

> the common destiny of all humanity: their common subjection to the sovereignty of the one Creator and the saving providence of the triune God, their fundamental equality as creatures before God, their common redemption through the one mediator, Jesus Christ, their common eschatological call to share in the communion of the triune God as members of the Body of Christ, their social interdependence with one another in sin and grace. All human beings have been created in the likeness of the triune God and called to become, in the power and movement of the Holy Spirit, brothers and sisters of Christ the Son and in him sons and daughters of the Father and therefore also brothers and sisters of one another.[21]

Min goes on to highlight three aspects in which migrants, especially undocumented migrant workers, are "the paradigmatic symbol of our eschatological destiny today":

1) The migrant workers, insofar as they are refused universal solidarity by the people of the host countries, are "the judge of our unworthiness to enter into the eschatological fulfillment in the community of the triune God."
2) The migrants urge us to "return to our most profound eschatological identity as sisters and brothers of one another in Christ the Son, and sons and daughters of the father of the father in the power and movement of the reconciling Spirit."

3) The migrants remind us that "we are all migrants to our eschatological destiny, and the success of that destiny depends on what we do now to the migrant worker, especially the undocumented."[22]

Migration and Christian Existence

Min's last point leads us to a cluster of issues that require consideration in a Catholic theology of migration and can be grouped under the general rubric of "Christian existence." They include the question of who human beings are today (anthropology), how Catholics should worship in a way that fosters solidarity with migrants (liturgy), and which virtues are especially apposite in the age of migration (ethics). A brief word on each of these by way of conclusion is in order.

Victorino A. Cueto describes human life in general today, and not only that of migrants, as "exilic existence in a hyperglobalized world."[23] In the globalized world, where persons often belong to more than one social and cultural grouping, existence is necessarily hybrid: it is lived "out of place," in "exile," "in-between worlds." We all are migrants, or better, co-migrants now. As such, when we welcome, protect, and love the foreigners, the strangers, and the migrants among us, we not only welcome, protect, and love them as we embrace, protect, and love ourselves, but also welcome, protect, and love ourselves in and through them. Together, as natives and migrants—the distinction has now become otiose—we are all pilgrims, not back to where we came from (the countries of origin) nor to the foreign lands (the countries of destination) because neither is our true home. As the celebrated *Letter to Diognetus*, already cited above, puts it most eloquently, "[Christians] live in their own countries, but only as aliens (*paroikoi*). They have a share in everything as citizens (*politai*), and endure everything as foreigners (*xenoi*). Every foreign land is their fatherland, and yet every fatherland is a foreign land."

Christian life is also ecclesial existence. Migration is a permanent feature of the church, and not just a historical phenomenon in its history.[24] Like unity, catholicity, holiness, and apostolicity, "migrantness," to coin a neologism, is a note of the true church because only a church that is conscious of being an institutional migrant on the way to the kingdom of God, and takes care of all the migrants in this common journey, truly practices faith, hope, and love.

Because of its intrinsic migrantness, the church must worship in its liturgical celebrations the Deus Migrator in Jesus, the Paradigmatic Migrant, and by the "push" and "pull" power of the Holy Spirit.

In this way not only are the migrants fully integrated into the local churches and able to participate as equals in their activities, but migration also becomes the spirit animating church worship.

Daniel Groody has offered insightful reflections on the link between the Eucharist and immigration, highlighting the connection between Jesus' actions and words at the Last Supper and the migrant's life: between "He Took the Bread" and the migrant's decision to migrate; between "He Broke the Bread" and the migrant's broken body; between "And Gave It to His Disciples" and the migrant's self-sacrifice for the good of others; between "Do This in Memory of me" and the church's "option for the poor/migrant."[25]

Finally, "welcoming, protecting, and loving" the stranger and the migrant entail an appropriate ethical behavior. Kristin E. Heyer has proposed a Christian ethic of immigration in which "civic kinship" and "subversive hospitality" serve as the guiding principles for our relationship with migrants. "Welcoming" the migrants takes the form of generous hospitality, a virtue to which all Catholic theologians of migration have given pride of place.[26] "Protecting" the migrants takes the form of defending human rights.[27] "Loving" the migrants takes the form of compassion (suffering with) and solidarity. In this compassionate solidarity, not only do I love the migrant *as*—in the sense of *in the way* that and *as much as*—I love myself (as enjoined by the command: "Love thy neighbor like yourself"), but I also love the migrant because *the migrant is myself* inasmuch as *I myself am a migrant* (as implied in Dt 24:17–18: "You shall not violate the rights of the alien or of the orphan, nor take the clothing of a widow as a pledge. For, remember, you were once slaves in Egypt"). The migrant is the person in and through whom I can discover my true identity, that is, who I am: a migrant, or better still, a *co-migrant* with Jesus. the Paradigmatic Migrant, and other fellow migrants, in the journey back to Deus Migrator.[28]

Notes

1. On Jewish theology of migration and ethical teaching on the treatment of migrants, see the essays by Melissa Raphael and Devorah Schoenfeld in this volume.
2. For a helpful survey of the New Testament perspectives on migration, see Donald Senior, "'Beloved Aliens and Exile': New Testament Perspectives on Migration," in *A Promised Land, A Perilous Journey,*" eds. Daniel Groody and Gioacchino Campese, 20–34 (Notre Dame: University of Notre Dame Press, 2008).

3. For *Letter to Diognetus* and a study of migration in the patristic era, see Peter C. Phan, "Migration in the Patristic Era: History and Theology," in *A Promised Land, A Perilous Journey*, 35–61.
4. The most comprehensive and best treatment of Catholic understanding of migration is *Migrazione: Dizionario Socio-Pastorale*, ed. Graziano Battistella (Chinisello Balsamo, Milan: Edizioni San Paolo, 2010). It is 1119-page long.
5. For excellent collections of official church documents on migration, see *Chiesa e mobilità umana. Documenti della Santa Sede dal 1883 al 1983*, ed. Giovanni Graziano Tassello and L. Favero (Rome: Centro Studi Emigrazione, 1985); and *Enchiridion della Chiesa per le migrazioni. Documenti magisteriali ed ecumenici sulla pastorale della mobilità umana (1887–2000)*, ed. Giovanni Graziano Tassello (Bologna: Centro Editoriale Dehoniano, 2001). Also the website of the Pontifical Council for the Pastoral Care of Migrants and Itinerants contains important official documents on migration (http://www.vatican.va/roman_curia/pontifical_councils/migrants). For an informative study of papal teachings on migration, see Lorenzo Prencipe,"I papi e le migrazione," in *Migrazioni: Dizionario Socio-Pastorale*, 746–783; G. Manzone, "Le migrazioni umane nel magistero della Chiesa," *Nuntium* 30, 3 (2006), 257–263; and idem, "Le migrazioni nella dottrina sociale della Chiesa," *Rivista della teologia morale* 160 (2008), 487–496.
6. For a survey of recent migration in the United States of America, Europe, Asia, Australia, and Africa, see Leonore Loeb Adler and Uwe P. Giellen, eds., *Migration: Immigration and Emigration in International Perspective* (Westport, Conn.: Praeger, 2003); and Stephen Castles, Hein de Hass, and Mark J. Miller, *The Age of Migration: International Population Movements in the Modern World*, 5th ed. (New York: Guilford Press, 2013). For a highly readable study of migration in general, see Paul Collier, *Exodus: How Migration Is Changing Our World* (Oxford: Oxford University Press, 2013).
7. For a study of the teaching of Vatican II on migration, see Velasio De Paolis, "Concilio Vaticano II," in: *Migrazioni: Dizionario Sociale-Pastorale*, 176–182.
8. The text of *Exul Familia* as well as other papal documents are available at www.papalencyclicals.net/all.htm. For a study of this instruction, see Giovanni Terrani, "*Exul Familia,*"in *Migrazioni: Dizionario Socio-Pastorale*, 485–495.
9. The text of this instruction is available in *Acta Apostolicae Sedis* 61 (1969), 614–643.
10. The text of this instruction is available at http://www.vatican.va/roman_curia/pontifical_councils/migrants/documents/rc_pc_migrants_doc_20040514_erga-migrantes-caritas-christi_en.html. For a study of this instruction, see Angelo Negrini, "*Erga Migrantes Caritas Christi,*" in *Migrazioni: Dizionario Socio-Pastorale,*" 451–460.

11. Space does not permit a consideration of the documents of various national episcopal conferences. Of special importance are those episcopal conferences representing Africa, Asia, Latin America, Europe, and Australia. Of episcopal conferences of individual countries (where migration constitutes a serious issue), the following have issued significant documents: Argentina, Belgium, Brazil, Korea, The Philippines, France, Germany, Italy, Mexico, Portugal, Spain, and Switzerland. Of course, the American Catholic Church has been very concerned about migration and the welfare of migrants, from the establishment of the National Catholic Welfare Council to the reorganization of the Unites Catholic Conferences of Catholic Bishops (USCCB). Three documents deserve mention: *Asian and Pacific Presence: Harmony in Faith* (2001); *From Newcomers to Citizens: All Come Bearing Gifts* (2003); *Strangers No Longer: Together on the Journey of Hope* (2003, together with the Catholic Bishops of Mexico). For an analysis of the documents on migration by the episcopal conferences mentioned above, see *Chiesa e migrazioni* (Agenzia Scalabriana per la Cooperazione allo Sviluppo (ASCS Onlus). Piazza del Carmine 2–20121 Milano). Available at: www.scalabrinini.org.
12. Vatican II, *Pastoral Constitution on the Church in the Modern World* (*Gaudium et Spes*) no. 4.
13. For an extensive elaboration of this methodology, see Peter C. Phan, "The Experience of Migration as Source of Intercultural Theology," in *Contemporary Issues of Migration and Theology*, eds. Elaine Padilla and Peter C. Phan (New York: Palgrave Macmillan, 2013), 179–209. See also Jorge E. Castillo Guerra, "A Theology of Migration: Toward an Intercultural Methodology," in *A Promised Land, A Perilous Journey*, 243–270.
14. Among works on a Catholic theology of migration, the following deserve notice: Daniel G. Groody *Border of Death, Valley of Life: An Immigrant Journey of Heart and Spirit* (Lanham: Rowman & Littlefield, 2002); Gioacchino Campese and Pietro Ciallella, eds., *Migration, Religious Experience, and Globalization* (Staten Island, N.Y.: Center for Migration Studies, 2003); Daniel G. Groody and Gioacchino Campese, eds., *A Promised Land, A Perilous Journey: Theological Perspectives on Migration* (Notre Dame: University of Notre Dame Press, 2008); Donald Kerwin and Jill Marie Gerschutz, eds., *And You Welcome Me: Migration and Catholic Social Teaching* (Plymouth, UK: Lexington Books, 2009); and Fabio Baggio and Agnes M. Brazal, eds., *Faith on the Move: Toward a Theology of Migration in Asia* (Quezon City, Philippines: Ateneo de Manila University Press, 2008). Along with Daniel Groody, Gioacchino Campese is among the most ardent advocates for a theology of migration. See his "The Irruption of Migrants, Theology of Migration in the 21st Century," *Theological Studies* 73 (2012), 3–32; "Mission

and Migration," in *A Century of Catholic Mission: Roman Catholic Missiology 1910 to the Present*, ed. Stephen B. Bevans, 247–260 (Oxford: Regnum Publications, 2013); " La théologie et les migrations: La redécouverte d'une dimension structurelle de la foi chrétienne," *Dossier: Les catholiques et les migrations* 24, no. 139 (2012): 135–155.

15. Aristotle, *Metaphysics*, Bk XII,1072b. English translation by W. D. Ross in *The Complete Works of Aristotle: The Revised Oxford Translation*, ed. Jonathan Barnes (Princeton: Princeton University Press, 1995), 1695.

16. Of course not all thinkers ground the human rights in the fact that humans are created in the image and likeness of God. This claim for human rights is unique to the Abrahamic religions.

17. Daniel G. Groody, one of the few Catholic theologians who have written extensively on the theology of migration, makes an eloquent and forceful case for the migrant's human rights based on the fact that the migrant is the *imago Dei*. Groody elaborates on the need to cross over the four divides separating migration from theology by (1) moving from treating the migrant as a problem to seeing the migrant as the imago Dei; (2) joining the divine with the human by seeing Jesus as *Verbum Dei* (3) uniting the human with the divine in understanding Christian mission as *missio Dei*, and (4) overcoming xenophobia by subordinating nation/country to the kingdom of God by considering the goal of human existence as *visio Dei*. See his "Crossing the Divide: Foundations of a Theology of Migration and Refugees," in *And You Welcome Me: Migration and Catholic Social Teaching*, ed. Donald Kerwin and Jill Marie Gerschutz, 1–30.

18. Though the history of God's migration with Israel—with the patriarchs and during the covenanted people's exodus out of Egypt, exile, and return from exile—is an intrinsic part of the Christian faith, I leave it out of consideration here since it has been treated in other chapters of the book; I concentrate instead on the distinctive beliefs of the Christian faith.

19. See Michael J. Piore, *Birds of Passage: Migrant Labor in Industrial Societies* (Cambridge: Cambridge University Press, 1979). On theories of migration, see Karen O'Reilly, *International Migration and Social Theory* (New York: Palgrave Macmillan, 2012) and Caroline B. Brettle and James F. Hollifield, eds., *Migration Theory: Talking across Disciplines* (New York: Routledge, 2008).

20. For an insightful study of eschatology from the perspective of migration, see Anselm Kyongsuk Min, "Migration and Christian Hope: Historical and eschatological Reflections on Migration," in *Faith on the Move*, 177–202.

21. Ibid., 190.

22. Ibid., 199.

23. See his "'Out of Place': Exilic Existence in a Hyperglobalized World," in *Faith on the Move*, 1–19.
24. On church as a migratory community, see Emmanuel Serafica Guzman, "The Church as 'Imagined Communities' among Differentiated Social Bodies," in *Faith on the Move*, 118–154.
25. See his "Fruit of the Vine and Work of Human hands: Immigration and the Eucharist," in *A Promised Land, a Perilous Journey*, 299–315.
26. See William O'Neill, "Christian Hospitality and Solidarity with the Stranger," in *And You Welcome Me*," 149–155.
27. See Graziano Battistella, "The Human Rights of Migrants: A Pastoral Challenge," in *Migration, Religious Experience, and Globalization*, 76–102; Graziano Battistella, "Migration and Human Dignity: From Politics of Exclusion to Politics Based on Human Rights," in *A Promised Land, A Perilous Journey*, 177–191; Donald Kerwin, "Rights, the Common Good, and Sovereignty of Service," in *And You Welcome Me*," 93–121; Donald Kerwin, "The Natural Rights of Migrants and Newcomers: A Challenge to United States Law and Policy," in *A Promised Land, A Perilous Journey*, 192–209; and Agnes M. Brazal, "Cultural Rights of Migrants: A Philosophical and Theological Exploration," in *Faith on the Move*, 68–92.
28. See Giovanni Zevola, "'What are you talking about to each other as you walk along?'(Lk 24:17): Migration in the Bible and Our Journey of Faith," in *Faith on the Move*, 93–117.

Chapter 6

Protestantism in Migration: *Ecclesia Semper Migranda*

Nancy Bedford

The very word "Protestantism" brings with it cognitive dissonance for many Protestants across the world, who often prefer to describe themselves using other terms. In the Spanish-speaking world, for example, Christians across the confessional and denominational spectrum who are neither Roman Catholic nor Eastern Orthodox refer to themselves most often not as Protestants, but as *evangélicos* and *evangélicas* (which does not necessarily mean "evangelical" in the English-language sense). As Argentine Methodist theologian José Míguez Bonino puts it, "I have been catalogued variously as conservative, revolutionary, Barthian, liberal, catholicizing, moderate, liberationist. Probably all of it is true...But if I try to define myself in my most intimate being, what 'comes out' from my heart is that I am *evangélico*."[1] By contrast, *protestante* has often been used as a derogatory term. To make matters even more confusing, many Protestants all over the world belong to groups that do not trace their historical origins directly back to the European Protestant Reformation of the sixteenth century, though in indirect ways they have all been touched by that movement, so that it truly can be said that they have a Protestant genealogy. Rather than a single Protestant family tree, perhaps one should speak of a variety of "Protestant trees" with a somewhat similar genus, though growing on many different soils and in all sorts of climates.

In some contexts, there is a good bit of distrust between "classical" Protestants (such as Lutheran or Reformed churches) and groups that came about later, sometimes called neo-Protestants (such as Baptists, Brethren or Pentecostals); these tensions sometimes flare up even where Protestantism is a minority in a majority Roman Catholic or

Orthodox society.[2] Nevertheless, in recent decades, there has been much cross-fertilization between these different ecclesial bodies and movements, especially in the global South. For example, neo-Pentecostal liturgical styles, as well as its theological emphases on healing, exorcism and spiritual warfare, have now influenced at least in some measure a majority of Protestant churches in Latin America, in part as a result of shared evangelistic campaigns, transforming—or, as one author puts it, "defeating"—denominational cultures.[3] At the same time, the so-called "historic" Protestant denominations in Latin America (somewhat equivalent to the "mainline" Protestants in the United States) have had an influence disproportionate to their numbers on theological education, the defense of human rights, biblical scholarship, and interreligious dialogue, all of which also help shape the Protestant landscape and civil society more generally.[4]

As Mark Noll points out, "contemporary Protestant diversity is much more than just geographical." He speaks in this sense of the "multiform character" of contemporary Protestantism, and of the existence of both "Protestant" and "Protestant-like" churches. Among these are traditions that pre-date the Reformation (such as the Waldensians), others that trace their origins directly to various strands of the European Reformation movements of the sixteenth century (such as Lutherans, some Reformed denominations, Mennonites and Anglicans) or to dissident movements a century or two later in Europe or the United States (such as Congregationalists, Baptists, and Methodists). Starting in the early twentieth century, we witness the emergence of Pentecostalism and of local independent churches all over the world. Many of the strongest Protestant movements are now found outside of Europe and North America, and show both continuities and discontinuities with the Protestant past.[5] The countries with the highest number of Protestants at present are the United States, Nigeria, China, Brazil, and South Africa, in that order, none of which are located in the continent that gave birth to Martin Luther, John Calvin, Menno Simons, and John Wesley.[6] At the same time, in the Global North, particularly in Europe, the face of traditional Protestant denominations is changing rapidly as a result of the influx of migrants. In some countries, minority Protestant churches are growing because of migration, as is happening in Italy, where well over half of the members of Protestant churches are now transnational migrants, primarily Africans.[7]

Despite the multi-faceted realities of contemporary Protestantism, there is enough common ground among these various ecclesial bodies to come up with a number of characteristic marks, beyond the common bond of not being Roman Catholics or Orthodox. Protestant groups proclaim "salvation as a gift from God that brings reconciliation with God and among people on earth," their primary authority is the Bible, and their forms of ecclesial organization "tend to the local and the participatory," with activities that "feature individual activity and responsibility."[8] Related to the latter is the important notion of the "priesthood of all believers," which pushes toward a horizontal ecclesiology, but can also lead to fragmentation.[9] Likewise, the hermeneutical license implicit in the priority of Scripture, coupled with the priesthood of all believers, can lead to a great deal of creative freedom, but also to an individualistic approach to interpretation. Protestantism is a "religion of freedom," something that entails many advantages, including freedom of conscience within and without the church, but also its own perils, whenever that freedom is construed selfishly or narrowly.[10] It seems that Protestantism is at its best when it is lived out as a movement rather than as an institutional system or a collection of dogmas. By nature, it is continually in the making, since it is not "definitive" but rather a multifaceted ecclesial movement in the way of Jesus Christ, in ways actualized by the Holy Spirit in the service and anticipation of God's reign or commonweal. Protestantism understands the church as needing continual renewal, something that has traditionally been expressed by the statement *ecclesia semper reformanda est* (the church is always being reformed).

An important dimension of the "glorious freedom of the children of God" (Rom. 8:21) as understood by Protestantism is the "Protestant Principle." Traditionally, the phrase was used by Protestant theologians to refer to the doctrine of justification through grace by faith. However, Lutheran theologian Paul Tillich, who migrated from Germany to the United States, rearticulated this principle in order to unleash its prophetic character, so as to help the church to critique its own idolatrous tendencies. The Protestant Principle in this Tillichian sense consists of opposing the identification of our "ultimate concern," that is God, with any "penultimate" creation of the church or of society.[11] In practice this means that Protestants have a theological justification for concluding that if certain customs or laws are hurtful to a particular group of people (such as migrants), obeying them is contrary to their confession of faith, and civil disobedience is called for. This is known as *status confessionis*. For example, in the face of apartheid in South Africa, both the Lutheran World Federation (1977) and the World Alliance of Reformed Churches (1982) declared it heretical, and churches belonging to these confessions that supported apartheid were suspended from membership.[12]

In this essay, I will focus primarily, though by no means exclusively, on the situation of Latino and Latina Protestant migrants in the United States as a way to get a grip on the theological ambiguities and possible contributions of a Protestant lens on migration. Because the United States is one of the main receiving countries for migrants in the world, as well as being a country profoundly marked by Protestantism both for good and ill, while its southern neighbor Mexico is one of the main sending countries in the world for migrants in general, and for Christian migrants in particular, the US migrant context can be particularly illuminating. Beyond these structural facts, on a personal level as a Latin American Protestant now living in *el Norte*, the Latino and Latina migrant reality in the United States is one I know from the inside. I have found in my own experiences of migration that what it means to be Protestant in different countries and contexts can be quite varied, so that my own sense of "Protestantism" has been marked by continuities and discontinuities even within similar confessional traditions. Protestantism is itself to a great extent "in migration," meaning that both what it is and what it may become are in flux and being shaped in pivotal ways by the concrete lives and experiences of migrants. When we look at Protestantism in migration, we discover a particular dimension of the church as *semper reformanda*, because migration and especially the lives of migrants in all their particularity, show us clearly that the church and theology are always contextual and embodied, and always on the move. In this sense, Protestantism is an expression of the church in migration: *ecclesia semper migranda est*.

Migration and Protestantism

Within the dominant culture in the United States, Protestantism has not always done well at shaping the imagination of its adherents on the matter of immigration. In the worst instances, Protestantism has fueled anti-immigrant sentiments in a framework of Christian nationalism linked to white supremacist ideas.[13] This is akin to the distorted "Protestant" ethos that during Jim Crow made the lynching of Black people by so-called upstanding white churchgoers a permissible Sunday afternoon pastime in areas of the US South. A mythical white Protestant past continues to be reenacted, for example through Fourth of July parades, sometimes conceived of as counter-symbolic gestures in the face of the public presence of Latino and Latina Roman Catholic Good Friday processions.[14] In this symbolic world, "Protestant" is melded with "Anglo" to form "Anglo-Protestant," as in the supposed "Anglo-Protestant" values that built the "American Dream." These values are then presented as imperiled by an influx of "non-assimilated" Latinos and Latinas.[15]

There are many problems associated with this perspective, not least a profound ignorance about the actual religious practices of Latino and Latina immigrants to the United States. The growth of Protestantism in Latin America in the last decades (especially outside of Mexico), as well as of Afro-Caribbean and Afro-Brazilian religions, makes it a mistake to presuppose that all Latin American migrants are necessarily adherents of the Roman Catholic faith. Even in heavily Roman Catholic Mexico, many indigenous groups, especially in the Chiapas region, are now predominantly Protestant.[16] Though a majority of Latinos and Latinas in the United States continue to be Roman Catholic (perhaps 30 million people), if we look closely at the numbers we will find that there are also a great many Protestant Latinos and Latinas (over nine million people). This means, for instance, that there are now more Latino and Latina Protestants in the United States than there are either Jews or Muslims.[17] Clearly, Latino and Latina immigration energizes not only Roman Catholic but also Protestant religious life. Indeed, all other factors being equal, it would seem that Latin American Protestants are more likely to migrate to the United States than their Roman Catholic counterparts, to the point that some scholars have spoken of the "Protestant effect" on migration.[18] Studies in urban anthropology show that the Latino and Latina "culturalization" of urban spaces in the United States, includes not only the ubiquitous *taquerías* and laundromats, but also a multiplicity of storefront Protestant churches.[19]

What is deeply disturbing about the imaginary of Anglo-Protestant nationalism is the link forged between whiteness and Protestantism: not only is this linkage hurtful to US society as a whole, and to those coded as "non-white" in US society in particular, but it also undermines Protestantism itself. It turns the Protestant faith at worst into a toxic, racist ideology, and at best into the irrelevant religiosity of an ever-smaller contingent of "white" people who have forgotten the "Protestant Principle." There are, at present, however, many encouraging and important attempts that work counter to such distortions, finding ways to "welcome the stranger" from within a Protestant framework.[20] Many church leaders in the United States across the Protestant spectrum, including a number of prominent white Evangelicals who are not known for being socially progressive, have been quite vocal in recent years about supporting comprehensive immigration reform and advocating for migrants.[21] This support is not limited to leaders; significantly, a Pew research study concluded that among white Protestants, "those who attend church most frequently tend to be more likely than their less-frequently-attending counterparts to share their religious leaders' pro-immigrant sentiments," regardless of other variables, such as gender and education.[22]

Some of the statements put out by Protestant denominational bodies clearly reflect internal tensions that are yet to be worked out, that put Protestantism to the test of its own convictions. Such is the case of the Southern Baptist Convention resolution, "On Immigration and the Gospel," of June 2011. Its language wavers between a defensive discourse and a wider sense of justice for all. For example, it states explicitly that "this resolution is not to be construed as support for amnesty for any undocumented immigrant" and asks "our governing authorities to prioritize efforts to secure the borders," a veiled reference to Mexican and Central American immigration. At the same time, it espouses a scripturally based understanding of hospitality to strangers and the explicit rejection of "any form of nativism, mistreatment, or exploitation" as "inconsistent with the gospel of Jesus Christ."[23]

These internal contradictions point to a larger systemic problem within Protestantism, whenever it flirts too closely with Christendom models: the inherent tension between any sort of nationalism (hence the need to "secure borders" from migrants while allowing capital, for instance, to flow freely) and the demands of the gospel for universal justice. As the symbolic hegemony of Protestantism is loosened in the United States, such tensions tend to become more evident. The question of migration, because it entails not only abstract principles, but actual bodies who come together to worship in church regardless of their immigration status, puts the Protestant Principle on the line: What is ultimate and what is penultimate? If God is ultimate, then an unjust immigration legal system is clearly penultimate, and the duty of Protestants is to work to reform it.

Marginal Protestantism in Migration

Perhaps the most promising hints for thinking through the migrant experience emerge from within the logic of what we might call "marginal Protestantism." I find the adjective "marginal" triply helpful. First, it points to a way of living out Protestantism that is not lodged in the "center" of power. Its *locus theologicus* is therefore, in a real sense, outside the city walls. This is a safeguard for the Protestant temptation to make alliances with political and economic power structures (as white Protestants did with US slavery or the "German Christians" did in Nazi Germany) rather than focusing on empowering the weakest (as in the US Civil Rights Movement and in Monday evening prayers for peace in East Germany in the 1980s).

Second, the concept has been theorized fruitfully in the context of migration by Methodist theologian Jung Young Lee. The reality of the periphery, or as he prefers to speak of it, of "marginality," becomes for Lee the "key to multicultural theology."[24] Lee's theology of marginality is, as he puts it, not based on the norm of "centralist" theology. It develops its own norm, method, and content, which emerge when "marginal" people (such as migrants) reflect creatively on Christian symbols emerging from marginality. The experience of such persons and of Lee himself, as a Korean who became a migrant and as such a Korean-American, includes the negative aspect of living "in-between" (belonging to neither culture) and the positive aspect of living "in-both" (belonging to both cultures).

The intersection of these two aspects creates a new interstice or margin, that Lee terms the "in-beyond." It refers to a margin, edge, or periphery that is not defined primarily by the center, but rather by the point at which negative and positive experiences of interculturality connect.[25] Lee's model parts from the experience of what he calls "hyphenated Americans," many of whom are migrants or are treated as strangers in their own land. (He mentions Asian-Americans, Native-Americans, African-Americans and Hispanic-Americans.) Lee's "marginality" is not a fixed reality existing in isolation. Like migration itself, "marginalities" are in motion, permeable, mutable, and often ambiguous, in touch with each other and with various "centers." Homi Bhabha has suggested that "the truest eye may now belong to the migrant's double vision."[26] What Lee's approach allows is a way to socialize within Protestantism more widely what migrants are able to see as part of the ecclesia semper migranda, without presupposing that they are somehow ontologically different from other people. They can see because they are walking in a given place, not because they have eyesight intrinsically different than that of other people.

Third, "marginal" is used by theologians such as Oscar García-Johnson to describe Latino and Latina migrant Protestant churches as agents of change within US Protestantism, for their capacity to produce contextual and local ecclesial forms while maintaining a transnational imaginary and strong ties to communities outside the United States.[27] Scholars from various disciplines in the social sciences who specialize in the area of migration sometimes speak of the "migrant imaginary" in the Americas and elsewhere. By this they refer to the capacity of transnational migrants with long-standing patterns of moving across political borders (such as the United States-Mexican border) to go beyond national boundaries, in order to find a sense of self. In other words, such migrants tend to privilege transnational forms of identification to a nation-based model of identity. More important for the migrants than national borders in themselves is the way that the borders affect their struggle for civil and human rights. In this process, material culture and the world of the imagination are highly significant, so that a reductive socioeconomic understanding is insufficient to understand the lives of migrants: creative imagination, cultural production, sustaining family ties across political borders, and speaking up privately and publicly can become political forces in daily life.[28] Religious faith often plays a central role in these processes, especially inasmuch as it allows migrants to exercise agency as they negotiate their identities in a new society, and to find meaning in their uprooted existence.[29]

In speaking of migration and migrants, it is always important to avoid the trap of naively celebrating their achievements in an individualistic manner, since that can disguise the unjust structures and the oppressive dynamics of contemporary capitalist globalization that can fuel migration. On the other hand, they should not be thought of as persons with no agency, simply tossed around by the winds of fortune. Migrants live immersed in the ambiguities and difficulties of the present age, and are forced to navigate them as best they can. Of particular interest to me as a Protestant theologian is whether and how Protestantism can become part of a liberating, empowering imaginary for some migrants, and what it can contribute positively, both to its adherents and to the wider community. Because of the centrality of congregational life in Protestantism, and the way that Protestant churches often provide believers with an extended family of faith, it is important first of all not to overlook the familial dimension of the Protestant *ecclesia semper migranda*.

Familial Ties in Migration

The Latino and Latina phenomenon in the United States is an amalgam of various cultural influences from Latin America coming together in ways indigenous to the US American context, and in that sense is quite different from cultural realities in the various countries of origin in Mexico, Central America, South America, and the Caribbean. Furthermore, in some parts of the country, such as

New Mexico and other regions of the US Southwest, many Latinos and Latinas are not "migrants" but have been present for generations, since before the arrival of English-speaking colonizers. This said, Latino and Latina Protestant churches often do provide a sense of familiarity to recent Latin American migrants, in part because of the use of Spanish in many regional varieties (often alongside English, which tends to be preferred by the children and young people, unless they are very recent arrivals).[30] To this is added the familial, and especially fraternal, dimension of congregational life, where members often refer to each other as *hermanos* (brothers) and *hermanas* (sisters). This extended family is supportive emotionally and also sometimes financially. Especially in the case of female migrants, struggling to make ends meet as heads of household, this concrete solidarity can be vital to well-being.[31]

Migration changes family dynamics, both for the migrants and children born to migrant families, and for those family members who are still in the country of origin. Because they are now somewhat removed geographically from their extended families and the religious dimensions of filial obligations, migrants often feel a greater freedom to innovate religiously, which may mean converting to a new religion altogether, becoming more involved or less involved in their faith of origin, or changing confessional allegiances. Migrants are sometimes attracted to Protestant church communities precisely because they find there a kind of familial support to which they now have access, as well as a degree of cultural continuity or familiarity, and the development of strong friendships and personal bonds because of migration. This can be seen in the Latino and Latina context in the United States, but also in many other contexts with internal and external migration, such as Taiwan, where a number of urban migrants have converted from traditional non-Christian religions to Protestantism, a minority religion.[32]

Add to this a sense of solidarity in the face of a shared "marginality" made evident, for example, in the United States by an anti-immigrant discourse linked to white nativism and a patchwork of emerging state laws that push undocumented immigrants further into the shadows and put their families at risk.[33] Church leaders are finding that an important part of pastoral care is helping undocumented members of the community make contingency plans for the care of their children, should the adults in the family be swept up in immigration raids, jailed, and deported. In these cases, children, unless they previously have been assigned a guardian in case of parental absence, are put into the foster care system, and parents (unable to show up to court) can even lose their parental rights. In the US state of Illinois, for example, an estimated 80,000 children, mostly Latinos and Latinas, have lost one or more parent to deportation since 2007.[34]

Parallel to this problem is the phenomenon of families fractured by migration when children are left behind with relatives, often grandmothers or aunts, in the country of origin, while parents or a mother cross the border in order to generate resources to sustain the family on both sides. When one or both of those parents are undocumented and unable to return to visit, the fracturing becomes even deeper.[35] The "familial" character of Protestant migrant churches, though real, is thus challenged to be lived out and reconfigured in sometimes extreme circumstances that include taking in and caring for the children of deported parents.

A Trinitarian Imaginary in Migration

Another expression of the familial dimension in migrant Protestant congregations is that metaphors used for God often also have filial connotations. God's paternal, maternal and fraternal love, parsed out in Trinitarian faith patterns, is a constant presence and comfort in times of need for a church in migration. This is not surprising, as one of the distinctive characteristics of Christian faith in God is the experience of God as Triune. Indeed, a Trinitarian confession of God is a core conviction that most Protestants share with Roman Catholics and Orthodox Christians. There are admittedly some Protestant or "Quasi-Protestant" confessions that are not fully Trinitarian, such as Unitarian Universalism and Oneness Pentecostalism, as well as many individual Protestants of various confessions who would be hard-pressed to articulate Trinitarian faith in detail.[36]

Still, at the heart of the Christian confession of God as made known in Jesus Christ as Lord, Liberator, and Friend, by the work of the Holy Spirit, is a dynamic that pushes toward Trinitarian expression. In a Protestant context, this Trinitarian confession is often communicated in narrative form, as the story of God's involvement with creation in an intensely personal way, with the children of Israel, and by means of the incarnation, life, death, resurrection and ascension of Jesus Christ. The sending of the Holy Spirit empowers Christians to remember and to follow Jesus in new and changing historical circumstances, bringing them closer to the mystery of God's love and justice. Karl Barth, for example, reimagined the parable of the "prodigal son" (Luke 15:11–32) in terms of migration, in order to frame his

Christology of reconciliation narratively as the journey of the Second Person of the Trinity into a "strange land" and then back home to the Father.[37]

A Trinitarian theology in migration, developed along the lines of a Protestant imaginary that gives priority to narrative structures for doctrine, can contribute to the wider discussion on migration by allowing the migrant experience to shed light on the doctrine of God, even as the confession of God as Triune sheds light on the migrant experience. One way to organize such reflection is to think through aspects of the migrant experience from the perspective of being sent, yet also choosing to go; of the work of receiving and recognizing the testimony of migrants in a given place; and of the hope for a home that goes through and beyond the melancholy of what was lost. These movements can be related to the work of the Three Divine Persons, not as exact analogies, but rather as contributory elements to a narrative Trinitarian imaginary in migration.

Being Sent and Sending Oneself to the Strange Land: Incarnation in Migration

Feminist theologians have long pointed to the problem inherent in a Christology that makes of the Son a passive victim, sent to the world to suffer, having little say in the matter. In the end, an adoptionist model of Christology such as is presupposed in such a scheme cannot be good news for those of us who find in Christ the Brother and Friend who became one of us, that we might become friends of God and participants in God's very nature (2 Pet. 1:4). If to be in Christ and to become like Christ were a matter of becoming passive pawns in the hands of an almighty "Father," the whole work of liberation and reconciliation would cave in upon itself, as we would be made into creatures with no creativity and agency, and therefore no capacity even to worship God meaningfully. A healthy, life-giving Christology robs neither the Son of creativity and agency, nor us as siblings of our Brother Jesus of our exercise of gifts and graces in the realms in which we move. By the work of the Spirit, we are becoming truly human (and also more like God) as we grow in the image of Christ. A life-giving Christology, then, sees that the Son not only was sent to the world, but also exercised "agency" in the incarnation. In Gal. 1:4, Paul expresses this dual dynamic of being sent and choosing to go by saying that the "Lord Jesus Christ gave himself" in order to "liberate us" according to the "will of God." Paul understands his own apostleship to the Gentiles analogously, as being called and sent by God to preach the good news, but also as a matter in which his own agency and discernment are actively involved (see Gal. 1:15–24). This process of being-sent and choosing-to-go is always lived out in the power of the Holy Spirit (see Gal. 4:6 and 5:5), even as the Spirit was involved in the sending and in the going of the Son—that is, in the "travels" of the Son.

In the incarnation, the eternal Son, born of a woman in the fullness of time (Gal. 4:4) becomes a "fellow-traveler" with all migrants. Julian of Norwich, the fourteenth century mystic who writes vividly of the motherhood of the Triune God as well as of the motherhood of Christ our Brother, makes the point that as our Mother, Christ is "in travail."[38] In Julian's Middle English, this word has a triple meaning: Christ labors to give birth to us, Christ sorrows with us (sharing in our travails), and in doing both, Christ "travels" (travails) with us.[39] This takes on special significance from within a migrant imaginary that entails suffering, joys, and travel in ways that bring forth a new life. The incarnation means that God in Christ has taken on, bodily and materially, the condition of a migrant, and is acutely aware of what it means to be a migrant "according to the flesh" (*kata sarka*). God takes into Godself the migrant condition, in order to make a place, a new creation, and a "rest" for all those migrants who hope for a home in God.

Lee's notion of Christ as the "margin of our marginality" is helpful here. Faith in Christ allows migrants as disciples to transfer from one kind of marginality (a negative kind determined by the "center") to another, more positive form of marginality, in the image of Christ.[40] In Christ, migrants participate in Christ's agency as sent and as choosing-to-go.

Migrant religiosity is explicitly embodied faith, because migrants are acutely aware of location: they are now here and not there, singing songs to God as strangers in a strange land (Psalm 137:4). There are emotional and physical costs related not only to the journey to their present location, but to making a life in a new place with strange sounds, sights, and smells. Within Protestantism as a whole, it is especially in variants of Pentecostalism that this sense of embodiment finds direct expression in prayer and worship. As Caroline Jeannerat points out in her study of the Pentecostal Nigerian migrant experience in South Africa, among Pentecostals it is often possible for the body to become a "positive and active conduit of religious practice and experience," as opposed to something to be controlled and subdued, as it often has been in traditional forms of Protestant worship. In the Pentecostal approach, which in the last few decades has become so influential in other variants of Protestantism, communication with God occurs not only through words, thoughts, or silent prayer, but explicitly through the positive employment of the body. In the context of migration, such a focus allows even the poorest migrants to use what they do have and are, namely their bodies, to communicate meaningfully and deeply with God.[41]

A spirituality of embodiment in migration allows for a deep sense of connection with the incarnate Christ, whose embodied life was dedicated to the service of the poor and marginalized, whose crucified and resurrected body is a locus of solidarity and hope, and whose symbolic bodily presence, shared regularly as bread and wine, is so central for the Protestant sense of the divine and for the shaping of the community of faith—also understood metaphorically as Christ's body.

Receiving and Recognizing the Testimony of Migrants: Empowerment in Migration

Place has a profound effect on how people are able to live out their faith. In order to "get a grip" on life in a new place, migrants have to reconfigure and reimagine their practices, forging connections and making use of resources both old and new in order to find the strength to make a new life in a different place. In the context of Latino Roman Catholic practices and Marian devotions in Miami, Ana María Bidegain describes this process as a "transnational spirituality." She rightly perceives that many migrants "find it necessary to re-model their spiritual life in a way that allows them to incorporate and give meaning to their past life as well as their present one."[42] This unleashes what we might call a "pneumatological creativity" in the community of faith. In Protestant migrant circles, this sort of transnational spirituality is often manifested in finding new meaning in Scripture and new strength in the relationships within the community of faith as well as in the exercise of speaking or giving "testimony."

An important ritual dimension of migrant Latino and Latina Christianity is indeed the practice of giving a *testimonio*, or witness. Elizabeth Conde-Frazier describes testimonios as public testimonies of faith that are personal but not individualistic, since they emerge as part of a shared collective search for meaning by the people of God. They arise from everyday situations, but are not privatized. As she points out, in the Latino and Latina Protestant context, such testimonies are shaped by Scripture, tradition, and experience. The latter does not belong only to the subjective realm, because the witness is put before the community for its discernment. The fact of giving testimony, and therefore having a voice, is related to the call of the Holy Spirit to ministry in the world and to the Spirit's giving of gifts.

Looked at from the perspective of gender, the synergy between testimony and call can be especially empowering for women, particularly as they articulate liberating narratives. Conde Frazier therefore also connects the practice of testimonios to agency and to the possibility of an "oppositional epistemology" within the churches.[43] This allows women, for instance, to question patriarchal structures within churches, and also opens up wider possibilities to question hegemonic common sense within society,

Personal testimonies and narratives elaborated in the idiom of Scripture can translate into effective political action on a structural scale, as well. Gastón Espinosa, for example, analyzes Evangelical Latino and Latina political activism in the struggle for comprehensive immigration reform in the United States, and finds that, like Martin Luther King Jr. and the civil rights movement before them, Latino and Latina Evangelicals use the Bible to appeal to a higher law, cultivate relationships with religious and political leaders based on a common faith, and seek to advocate on behalf of justice for immigrants on the basis of what they understand as a God-ordained mandate.[44] In this sense, they are applying the Protestant Principle, in the context of an ecclesia semper migranda, to a particular set of laws that are unjust, in order to help transform society.

Beyond the Melancholy of What Was Lost: Mystagogy in Migration

Protestants in migration are reorganizing the religious landscape in the societies where they have relocated, in at least two ways: by providing a safe space for migrants to reconfigure their cultures of origin in a new context, and by reaching out to evangelize the people around them. Claudia Währisch-Oblau, who has studied the self-perception and the missionary imaginary of Protestant migrants from the Global South in Western Europe, points out that mainline-style Protestant churches, such as most Korean Presbyterian groups in Germany, tend to focus their mission inward toward their own migrant communities living in diaspora. Evangelicals and Pentecostals by contrast, such as West African Pentecostals in Germany, are concerned also with reaching indigenous Europeans with the gospel. Währisch-Oblau thinks that the latter attitude allows the migrants to look forward and develop creative bicultural or internationalist ways to relate their old and new cultures. For the former, more inward-looking group, by contrast, identity "is defined by roots rather than by routes."[45]

The West African Pentecostals interviewed by Währisch-Oblau understand themselves as missionaries, and often as part of a spiraling movement of reciprocity: just as Africans received the gospel from European missionaries at an earlier time, it is now time for Europeans to receive the gospel from Africans. They offer access to Jesus in a way that they think is not only different but also more helpful for life than what is presented by Western Enlightenment logic. This means that they position themselves as agents of God's divine economy in reawakening Europe to the gospel.[46]

A similar dynamic can be seen among African migrant Protestants in the United States.[47] There is a racial and ethnic subtext here as well: the racist idea of the "curse of Ham" is subverted and turned into an African blessing. As a Protestant on the receiving end of migration, Bernard Coyault writes, "In the past they received the gospel from our missionaries. Are we now not to receive 'their' gospel?" He proposes engaging in fraternal, theological, and spiritual exchanges, manifested in concrete ways, such as meetings, singing, worship services, shared meals, reflection, prayer and Bible studies, the exchange of pastors, and shared financial contributions for common projects. All of this can help lead churches to a mutual transformation, a renewed vision of community, of the Christian life, and of evangelization.[48]

Though a sense of loss and of melancholy are part and parcel of the migrant experience, and the traumas of the past cannot simply be ignored or swept aside, hope in the living God does help migrants to imagine and live out new possibilities. Carmen Nanko Fernández rightly warns Latino and Latina theology not to get so wrapped up in idyllic ideas of what was lost, such as the mythical Aztec territory of Aztlán, that it risks becoming blind to the potential of what she calls "cosmo-politan" reality, at the intersection of *cosmos* and *polis*, of the world of creation and of the city, where many migrants live and find work.[49] Even migrant farm workers are producing food mostly for these cosmo-politan spaces, and migrants often literally revitalize urban spaces in decay.

Christian hope does not look back with regret on a lost garden to which it hopes to return, but rather looks forward to the future of God and to that better "city" promised by God (Heb. 11:16; 13:14)—presumably a city with many gardens, but not in itself constituting a return to "paradise." In a fallen reality—in which even mountains are no longer safe symbols of the majesty of creation and the strength of

God, but can be felled and sullied by strip mining—nature can no longer be thought of in isolation from the urban presence of human beings. Liberation from human destructiveness and the transformation of hegemonic common sense based on greed and accumulation has to happen in the city as well as outside of it, if the mountains are to continue to proclaim the glory of God and the trees are to be able to clap their hands for joy. In this context, migrants are not romantic exemplars of an unsullied nature that resides far away, but constructors of a new city in a shrinking world. As part of the ecclesia semper migranda, Protestants in migration are on a journey in God to God, simultaneously at home and on the way.

Conclusion: Ecclesia semper reformanda et semper migranda

There are many things global Protestantism will not or cannot do: it cannot speak in a single, unified voice, for instance, or enact the degree of common liturgical gestures that can be seen in Roman Catholic and Orthodox circles. Roman Catholic bishops in the United States, for instance, have, as a rule, been much more vocal and united in their defense of immigrant rights than Protestant leaders. The more horizontal, congregational, and patchwork nature of Protestantism makes any sort of a united voice much more difficult to achieve. On the other hand, what Protestantism can do, and do quite well, is to weave together migrants and non-migrants in a movement from below, constituting an ecclesia semper migranda that is always evolving. As a dynamic, multifaceted movement with a good bit of organizational leeway and many instances of horizontal forms of polity, it is well-equipped to embrace the continual need for reform and renewal of the church by God's Spirit. In the liturgical year, it is perhaps the feast of Pentecost that best serves as a symbol of this transformation and "migration" of the church, allowing for surprising forms of intercultural communication, the sharing of resources, and new ways of living out the way of Jesus in changing contexts.

Given its reality as a fragile, interconnected ecosystem of wildly varied churches, Protestantism has to trust the Spirit to make use of its diversity to the glory of God and for the flourishing of creation. The Spirit helps it with discernment when it becomes entangled with ways of being in the world that are harmful rather than helpful. Protestantism is at its best, paradoxically, when it is most conscious of its own provisional character, staying true to the Protestant Principle. Protestantism in migration is one way of putting flesh and bones on that principle: human beings are crossing borders, engaging in hospitality, maintaining links with those who have left, and engaging in the development of new transnational imaginaries. Their thriving is more important to God than any imperative to uphold the status quo, whether or not it is disguised in Protestant garb. It is perhaps easier for marginal Protestantism to grasp this, but all Protestants have the potential to embody this mission, especially as Protestant forms of Christendom lose their grip and make way for other forms of living out the Christian faith. As one of the migrants in my own congregation commented, when asked what was significant about Protestantism in migration, whenever the message of the gospel is taken seriously, migrants—regardless of their accent, appearance, gender and customs—can find equal footing with people from the receiving culture, something unusual under most other circumstances. The Triune God is engaged in the pneumatological reorientation of the church for service in God's work of healing, justice, and compassion. As an *ecclesia semper reformanda et migranda*, with all its potential and also its limitations, Protestantism is called to cooperate joyfully with God in that work, a calling that is not beyond its gifts and graces.

Notes

1. José Míguez Bonino, *Rostros del Protestantismo Latinoamericano* (Buenos Aires: Nueva Creación, 1995), 5. All references to non-English sources have been translated by the author.
2. *Cf.* Luka and Angela Ilić, "Protestant Identity In An Orthodox Context: The Example Of Serbia," in *Christian Identity*, ed. A.J.G. Van Der Borght, 467–480 (Leiden: Brill, 2008).
3. *Cf.* Matthew Marostica, "The Defeat of Denominational Culture in the Argentine Evangelical Movement," in *Latin American Religion in Motion*, ed. Christian Smith and Joshua Prokopy, 147–172 (New York: Routledge, 1999).
4. One example of this is the vocal (and dangerous) defense of human rights during the 1970s by some "historic" Protestant groups in Argentina, while conservative Evangelicals were largely compliant with the dictatorship; see Miguel Ponsati, *Praxis y obediencia: Derechos Humanos y teología en los Documentos y Declaraciones del Movimiento Ecuménico por los Derechos Humanos (1976–1984)* (Buenos Aires: Publicaciones del MEDH, 2009). A more recent example is the work by the largely "mainline" Instituto Universitario ISEDET in Buenos Aires, which was invited by Indigenous Evangelical and Pentecostal groups in the Argentine Chaco to help them develop contextual theological education, accessed March 1, 2014, http://www.isedet.edu.ar/quienes_somos/brief.html.

5. Mark A. Noll, *Protestantism: A Very Short Introduction* (Oxford: Oxford University Press, 2011), 2–4.
6. "Global Christianity: A Report on the Size and Distribution of the World's Christian Population," *Pew Forum for Religion and Public Life*, accessed March 1, 2014, http://www.pewforum.org/Christian/Global-Christianity-protestant.aspx.
7. *Cf.* Darrell Jackson and Alessia Passarelli, *Mapping Migration: Mapping Churches' Responses* (Europe Study, Churches' Commission for Migrants in Europe/World Council of Churches, 2008), 29, accessed March 1, 2014, http://europeanmission.redcliffe.org/2012/03/07/mapping-migration-mapping-churches-responses-europe-study/
8. Noll, *Protestantism*, 5.
9. This does not rule out the possibility of authoritarian excesses and micro-fascisms, often of an androcentric nature, which lamentably do exist in Protestant circles.
10. *Cf.* Jürgen Moltmann, "Protestantismus als 'Religion der Freiheit,'" in *Religion der Freiheit. Protestantismus in der Moderne,* ed. Jürgen Moltmann, 11–28 (München: Christian Kaiser, 1990).
11. *Cf.* Paul Tillich, *Systematic Theology,* vol. 1 (Chicago: University of Chicago Press, 1951), 37.
12. *Cf.* Lukas Vischer, "What does *status confessionis* mean?" in *Semper reformanda: World Alliance of Reformed Churches,* accessed March 1, 2014, http://web.archive.org/web/20070503184806/http://www.warc.ch/where/22gc/study/13.html.
13. Eric Leon McDaniel, Irfan Nooroodin and Allyson Faith Shortle, "Divine Boundaries: How Religion Shapes Immigrants' Attitudes Toward Religion," *American Politics Research* 39 (2011): 205–233.
14. Chad Searles, "Parades and Processions: Protestant and Catholic Ritual Performances in a Nuevo New South Town," *Numen* 55 (2008): 44–67.
15. Samuel Huntington, *The Clash of Civilizations and the Remaking of World Order* (New York: Touchstone, 2004), 1.
16. *Cf.* Virginia Garrard-Burnett, "'Like a Mighty Rushing Wind.' The Growth of Protestantism in Contemporary Latin America," in *Religion and Society in Latin America: Interpretive Essays from Conquest to Present,* ed. Lee M. Penyak and Walter J. Petry, 190–206 (Maryknoll: Orbis, 2009).
17. *Cf.* Gastón Espinosa, "'Salvation and Transformation': Latino Evangelical Political Activism and the Struggle over Comprehensive Immigration Reform," in *Wading Through Many Voices: Toward a Theology of Public Conversation,* ed. Harold J. Recinos, 133–151 (New York: Rowman & Littlefield, 2011); and Gastón Espinosa, Virgilio Elizondo and Jesse Miranda, "Introduction: US Latino Religions and Faith-Based Political, Civic, and Social Action," in *Latino Religions and Civic Activism in the United States,* ed. Gastón Espinosa et al (New York: Oxford University Press, 2005), 6.

18. *Cf.* Phillip Connor, "International Migration and Religious Selection," *Journal for the Scientific Study of Religion* 51 (2012): 184–194.
19. Alicia Re Cruz, "Taquerías, Laundromats and Protestant Churches: Landmarks of Hispanic Barrios in Denton, Texas," *Urban Anthropology* 34 (2005): 281–303.
20. From an evangelical perspective, *cf.* Matthew Soerens and Jenny Hwang, *Welcoming the Stranger: Justice, Compassion and Truth in the Immigration Debate* (Downer's Grove, IL: IVP, 2009).
21. See, for example, the institutional and personal signatories of the *Christians for Comprehensive Immigration Reform* "Statement of Principles," accessed April 6, 2012, http://faithandimmigration.org/content/statement-principles.
22. Gregory A. Smith, "Attitudes toward Immigration: in the Pulpit and the Pew," *Pew Research Center Publications* (April 26, 2006), accessed March 1, 2014, http://pewresearch.org/pubs/20/attitudes-toward-immigration-in-the-pulpit-and-the-pew.
23. The resolution can be read at http://www.sbc.net/resolutions/amresolution.asp?id=1213 accessed March 1, 2014. It is quite short, and makes reference to a number of scriptural passages from both testaments. The primary rationale put forth for defending immigrants is based on Rev. 7:9 as a description of "God's Kingdom," composed of people from "every tribe, tongue, nation and language." It is followed by a statement about "our ancestors in the faith," that is, the children of Israel, who were sojourners and strangers in the land, as well as about Jesus, "who lived his childhood years as an immigrant and refugee." These wide themes relating to salvation history and Christology are at the basis of the resolution's initial openness to undocumented immigrants. In the second part of the resolution, however, the wider theme of grace comes up against a narrow and rather legalistic interpretation of Rom.13:1–7, one that shuts down the possibility of deeply questioning the present-day laws of the United States, since "Christians are under biblical mandate to respect the divinely ordained institution of government."
24. Jung Young Lee, *Marginality: The Key to Multicultural Theology* (Minneapolis: Fortress Press, 1995), 2.
25. Lee, *Marginality*, 59ff.
26. Homi Bhabha, *The Location of Culture* (New York: Routledge, 1994), 5.
27. Oscar García-Johnson, "Las iglesias latinas y el 'nuevo' denominacionalismo estadounidense: Una perspectiva glocal," in *Vivir y servir en el exilio: Lecturas teológicas de la experiencia latina en los Estados Unidos,* eds. Jorge Maldonado and Juan F. Martínez, 187–212 (Buenos Aires: Kairós, 2008).
28. Marion Rohrleitner, "Who We Are: Migration, Gender and New Forms of Citizenship," *American Quarterly* 63 (2011): 419–429.

29. *Cf.* Jacob K. Olupona and Regina Gemignani, "Introduction," in *African Immigrant Religions in America,* eds. Jacob K. Olupona and Regina Gemignani (New York: New York University Press, 2007), 5.
30. Admittedly, not all Latin American migrants speak Spanish; in some Protestant churches, Quiché, Garifuna, or Portuguese is spoken, among other languages.
31. Re Cruz, "Taquerías, Laundromats and Protestant Churches," 294–295.
32. *Cf.* Hsing-Kuang Chao, "Conversion to Protestantism among Urban Immigrants in Taiwan," *Sociology of Religion* 67 (2006): 193–204.
33. Some examples are HB 1070 in Arizona (2010), HB 56 in Alabama (2011), and HB 87 in Georgia (2011).
34. These numbers are mentioned by the *Illinois Coalition for Immigrant and Refugee Rights* (ICIRR) in their "Know Your Rights Presentations" (unpublished).
35. In the United States, if an undocumented person has accumulated unlawful presence in the country for a year or more and then leaves, this triggers a ten-year reentry bar, something that becomes a burden for mixed-status families.
36. For the purposes of this essay, I am not including within "Protestantism" the Church of Jesus Christ of Latter-day Saints (Mormons) or Jehovah's Witnesses, who have historical connections and some overlap with Protestantism, but explicitly reject a Trinitarian faith. These groups, as well as Unitarians, are often faithful advocates of migrant rights.
37. See the *Kirchliche Dogmatik* IV/1, §59.
38. Julian of Norwich, *Showings,* trans. Edmund Colledge (Mahwah, NJ: Paulist Press, 1978), Long Text, §§ 57–63, 290–305.
39. Janet Soskice, *The Kindness of God: Metaphor, Gender and Religious Language* (Oxford: Oxford University Press, 2007), 149–151.
40. Lee, *Marginality,* 101–102.
41. Caroline Jeannerat, "Of Lizards, Misfortune and Deliverance: Pentecostal Soteriology in the Life of a Migrant," *African Studies* 68 (2009): 251–271.
42. Ana María Bidegain, "Living a Trans-national Spirituality: Latin American Catholic Families in Miami," in *Migration in a Global World,* ed. Solange Lefebvre and Luiz Carlos Susin, 95–107 (London: SCM Press, 2008).
43. Elizabeth Conde-Frazier, "Testimonios: Relato, agencia y la mujer latina," 125–148.
44. Espinosa, "Salvation and Tranformation," 150–151.
45. Claudia Währisch-Oblau, *The Missionary Self-Perception of Pentecostal/Charismatic Church Leaders from the Global South in Europe: Bringing Back the Gospel* (Leiden: Brill, 2009), 225–229.

46. Währisch-Oblau, *The Missionary Self-Perception*, 259–262.
47. *Cf.* Olupona and Gemignani, *African Immigrant Religions*, 8–9 and *passim*.
48. Bernard Coyault, "Les communautés chrétiennes étrangères: enjeux et collaborations," in *Proceeding Documents of the Conference Essere Chiesa Insieme / Uniting in Diversity (Italia and Churches' Commission for Migrants in Europe)*, eds. Annemarie Dupré, Thorsten Leisser and Patrizia Tortora, Federazione delle chiese evangeliche (Ciampino-Sassone: March 26–28, 2004), 28–32, accessed March 1, 2014, http://fedevangelica.it/documenti/3/6fcc1ff4f3dced3926874551 1a97a6f0.pdf.
49. Carmen Nanko Fernández, "Creation: A Cosmo-politan Perspective," in *In Our Own Voices. Latino/a Renditions of Theology*, ed. Benjamín Valentín, 41–63 (Maryknoll: Orbis, 2010).

Chapter 7

The Im/migrant Spirit: De/constructing a Pentecostal Theology of Migration

Amos Yong

Im/Migration: A Testimony and an Introduction

In typical pentecostal style, I begin with a testimony. I was born in Malaysia to a family of Chinese pentecostal pastors and raised as a preacher's kid (PK), the eldest of three boys. When I was ten, my parents moved us to California, where they had been called to take over the pastorate of a small congregation of Cantonese-speaking immigrant families, predominantly from Hong Kong, and I became a missionary kid (MK)—To the United States![1] I then went to a mostly white, small liberal arts pentecostal-affiliated college where I met my wife, a fifth generation Mexican American who was born in Wisconsin during harvest season to migrant farm workers from Texas, grew up in the Eastern Washington basin, and was raised partly as a Catholic and then later in pentecostal churches in her teens. Our three children have had the perennial problem of checking the proper box to identify their racial and ethnic profile, since there isn't one that fits them on most forms.

As a family, we have migrated around the country on several occasions as well. For eight years, we lived in the Vancouver, Washington / Portland, Oregon area where I went to a Wesleyan Holiness seminary and a secular university. Then, we moved our family across the country to an old European-dominated suburb of Boston, in Massachusetts, where I did my PhD, and then landed a teaching position in St. Paul, Minnesota. Our six years at Bethel University introduced us to the Swedish pietist tradition of the Baptist General Conference, even as our sojourn in the upper Midwest gave us insight into the Scandinavian migration of the nineteenth century into the area, a migration that has by now left a deep imprint on the region. In 2005, we moved to the Hampton Roads area of southeast Virginia (to teach at Regent University), and we felt palpably for the first time the history of racism that has long marked Southern life (even though Virginia is one of the northernmost states of the former Confederacy).[2]

In looking back over my life journey so far (there may be more moves in the future), as a pentecostal, I map it onto the experience of the earliest Christians.[3] At the heart of the modern pentecostal experience remains the Lukan text, especially the promise regarding the outpouring of the Spirit from on high: "But you will receive power when the Holy Spirit has come upon you; and you will be my witnesses in Jerusalem, in all Judea and Samaria, and to the ends of the earth" (Acts 1:8).[4] This text indicates, in light of my own personal history and experience of migration, the migratory nature of the earliest followers of Jesus as messiah. Yet I am unaware of any theological reflections to date about what it means to think about migration from an explicitly pentecostal perspective.[5]

This essay outlines just such a pentecostal theology of migration. We begin with a brief overview about the appropriateness of such a theological task for pentecostalism. The middle and longest section of this essay attempts to tease out from the book of Acts a basic framework for thinking theologically about migration. We conclude with some overarching theological reflections on migration that fuses the first century horizons of the apostolic migrant experiences with the contemporary perspectives of the global pentecostal and charismatic renewal movement. Our goal is to suggest how pentecostal perspectives might help us think constructively about migration in ways that simultaneously interrogate and, where necessary, deconstruct discursive practices that are "too heavenly minded but not sufficiently of earthly good," as the saying goes.[6] Insofar as the forces of globalization and the continuously shrinking global village have touched all of us in various respects, perhaps the pentecostal perspective can enable not just pentecostals, but all Christians, and even all migrants, to adapt as aliens and strangers in foreign lands.

Pentecostal Migration: An Overview

To be sure, pentecostals are not the only group of contemporary migrants. However, in order to fill out the broader socio-historical contexts within which my own experiences of migration have unfolded, and to further set the table for the exegetical and theological reflections to come, I need to provide a brief portrait of the migratory character of pentecostalism as a renewal movement. Three aspects of pentecostal migration are especially noteworthy for our purposes: its missionary heart, its global extent, and its translatability.[7]

First, pentecostalism is, in many respects, a missionary religion. Yes, at its core, Christianity itself is driven by a missionary impulse, so in that sense, there is nothing distinctive to this claim. Yet on the other hand, it is also practically undisputable that whereas the nineteenth century featured the missionary emergence of Christianity as a world religion, the twentieth century has seen the missionary "pentecostalization" of world Christianity.[8] In that sense, the missionary mantle for contemporary Christianity has been donned, like it or not, by pentecostalism. And it has been precisely its missionary spirit that had led pentecostals along the path of transnational migration, going here and there, wherever it is that they believe God has called them to the work of mission and evangelism.

More specifically, there are two aspects—historical and contemporary—to understanding the missionary identity of pentecostalism. Historically, we must register the missionary impulses that launched the movement as a global phenomenon.[9] More than anything else, early pentecostals were motivated as missionaries because they believed that they also, like the apostles, had received the power of the Spirit to take the gospel to the ends of the earth. Thus from Azusa Street, one of the earliest pentecostal centers, missionaries went to Asia, Africa, and Latin America, believing that they had been called by God to preach the gospel in order to make way for Christ's imminent return. On the contemporary scene, this missionary impulse has fed ever more intense initiatives directed toward the evangelization of the world. Thus have pentecostals ventured courageously into unevangelized areas, obeying the call of God to bear witness to the gospel to every creature under heaven (Col. 1:23). Many observers of the Christian mission have therefore recognized pentecostals to have been at the vanguard of global mission and evangelism projects, even if pentecostals themselves have not, at least to date, produced the widest circulating missiology textbooks.[10]

Second, and related to the first point, concerns the spread and extent of pentecostal migration. If its missionizing heart has driven pentecostals ever outward from their comfort zones, the result has been literally the globalization of the renewal movement over the last century.[11] There are various aspects of this global and globalizing phenomenon. Sociologically, globalization experts have noted recurring patterns—for instance, the migration of people from rural to urban areas—in many cases reflecting a response to labor and market demands and fluctuations, the movements across established transnational routes, and the usual shifts forced by wars (civil and otherwise), famines, and other tragic developments.

Economically, pentecostal entrepreneurship has not been overlooked.[12] Pentecostal boldness in witness, evangelism, and missions has transferred over into their economic lives: many are adventurous in launching business initiatives and creative in expanding opportunities variously to engage with developments locally and globally. Often, they are also at the forefront in taking advantage of and extending the new media and communications technologies, both with regard to mission and evangelism on the one hand, and with regard to economic mobilization and expansion on the other.[13] What this means is that alongside mission-related migration, pentecostals fully inhabit our globalized world: socially, economically, and telecommunicatively. These developments mean that even those who "stay at home" are touched by migration, experiencing globalization through their friends and families who emigrate for whatever reason.

All of this pentecostal mobility, however, raises the question about its adaptability. This concerns the third aspect of pentecostal migration I wish to highlight: its translatability across cultures. Scholars like Lamin Sanneh have called attention to the translatability of the Christian faith as a whole and how the emergence of world Christianity is itself a reflection of the religion's capacity to be contextualized and acculturated across time and space,[14] so again, I am not saying that this is a feature only of pentecostalism. My claim, however, is that pentecostalism is in a certain sense uniquely indigenizable across vastly different languages, cultures, and environments, in part because the center of pentecostal spirituality itself is deeply shaped by the many tongues of the Day of Pentecost experience.

Harvey Cox refers to this as the primal spirituality of pentecostalism, one that touches and more easily connects with the primal speech and primal piety of the indigenous cultures that underlies much of the cultural-religious traditions of the world.[15] In short, as pentecostal scholars Murray Dempster, Byron Klaus, and Douglas Petersen have suggested, pentecostalism is itself uniquely suited as "a religion made to travel."[16]

All this movement, expansion, and translation beg for more formal theological consideration on the phenomenon of migration. Pentecostals have begun to reflect theologically on the missiological implications of their spirituality, but this has yet to translate into a theology of migration. My suggestion, in the remainder of this essay, is that the distinctive character of pentecostal spirituality and missionary sensibility can be mined for insights that can contribute to the emerging discussions on theologies of migration. As should be clear from the foregoing, however, I am thinking about migration in exceedingly broad terms, across the spectrum of perspectives from those moving from a region or nation (emigrants) to those settling into a new country (immigrants) as well as including vastly different experiences of voluntary labor movements (migrants) and forced movements due to especially political turmoil (refugees, exiles, asylum seekers, etc.).[17] Yet I will return in my conclusion to suggest why we can think theologically more specifically about a pneumatology of *im*migration, following the work of the Spirit who always seeks to arrive and rest in human hearts, lives, and communities.

Lukan Migration: Early Christianities— Migrant Communities

As a springboard for our thinking about migration, I turn to the pentecostal canon-within-the canon, the book of Acts.[18] The following unfolds in three acts, according to the division that the author outlines in the verse, the first part of which has become central to the modern pentecostal movement's self-understanding: "But you will receive power when the Holy Spirit has come upon you; and you will be my witnesses *in all Judea and Samaria, and to the ends of the earth*" (Acts 1:8, italics added). My intention is to unpack this three part migration of the apostolic experience in light of contemporary globalization trends.[19] I will argue that the early messianic movement was constituted essentially by its migration experiences, and that such movement enabled the incarnation of Christian faith in a diversity of forms on the one hand, yet also allowed the subversion of local hegemonic structures, on the other.

Act 1: The Early Church in Jerusalem as a Migrant Community

I want to make three broad observations about the migratory nature of the earliest messianic community that is described in the initial chapters of the book of Acts. First, it is clear that the initial followers of Jesus as the messiah were mostly Jews and godfearers from around the Mediterranean who had come "home" to celebrate the Feast of Pentecost (Acts 2:5–11). Luke states that the original "congregation" of 3,000 was constituted by these migrants "from every nation under heaven" (cp. Acts 2:5 and 2: 41).[20] Within a short time, the number of messianists had grown to over 5,000, not including women and children (Acts 4:4), although their numbers were being added to by those from the countryside around Jerusalem (Acts 5:16). It appears, as a result of the revival, that most of those who had returned from around the Mediterranean world to Jerusalem and the surrounding regions decided to stay in the area, leading to major long-term organizational challenges to house and feed so many families.

Thus, second, the earliest Christian community was confronted with its most severe challenge, and opportunity, because of its migrant constitution. As Luke records it, "during those days, when the disciples were increasing in number, the Hellenists complained against the Hebrews because their widows were being neglected in the daily distribution of food" (Acts 6:1). On the surface, this "problem" can be understood as no more or less than an economic one: migration brings with it economic risks and challenges. However, we have already been told that somehow, there were sufficient resources that the growing community pooled together to meet the needs of all (Acts 2:45, 4:34). Something more is going on, reflecting perhaps the inequalities common to migration experiences from the beginning of time. In this case, the local Hebrew widows, who spoke Aramaic, appeared to have been able to control the distribution of food, resulting in the neglect of the "outsiders": the Greek-speaking or Hellenist widows. Note though, that the problem was not so much that Hellenist widows were not getting food, but that they were not participants in the distribution of food, resulting, perhaps, in the lack of food not only for Hellenist widows but also for Hellenist families as a whole.[21]

Why should we be surprised that factions had developed in the early messianic community? No doubt there were miscommunications, misunderstandings, and even jealousies that characterized such a diverse community, drawn together by Jewish and messianic commitments to some extent, yet deeply diverse in terms of linguistic, customary, and cultural differences that inevitably emerged over time. Just as inevitably, when such disagreements boiled over, those "in charge," the Aramaic-speaking messianists, acted exclusively and maybe even condescendingly, vis-à-vis the migrants in their midst. After all, outsiders, or at least those whose ties to the local area had been stretched or even broken for a time, did not deserve the same level of treatment as insiders. That has been the undeniable experience of migrants since human beings have launched out or been cast out (as the case may be) from their home regions in search of a better tomorrow.[22]

This leads to my third observation about the burgeoning messianic community: that they worked hard to develop an egalitarian leadership by putting migrants in charge. The apostles appointed seven deacons, all apparently—if their names are any indication—leading members of the migrant Hellenist Jews, one of whom, Nicholas, was said explicitly to have been from the diaspora: that is, from Antioch in what is today called Asia Minor (Acts 6:5). Herein I think we learn a further lesson about theological indigenization commensurate with the Day of Pentecost narrative. If the outpouring of the Spirit empowered the speaking of many tongues and languages to declare "God's deeds of power" (Acts 2:11), then part of the outworking of this dynamic gift of the Spirit should be the empowering of people from many cultures to incarnate the gospel on their own terms. The Pentecost event did not erase the diversity of tongues but redeemed it, in fact, loosing the plurality of human expressions while orchestrating such dissonance miraculously for the glory of God. Similarly, then, the experience of migration, which brings very different people together, should not result in a homogenization of the messianic community but in its diversification instead. And appreciation for such diversity and pluralism depends on our following the Spirit's lead in empowering leadership across the spectrum, even when that means putting migrants in charge![23]

Of course, this is not to say that the apostolic leaders had made all of the right decisions in empowering the Hellenist Jews to take responsibility for their widows. In point of fact, initially there remained a distinction between the authority of the apostles themselves, as prayers and preachers/proclaimers, and that of the deacons, "to wait on tables" (Acts 6:2–4). Yet once released as deacons, the empowerment of the Spirit, which ultimately sought to take the gospel beyond the confines of Jerusalem and Judea, began to move upon these Hellenist Jewish leaders to undertake tasks beyond that of their initial assignment. It was Stephen, the deacon, who began to see, and to proclaim under the Spirit's inspiration, that the scope of the presence and activity of God's Spirit was not limited to Jerusalem or to the temple. Here was a Hellenist Jew who began to discern that this eschatological outpouring of the Spirit had diasporic implications.

The entire history of Israel pointed to the universal character of God's redemptive activity (Acts 7). Stephen upbraided the Sanhedrin and other Jerusalem- and temple-centered Jews, about their parochial perspectives, and as a result, he was stoned as punishment for blasphemy against Moses and the temple (Acts 7:44–53). Is it too much to say that it was Stephen's migrant point of view—from the margins—that allowed him to realize the extent of the salvation in Christ that the more centrally located apostolic leaders might have discerned but failed to act on?[24]

Act 2: Philip, the First Migrant Evangelist to Samaria

In the aftermath of the tragedy that ended Stephen's life and ministry, the local Jewish intelligentsia launched a severe persecution "against the church in Jerusalem, and all except the apostles were scattered throughout the countryside of Judea and Samaria" (Acts 8:1). Interestingly, while the Judean- and Galilean-based apostolic leadership hunkered down in Jerusalem, it was the migrant Hellenist Jewish deacons who gave no second thought to the doors that appeared closed—that is, in Jerusalem—and moved to take advantage of open doors: in the wider countryside and, God forbid, in the land of Samaria. Recall that during that time, it was clearly known that "Jews do not share things in common with Samaritans" (John 4:9). In fact, relationships had so degenerated between Jews and Samaritans that the former had already begun to engage in the rhetorical demonization of the latter; thus does John record the Jewish leadership's polemic against Jesus: "You are a Samaritan and have a demon" (John 8:48)! In light of this background, let me proffer four sets of comments about the migration of the gospel to the region of Samaria and beyond.

First, Luke records, "Those who were scattered went from place to place, proclaiming the word. Philip went down to the city of Samaria and proclaimed the Messiah to them" (Acts 8:4–5). Although Jesus was himself an itinerant evangelist, the apostles he personally instructed did not initially follow in his footsteps. But migrants like Philip had embraced a messianic message with a much more extensive reach that was not geographically bound. Not even the despised Samaritans were beyond the pale of the gospel's offering.

Second, Hellenist migrants like Philip had developed a repertoire of skills by learning how to survive in hostile and foreign situations. Upon arrival in Samaria, then, he was able to engage with the locals in ways that the apostles may not have been able to. Along the way, he attracted the attention of Simon, the sorcerer, who "for a long time ... had amazed them [the Samaritans] with his magic" and commanded their attention (Acts 8:10–11). With skills honed from a life of migration, Philip was able to both engage the people and to interact calmly and extensively with Simon—who "stayed constantly with Philip" (Acts 8:13)—even to the point of baptizing him into the faith. To be sure, when the apostles finally arrived from Jerusalem, they were much more forthright with Simon, but this was only possible because the groundwork had been laid by Philip. Still, the result was essentially a two-fold subversion: first of the local Samaritan dynamics, with the authority of Simon being displaced by that of Hellenist and Jewish followers of the messiah, and second of the apostles themselves, by a migrant deacon who, while running for his life, had not known better than to act politically incorrectly by building bridges with the perennial enemies of Israel.

But third, while the apostolic leaders returned to Jerusalem even after the relatively successful mission to Samaria (Acts 8:25), Philip was not done, emboldened instead to venture into the region of Gaza (Acts 8:26). Along the way, he met another migrant, one who had become adept at crossing boundaries and borders: sexual boundaries, no doubt intimidating for a eunuch who worked for a queen in a male-dominated world; ethnic boundaries, as an Ethiopian on sojourn far from home, in Palestine; international and political borders, as "a court official of the Candace, queen of the Ethiopians" (Acts 8:27a); socioeconomic borders, as one in charge of the treasury of Candace and of the Ethiopian people (Acts 8:27b); religious borders, as (in all probability) a gentile who "had come to Jerusalem to worship" (Acts 8:27c); and personal/relational borders, as one perhaps without family, certainly without descendants, who felt alone in the world.[25] Maybe it was precisely because of his reflection on his own existential state that what he was reading resonated with him: "In his humiliation he was deprived of justice. *Who can speak of his descendants?* For his life was taken from the earth" (Acts 8:33, citing Isa. 53:8, New International Version; italics added). Perhaps the eunuch empathized with this stranger, who even as he "was led like a sheep to the slaughter...did not open his mouth" (Acts 8:32, citing Isa. 53:7, NIV).

Philip, "starting with this scripture...proclaimed to him the good news about Jesus" (Acts 8:35). This migrant Hellenist told the migrant Ethiopian all about the migrant Jew named Jesus, who not only had no descendants but also "nowhere to lay his head" (Luke 9:58). Thus, here was a boundary- and border-crosser the Ethiopian could identify with, one who was indeed rejected by his generation, as the Ethiopian felt himself to be. Yet as this migrant evangelist recounted, the one who had no descendants, through the gift of the Holy Spirit to all who would receive him, had formed a new people of God, called after his name, and into this new family even eunuchs, Ethiopians, the sociopolitical elite, and the economically affluent, were welcome.

We are not told what happened to the eunuch after his encounter with Philip, except that he "went on his way rejoicing" (Acts 8:39b).

Tradition says that the church in Ethiopia can be traced, at least in part, to this migrant's experiences on the road from Jerusalem to Gaza. If so, then from its inception, the migrating power of the gospel was manifest in Ethiopia, embodied by a migrant, without descendants, but with the power of the Spirit of God whose community saw no bounds.[26]

Last but not least, however, this narrative ends with a migration experience for which nothing Philip had previously encountered would have prepared him. Upon baptizing the eunuch, suddenly "the Spirit of the Lord snatched Philip away; the eunuch saw him no more, and went on his way rejoicing. But Philip found himself at Azotus, and as he was passing through the region, he proclaimed the good news to all the towns until he came to Caesarea" (Acts 8:39b-40). What is amazing is that Philip the migrant simply continued up the coastline, toward Caesarea, perhaps anticipating that this was simply one more stop in following the call to take the gospel back to the ends of the earth from which he had come.

Act 3: Peter, Paul, and the Ends of the Earth

There is too much to comment on here, so I had better make a few general observations. We begin with Peter, who we saw was willing to venture at least into Samaria, following Philip, but who appears to have reconsidered his decision to remain in Jerusalem after all. Thus, later on, he embarked on his own itinerant trek, at least in the surrounding regions of Lydda and Joppa, and later up to Caesarea (Acts 9:32–10:24 and passim). From here on, the horizons and borders of his own ministry expanded. Over time, he must have revisited his relationship with the migrant Hellenistic community that had become part of the fabric of the early messianic movement, to the point of establishing connections with the diasporic communities represented by these migrants. Thus, later he writes to "exiles of the Dispersion in Pontus, Galatia, Cappadocia, Asia, and Bithynia" (1 Pet. 1:1). If in fact the author of this epistle is the same person—and there are no good reasons to doubt the letter's authenticity[27]—Peter had clearly come to claim for himself a migrant identity, urging his readers, "as aliens and exiles to abstain from the desires of the flesh that wage war against the soul" (1 Pet. 2:11). In short, migrancy is not just an accidental feature of the lives of those who have crossed humanly construed borders; rather, it characterizes the pluralistic nature of what it means to be the people of God at its core.[28]

Paul, of course, was a cosmopolitan figure who was raised in Tarsus but also felt at home throughout the Pax Romana. He exercised his travel rights as a Roman citizen, but did so by taking advantage of his educational achievements and elite status, possibly as one of the leading members of the Synagogue of the Freedman (Acts 6:9). Of course, Paul's legacy has been as the missionary par excellence during the first generation of the messianic Christian movement. He made multiple missionary excursions around the Mediterranean world (which are recorded in Acts), even visited Rome (albeit as a prisoner in chains)—Rome was considered to have been the heart of the empire, and, from the standpoint of Jerusalem, represented the "ends of the earth"—and long had aspirations to evangelize in Spain (Rom. 15:28). In short, after coming to embrace the Hellenist interpretations (by Stephen, et al.) of the message and meaning of Christ, Paul himself came to see the universal implications of the gospel. Yes, it was borne from out of the heart of God's covenant with the Jews, but it had from the beginning been intended to bless all the nations of the earth, as had been promised originally to Abraham.

My claim, however, is that Paul the migrant was not merely an itinerant evangelist or a peripatetic apostle. Rather, because he recognized that the power of a migrating gospel was only as strong as its roots in any local region, Paul established churches and worked to ensure that they were competently led and nurtured. Such local congregations were not explicitly subversive of the peace of Rome—after all, it was precisely such peace that enabled evangelical migration!—yet neither were they completely without imperial effect.[29] These effects could be measured economically, as exemplified in the communal way of life in the earliest days in Jerusalem; politically, as in how the followers of the messiah could respect and pray for their political leaders, but pledge their allegiances only to Jesus as Lord, rather than to Caesar; and socially, as represented by Peter's admonition to live differently from the world, especially when the world lives after the flesh.

Beyond this, there were also more direct imperial engagements. Following Jesus, Paul mounted no revolutionary assault against the imperial regime. However, he confronted the forces of empire personally when opportunities arose, challenging its various manifestations in different domains. Economically, for instance, Paul did not shy away from burning scrolls devoted to sorcery and from exposing the character of local deities to the extent that it came to have a negative impact on the political economy of Ephesian craftsmen (Acts 19:17–27). Politically, Paul regularly appealed to his rights as a citizen, and did not shy away from engaging with local leaders (i.e., Sergius

Paulus of Paphos, the Philippian magistrates, Publius on Malta) and politicians about matters related to "justice, self-control, and the coming judgement" (Acts 24:25). Throughout, he talked about the kingdom of God (Acts 14:22, 19:8, 20:25, 28:23), no doubt a subversive idea indeed, when understood against the backdrop of Caesar's claims to lordship.[30]

In all of this, I submit that Paul was simply following in the footsteps of his migrant savior. Jesus himself consistently crossed boundaries and borders: interacting with social pariahs like tax collectors and prostitutes; touching the religiously polluted like lepers, those hemorrhaging blood, or the bodies of dead people; and welcoming the poor and other unclean people, including Gentiles and Samaritans.

No, Jesus never left Palestine—unless one believes the apocryphal story of his visit to India—but once emergent on the public scene, he was constantly on the move, "through cities and villages" (Luke 8:1), relying on the goodwill, provisions, and resources of others. Thus also did he commission his followers as migrant evangelists: "Take nothing for your journey, no staff, nor bag, nor bread, nor money—not even an extra tunic. Whatever house you enter, stay there, and leave from there. Wherever they do not welcome you, as you are leaving that town shake the dust off your feet as a testimony against them" (Luke 9:3–5; cp. 10:3–12). Is it any wonder then that the earliest followers of Jesus set out as migrants, even to the very ends of the earth?

Theology of Im/migration: Lukan and Pentecostal Intonations

In these concluding paragraphs, I want to sketch the rudiments of a theology of migration as informed by my pentecostal rereading of the book of Acts. There are three dimensions to my summary reflections: missiological, political, and theological.

Missionally: Any pentecostal theology of migration must begin with the missional character of the Spirit-filled life. On this matter, mission involves migration, and migration is undertaken for missional purposes.[31] Yet as our overview of the early messianic experience shows, at some point, roots are planted, and in those cases, migrants need to find homes. Note that the apostolic decision to receive leadership from migrants reflects the discernment that in that case, at that place and time, these migrants, who were far from home (although as diaspora Jews they had in other respects returned home to Judea), needed their own leaders. Here was a case of enabling local leaders on foreign soil, so to speak. Along the way, at least at the dawn of the modern world, including the beginnings of the modern missionary movement, we have forgotten such truths, so that the missional task of Christianization has been co-opted by the colonial project of Westernization instead. Hence, over the last century, we have had to relearn the hard way many lessons about the importance of recognizing and empowering indigenous leaders.[32]

Yet such should not be understood only in terms of what happens "out there," abroad, in the Global South; it may also be relevant here, "at home," in the Euro-American West, particularly in light of the reverse missionary movement from the rest to the West. Pentecostals have usually been alert to the need to establish indigenous churches that are, following the famous missionary model of Roland Allen, self-supporting, self-governing, and self-propagating, at least in (missiological) theory, if not in (evangelistic) practice.[33] Yet the current task for any theology of migration, relative to the needs of the twenty-first century, must be sensitive to the challenges experienced by migrant communities and their churches, wherever they may be found.

Politically: Our review of the Acts narrative also highlights what we might not often hear much about in pentecostal circles—the political dimension of missional migration. Pentecostals have been, in general, so focused on the evangelistic dimension of missions that they have neglected to reflect more intentionally about the political relevance of their practices. In this respect, my initial efforts to construct a pentecostal theology of migration in this essay involve also an element of deconstruction of pentecostal assumptions about missional migration. What needs to be interrogated is the widely assumed notion in pentecostal mission and evangelism that the gospel is meant for human souls rather than for human lives in all of their political complexity. By political, of course, I am referring to the public aspects of human life, which includes not only the political, as narrowly conceived in relationship to the state, but also the economic, social, cultural, and civic domains.

Pentecostals are right to insist that neither Jesus nor Paul were directly concerned with such public structures in their migration. However, this does not mean that migrants have nothing to say about or contribute to the political formation of human lives. In fact, the subversive power of the gospel is precisely its capacity to interrogate the status quo of our political, social, and economic practices, even to the point of undermining the very nature of these presumed realities insofar as they do not measure up to the peace, justice, and righteousness of the coming kingdom.[34] The power of migration is that it injects fresh perspectives into local situations, perspectives that can generate new insights into underlying causes of what needs to be fixed and that can identify what needs to be done. There just needs to be structures in place that welcome migrants and enable their settling into a new home, yet that do not assimilate them to the point that they can no longer maintain a critical perspective.[35] The result should be a transformation of the margins, so that new centers emerge in a globalized and post-Christendom world.[36]

Finally, theologically: My pentecostal perspective that begins with the experience of Spirit-infilling and empowerment for mission realizes that our migration is modeled on that of the Holy Spirit's. The Spirit's migration, however, is also more precisely, from our perspective, an *immigration*, a movement of the Spirit that is incomplete until the Spirit takes up residence upon our heads, blows between our ears, enlivens our tongues, and gushes forth from within our hearts. Thus does Luke write,

> And suddenly from heaven there came a sound like the rush of a violent wind, and it filled the entire house where they were sitting. Divided tongues, as of fire, appeared among them, and a tongue rested on each of them. All of them were filled with the Holy Spirit and began to speak in other languages, as the Spirit gave them ability." (Acts 2:2–4)

The movements of the Spirit are thus outward, from the Father on high (Luke 24:49) through the Son at his right hand (Acts 2:33), and then inward, into us, so as to redeem us as the people of God. No wonder we are a migrant people, caught up in the migrations of the Spirit. Yet simultaneously, we are also an immigrant people, following the immigrations of the Spirit. But if the Spirit immigrates into human hearts, so do we, as living epistles, immigrate into the proximity of the lives of strangers, and there seek to take root, not in the sense of making their world our home, but in the sense of enabling the gospel to flourish deep in the hearts and lives of our hosts. Thus, the call of the Spirit is the empowerment to leave our homes and our comfort zones, to be guests of others in strange places, so that the gospel can become the home for us all. Herein is accomplished our own transformation, achieved through the Spirit by the differences represented in the hearts and lives of others. The Spirit immigrates betwixt, between, and through our own diasporic crossing over (emigration) and returning from (immigration) the borders and margins that had previously divided "us" from "them."[37]

When all of this finally happens, the eschatological transmigration will occur, one in which the new Jerusalem will come down from out of heaven, and the heavens and the earth will be renewed, so that it, and all its inhabitants, can become the final dwelling place of the living God.[38]

Notes

1. This phenomenon of missionaries coming from the Global South to the Euro-American West is no longer new, especially not since the repeal of the immigration law in 1965 opened up the flow of traffic to the United States—the end of the first wave of which washed me and my family ashore in the mid-1970s—and since the formation of the European Union allowed for easier travel within its borders. For introductions to pentecostal "reverse flow" missions, as it has come to be known in missiological circles, see Larry D. Pate, "Pentecostal Missions from the Two-Thirds World," in *Called and Empowered: Global Missions in Pentecostal Perspective*, eds. Murray Dempster, Byron D. Klaus, and Douglas Petersen, 242–58 (Peabody, Mass.: Hendrickson, 1991); and Daniëlle Koning, "Bringing Back the Gospel to Europe: Immigrant Churches as New Missionaries," in *A Moving God: Immigrant Churches in the Netherlands, International Practical Theology* 8, eds. Mechteld Jansen and Hijme Stoffels, 103–14 (Zürich and Berlin: Lit Verlag, and New Brunswick, NJ, and London: Transaction Publishers, 2006). An excellent recent study is Claudia Währisch-Oblau, *The Missionary Self-Perception of Pentecostal/Charismatic Church Leaders from the Global South in Europe: Bringing Back the Gospel* (Leiden and Boston: Brill, 2009).
2. I have written intermittently about myself in various places, including in introductory vignettes to chapters of my various books. The most theologically substantive of my personal reflections is "Between the Local and the Global: Autobiographical Reflections on the Emergence of the Global Theological Mind," in *Shaping a Global Theological Mind*, ed. Darren C. Marks, 187–94 (Aldershot, UK: Ashgate, 2008).
3. I explicate the "this-is-that" hermeneutic that enables pentecostals to intuitively correlate their experiences of the Spirit with that of the apostolic Christians, and vice-versa, in my article, "The 'Baptist Vision' of James William McClendon, Jr.: A Wesleyan-Pentecostal Response," *Wesleyan Theological Journal* 37, no. 2 (Fall 2002): 32–57.
4. Unless otherwise noted, all biblical citation will be from the New Revised Standard Version of the Bible and references will be made parenthetically in the text.
5. Leading the way in the theology of migration are Roman Catholic scholars—for example, Peter C. Phan, "The Experience of Migration

as Source of Intercultural Theology in the United States," in *Christianity with an Asian Face: Asian American Theology in the Making* (Maryknoll: Orbis, 2003), 3–25; Donald Kerwin and Jill Marie Gerschutz, eds., *And You Welcomed Me: Migration and Catholic Social Teaching* (Lanham, MD: Rowman & Littlefield, 2009); and Gemma Tulud Cruz, *An Intercultural Theology of Migration: Pilgrims in the Wilderness*, Studies in Systematic Theology 5 (Leiden: Brill, 2010).

6. This is in part a reference to the by and large apolitical character of much of the global renewal movement. Things, however, are changing, as I discuss in my "Salvation, Society, and the Spirit: Pentecostal Contextualization and Political Theology from Cleveland to Birmingham, from Springfield to Seoul," *Pax Pneuma: The Journal of Pentecostals & Charismatics for Peace & Justice* 5, no. 2 (2009): 22–34. More on this below.

7. In the following, I use "pentecostal," "charismatic," and "renewal" fairly synonymously. There are technical nuances in the literature for each of these labels, but for our purposes, these do not matter. For my own fairly inclusive definition of "pentecostalism"—which is why I do not capitalize it—see Yong, *The Spirit Poured Out on All Flesh: Pentecostalism and the Possibility of Global Theology* (Grand Rapids: Baker Academic, 2005), esp. 18–22.

8. For example, Cephas Omenyo, "From the Fringes to the Centre: Pentecostalization of the Mainline churches in Ghana," *Exchange* 34, no. 1 (2005): 39–60; Gastón Espinosa, "The Pentecostalization of Latin American and U.S. Latino Christianity," *Pneuma* 26, no. 2 (2004): 262–92; Damaris Seleina Parsitau, "From the Periphery to the Centre: The Pentecostalisation of Mainline Christianity in Kenya," *Missionalia* 35, no. 3 (2007) 83–111; and Douglas L. Rutt, "The 'Pentecostalization' of Christianity," *Concordia Theological Quarterly* 70, nos. 3–4 (2006): 371–73. See also Philip Jenkins, *The Next Christendom: The Coming of Global Christianity* (Oxford: Oxford University Press, 2002).

9. As documented by James R. Goff, Jr., *Fields White Unto Harvest: Charles Fox Parham and the Missionary Origins of Pentecostalism* (Fayetteville, Ark.: University of Arkansas Press, 1987); Cecil M. Robeck, Jr., *The Azusa Street Mission and Revival: The Birth of the Global Pentecostal Movement* (Nashville: Nelson Reference & Electronic, 2006); Allan Anderson, *Spreading Fires: The Missionary Nature of Early Pentecostalism* (London: SCM Press, 2007); and David D. Bundy, *Visions of Apostolic Mission: Scandinavian Pentecostal Mission to 1935* (Uppsala: Uppsala University Library, 2009).

10. Which is not to say that there have not been pentecostal missiologies written. For some of the leading pentecostal missiologies in the last two-plus decades, see Paul Pomerville, *The Third Force in Missions: A Pentecostal Contribution to Contemporary Mission Theology* (Peabody,

Mass.: Hendrickson, 1985); L. Grant McClung, *Azusa Street and Beyond: Pentecostal Missions and Church Growth in the Twentieth Century* (South Plainfield, NJ: Bridge Publications, 1986); Vinson Synan and Ralph Rath, *Launching the Decade of Evangelization* (South Bend, IN: North American Renewal Service Committee, 1990); Edward K. Pousson, *Spreading the Flame: Charismatic Churches and Missions Today* (Grand Rapids, MI: Zondervan Pub. House, 1992); Harold D. Hunter and Peter Hocken, eds., *All Together in One Place: Theological Papers from the Brighton Conference on World Evangelization* (Sheffield, England: Sheffield Academic Press, 1993); Andrew Lord, *Spirit-Shaped Mission: A Holistic Charismatic Missiology* (Bletchley, UK, and Waynesboro, GA: Paternoster, 2005); and Gary B. McGee, *Miracles, Missions, and American Pentecostalism* (Maryknoll: Orbis Books, 2010).

11. See David Martin, *Pentecostalism: The World Their Parish* (Malden, MA, and Oxford, UK: Wiley-Blackwell, 2002). As the title of his book suggests, pentecostals consider the world to be their parish. For more on the global character of pentecostalism, see Karla O. Poewe, ed., *Charismatic Christianity as a Global Culture* (Columbia, SC: University of South Carolina Press, 1994); Walter J. Hollenweger, *Pentecostalism: Origins and Development Worldwide* (Peabody, MA: Hendrickson, 1997); and Allan Anderson, *An Introduction to Pentecostalism: Global Charismatic Christianity* (Cambridge: Cambridge University Press, 2004).

12. I discuss the economic dimensions of global renewal in my *In the Days of Caesar: Pentecostalism and Political Theology* (Grand Rapids, MI: William B. Eerdmans Publishing Company, 2010), §§1.2 and 7.1.

13. For example, Simon Coleman, *The Globalization of Charismatic Christianity: Spreading the Gospel of Prosperity* (Cambridge: Cambridge University Press, 2000); Pradip N. Thomas, *Strong Religion, Zealous Media: Christian Fundamentalism and Communication in India* (Thousand Oaks, Calif.: Sage Publications, 2008); and David Edwin Harrell, Jr., *Pat Robertson: A Life and Legacy* (Grand Rapids, MI: William B. Eerdmans Publishing Company, 2010), esp. chs. 6–7.

14. His classic text is Lamin O. Sanneh, *Translating the Message: The Missionary Impact on Culture* (Maryknoll: Orbis Books, 1989); more recently, see Sanneh, *Disciples of All Nations: Pillars of World Christianity* (Oxford and New York: Oxford University Press, 2008). See also my essay, "The Church and Mission Theology in a Post-Constantinian Era: Soundings from the Anglo-American Frontier," in *A New Day: Essays on World Christianity in Honor of Lamin Sanneh*, ed. Akintunde Akinade, 49–61 (New York: Peter Lang, 2010).

15. Harvey G. Cox, *Fire from Heaven: The Rise of Pentecostal Spirituality and the Reshaping of Religion in the 21st Century* (Reading, MA: Addison-Wesley, 1995).

16. Murray W. Dempster, Byron D. Klaus, and Douglas Petersen, eds., *The Globalization of Pentecostalism: A Religion Made to Travel* (Oxford, UK, and Irvine, CA: Regnum Books, 1999).
17. The case of illegal immigration presents special theological challenges. For an excellent theological introduction to the issues, see M. Daniel Carroll R., *Christians at the Border: Immigration, the Church, and the Bible* (Grand Rapids: Baker Academic, 2008). I have begun to sketch my own thoughts on the topic from an Asian American perspective in "Informality, Illegality, and Improvisation: Theological Reflections on Money, Migration, and Ministry in Chinatown, NYC, and Beyond," in Eleazar S. Fernandez, ed., *New Overtures: Asian North American Theology in the 21st Century—Essays in Honor of Fumitaka Matsuoka* (Upland, Calif.: Sopher Press, 2012), 248–68, originally published in the *Journal of Race, Ethnicity, and Religion* 3:2 (2012) [http://www.raceandreligion.com/JRER/Volume_3_%282012%29.html].
18. My work in pentecostal theology has repeatedly been developed from out of the Acts narrative; I provide an extended rationale for this in my *In the Days of Caesar*, ch. 3.1–3.2. See also Zevola Giovanni, "'What are you talking about to each other, as you walk along?' (Lk 24:17): Migration in the Bible and Our Journey of Faith," in *Faith on the Move: Toward a Theology of Migration in Asia*, eds. Fabio Baggio and Agnes M. Brazal, 93–117 (Manila: Ateneo de Manila University Press, 2008), which also uses Luke-Acts as a springboard for sketching a biblical theology of migration.
19. The following thus complements and extends 1) my articulation of a theology of hospitality from Luke-Acts that emphasizes being both guests and hosts vis-à-vis people of other faiths, and 2) various aspects of my pneumatological theology of the public square developed from out of the Acts narrative; see Yong, *Hospitality and the Other: Pentecost, Christian Practices, and the Neighbor* (Maryknoll: Orbis Books, 2008), esp. 100–08, and Yong, *Who is the Holy Spirit: A Walk with the Apostles* (Brewster, MA: Paraclete Press, 2012), respectively.
20. I assume the traditional and scholarly consensus about Luke being the author of Acts and thus will refer to him in shorthand vis-à-vis the responsibility for this early Christian historical narrative; however, the thrust of my exegetical and theological reflections does not depend on any naïve one-to-one correlation between "Luke" and the authorship of Acts.
21. See Reta Halteman Finger, *Of Widows and Meals: Communal Meals in the Book of Acts* (Grand Rapids, MI and Cambridge, UK: Eerdmans, 2007), ch. 11, for details of this argument.

22. See Robert D. Goette and Mae Pyen Hong, "A Theological Reflection on the Cultural Tensions between First-Century Hebraic and Hellenistic Jewish Christians and between Twentieth-Century First- and Second-Generation Korean American Christians," in *Korean Americans and Their Religions: Pilgrims and Missionaries from a Different Shore*, eds. Ho-Young Kwon, Kwang Chung Kim, and R. Stephen Warner, 115–23 (University Park, Penn.: The Pennsylvania State University Press, 2001).
23. This builds off my discussion of the early church's ministry in "From Demonization to Kin-domization: The Witness of the Spirit and the Renewal of Missions in a Pluralistic World," in *Global Renewal, Religious Pluralism, and the Great Commission: Toward a Renewal Theology of Mission and Interreligious Encounter*, eds. Amos Yong and Clifton Clarke, 157–74 (Lexington, KY: Emeth Press, 2011).
24. I came upon Justo L. González, "Reading from My Bicultural Place: Acts 6:1–7," in *Reading from This Place*, vol. 1: *Social Location and Biblical Interpretation in the* United States, eds. Fernando F. Segovia and Mary Ann Tolbert, 139–47 (Minneapolis: Fortress Press, 1995), after I completed this section, but am happy to note that our observations are largely consistent, although I come at this from a different angle than González's Latin American point of view. I did, however, nuance my discussion in a few places in light of González's chapter.
25. Abraham Smith, "A Second Step in African Biblical Interpretation: A Generic Reading Analysis of Acts 8:26–40," in *Reading from This Place*, 213–28, esp. 225–27.
26. Yet it is precisely the openendedness of the story of the eunuch that constitutes it as a migration story par excellence; to see further how the characterization of the eunuch and the narrative location of this pericope deepen its function as a liminal account of what I would call the betwixt-and-between reality of the ongoing migration of the gospel to the ends of the earth, see Scott Shauf, "Locating the Eunuch: Characterization and Narrative Context in Acts 8:26–40," *Catholic Biblical Quarterly* 71, no. 4 (2009): 762–75.
27. See, e.g., Rebecca Skaggs, *The Pentecostal Commentary on 1 and 2 Peter and Jude*, Pentecostal Commentary Series 17 (Sheffield: Sheffield Academic Press, 2004), 3–7.
28. For Asian American reflections on 1 Peter, see Russell G. Moy, "Resident Aliens of the Diaspora: 1 Peter and Chinese Protestants in San Francisco," in *The Bible in Asian America*, eds. Tat-Siong Benny Liew and Gale A Yee, *Semeia* 90–91, 51–67 (Atlanta: Society of Biblical Literature, 2002), reprinted in *Asian American Christianity: A Reader*, eds., Viji Nakka-Cammauf and Timothy Tseng, 267–78 (Castro Valley, CA: The Institute for the Study of Asian American Christianity, 2009).

29. Here I summarize what I have elsewhere argued at length—that is, in *In the Days of Caesar* and *Who is the Holy*—about the public or political dimensions of the early messianic experience. See also, for example, Warren Carter, *The Roman Empire and the New Testament: An Essential Guide* (Nashville: Abingdon, 2006), and Christopher Bryan, *Render to Caesar: Jesus, the Early Church, and the Roman Superpower* (Oxford: Oxford University Press, 2005). For a briefer explications from very different perspectives, consult N. T. Wright, "Paul and Caesar: A New Reading of Romans," in *A Royal Priesthood? The Use of the Bible Ethically and Politically—A Dialogue with Oliver O'Donovan, Scripture and Hermeneutics Series* 3, eds. Craig Bartholomew, Jonathan Chaplin, Robert Song, and Al Walters, 173–93 (Carlisle, UK: Paternoster, 2002), and Richard A. Horsley, "Renewal Movements and Resistance to Empire in Ancient Judea," in *The Postcolonial Bible Reader*, ed. R. S. Sugirtharajah, 69–77 (Malden, Mass., and Oxford: Blackwell Publishing, 2006).
30. See Robert G. Reid, "'Savior' and 'Lord' in the Lukan Birth Narrative: A Challenge to Caesar?" *Pax Pneuma: The Journal of Pentecostals and Charismatics for Peace & Justice* 5, no. 1 (2009): 46–61.
31. See William LaRousse, "'Go…and Make Disciples of All Nations': Migration and Mission," in *Faith on the Move: Toward a Theology of Migration in Asia*, eds. Fabio Baggio and Agnes M. Brazal, 155–76 (Manila: Ateneo de Manila University Press, 2008); and Jehu J. Hanciles, "Migration and Mission: The Religious Significance of the North-South Divide," in *Mission in the Twenty-First Century: Exploring the Five Marks of Global Mission*, eds. Andrew Walls and Cathy Ross, 118–29 (Maryknoll: Orbis Books, 2008).
32. Elsewhere, I sketch the broad contours of a postcolonial approach to the missionary task: Yong, "The Missiology of Jamestown: 1607–2007 and Beyond—Toward a Postcolonial Theology of Mission in North America," in *Remembering Jamestown: Hard Questions about Christian Mission*, eds. Amos Yong and Barbara Brown Zikmund, 157–67 (Eugene, OR: Wipf & Stock, 2010).
33. See Yong, "Many Tongues, Many Practices: Pentecost and Theology of Mission at 2010," in *Mission after Christendom: Emergent Themes in Contemporary Mission*, eds. Ogbu U. Kalu, Edmund Kee-Fook Chia, and Peter Vethanayagamony, 43–58 (Louisville, KY: Westminster John Knox Press, 2010), esp. 47–48.
34. As I try to suggest, with Samuel Zalanga, in "What Empire? Which Multitude? Pentecostalism & Social Liberation in North America & Sub-Saharan Africa," in *Evangelicals and Empire: Christian Alternatives to the Political Status Quo*, eds. Bruce Ellis Benson and Peter Goodwin Heltzel, 237–51 (Grand Rapids: Brazos Press, 2008).
35. Or, to facilitate what Andrew Sung Park calls "transmutation," which is not assimilation (wherein the emigrating identity is lost),

amalgamation (wherein the emigrating and the new cultural identities are improperly syncretized), or mere co-existence (perpetuating ethnic enclaves and ghettos), but where there is the possibility of the mutual enhancement, enrichment, and deepening of all groups by one another. See Park, "A Theology of Transmutation," in *A Dream Unfinished: Theological Reflections on America from the Margins America*," eds. Eleazer S. Fernandez and Fernando F. Segovia, 152–66 (Maryknoll: Orbis Books, 2001).

36. As argued by Jehu H. Hanciles, *Beyond Christendom: Globalization, African Migration, and the Transformation of the West* (Maryknoll: Orbis Books, 2008).
37. This life betwixt and between has been brilliantly captured by my fellow Asian American theological colleagues in Peter C. Phan and Jung Young Lee, eds., *Journeys at the Margins: Toward an Autobiographical Theology in American-Asian Perspective* (Collegeville, Minn.: Liturgical Press, 1999), and Fumitaka Matsuoka and Eleazar S. Fernandez, eds., *Realizing the American of Our Hearts: Theological Voices of Asian Americans* (St. Louis: Chalice Press, 2003).
38. As beautifully argued, in the thesis that the cosmos is destined to become the dwelling place of the Spirit and the inhabitation of the Triune God, by Frank D. Macchia, *Justified in the Spirit: Creation, Redemption, and the Triune God* (Grand Rapids: William B. Eerdmans Publishing Company, 2010).Thanks to Peter Phan and Elaine Padilla for the invitation to write this essay, and for their feedback on it. Thanks also to my fellow South East Asian migrant and graduate assistant, Tim Lim (from Singapore), for his comments on an earlier draft. I take, however, full responsibility for what follows.

Chapter 8

Migration: An Opportunity for Broader and Deeper Ecumenism

Deenabandhu Manchala

If migration is described as a phenomenon that is radically changing the social and ecclesial landscapes of the twenty-first century world, then ecumenism, as a movement of churches, has not been exempt either. It is constantly evolving, assuming new meanings and expressions. What began as an attempt to seek *unity for witness* or for the evangelization of the world in the early part of the twentieth century,[1] soon evolved into one seeking *unity as an expression of witness*, particularly as churches, predominantly Western, recognized the contradiction of a fragmented Christian witness in a world that stood divided after two world wars. Since then, the purpose and scope of Christian understanding of unity have been constantly evolving, to include the unity of humankind and the whole of creation.

Along this journey, churches have strived hard to overcome a range of theological and ecclesiological differences in order to respond with more concrete expressions of the visible unity that our Lord prayed for: "That they all may be one" (John 17: 11). However, they soon discovered non-theological factors—national and ethnic identities, cultures, and practices such as racism and sexism—hindered the possibility of a united witness. Meanwhile, around the turn of the century, churches began to find themselves amidst increasing plurality, caused by large scale multidirectional movements of people, the complex realities of marginalization, the exclusion of millions of people from the coffers of progress on account of the effects of neo-liberal economic globalization, and the consequent intense, often more aggressive, struggles for justice, resources, liberation and identity. In addition, the reality of more Christians living in the diverse Global South has also necessitated the need to explore more people-based, wider ecumenical expressions in contrast to the twentieth century's Christian conciliar ecumenism.

Much has been said and written about ecumenism and the ecumenical movement. However much of it is drawn into preoccupation with Christian unity, the ecumenical movement has time and again upheld that its primary purpose is not to serve its own interests or those of the institutional structures of the churches, but to serve the cause of the transformation of the world through critical and creative engagement. The word "ecumenical" is derived from the Greek word "*oikoumene*," meaning the whole inhabited world as one household. It means that we live in, relate to, and share with one another as one people within the earthly home given to us by God. To that extent, ecumenism is not a church unity movement but a movement of churches together for life for all, countering the forces that deny and abuse life, and offering and holding forth alternative visions of the world. The worldwide spread of Christianity, the engagement of churches and Christian organizations in many people's initiatives, and the rise of experiential and people-based theologies from situations of struggle have enabled the search for broader and more inclusive expressions of ecumenism. It is against this backdrop that I would like to reflect on the theological significance of migration for our understanding of ecumenism and for ecumenical ways of being church.

Perhaps a brief account of the way in which the World Council of Churches (WCC), as an organisational expression of the global ecumenical movement, has responded to migration and its related issues, may be worthwhile. A more encompassing response to the issue of migration has been relatively new in the discussions within the WCC and its related ecumenical organisations. However, the issues and concerns of uprooted people, refugees, and migrant workers have continued to inspire WCC's responses since the 1956 Central Committee.[2] The New Delhi Assembly in 1961 and the Church and Society Conference in 1966 called for special campaigns to address these issues. The Programme to Combat Racism drew attention to the fact that migration is a result of discrimination and violence.[3] Consequently, the Churches' Commission on Refugees and World Service (CICARAWS) came into being in the 1980s, responding to a variety of concerns and needs of refugees and uprooted people in many parts of the world. Meanwhile, the Churches' Commission on Migration in Europe (CCME) became an active instrument of advocacy for the rights and protection of migrants, especially migrant workers. The 1995 Central Committee of the WCC issued a statement on uprooted people—"A Moment to Choose: Risking to be with Uprooted People."[4] Following the VIII Assembly in Harare in 1998, a desk on Uprooted People was put in place to encourage and enable churches to respond to their concerns and rights. A particular emphasis since 2000 has been to put demands for migrants' rights in the context of broader struggles against racism.[5] Since then, WCC's response also assumed a new dimension in which it began to see the issue of migration not as a mere *diakonia* (practical service) but as an urgent theological and ecclesiological challenge. The 2005 Central Committee, commemorating the 1995 document, affirmed the practice of hospitality and the need to monitor the issue of migration closely. Its statement entitled "Practising hospitality in an era of new forms of migration" said,

> We challenge the churches worldwide to rediscover their identity, their integrity and their vocation as the church of the stranger. Service to uprooted people has always been recognized as *diakonia* although it has been peripheral to the life of many churches. But we affirm that it is also an ecclesial matter. We are a church of the Stranger—the Church of Jesus Christ the Stranger (See Matthew 25:31–46).

Further, it called on Christian believers "to create community with the uprooted by accompanying them, providing services for their needs, supporting their initiatives, being church together with them, and engaging in living in diversity."[6]

In response to the trends of economic globalisation, human trafficking, and xenophobia, the WCC called on the churches to practise a culture of encounter, hospitality, and cordial welcome for migrants, and to identify positive examples where churches have worked together effectively to offer alternatives to restrictionist policies.[7]

Meanwhile, the realities of the movement of Christians to other parts of the world, their options for non-denominational and informal expressions of ecclesial life, and more Christians living in the Global South prompted discussions on a number of issues in the WCC that had direct relevance to ecclesial and ecumenical relationships. Churches' efforts toward unity—seeking convergence on doctrines and ecclesiastical traditions—did not seem adequate enough as migration posed the necessity to examine and address certain non-theological but crucial issues: the interplay of social, national and ethnic identities, anthropological presuppositions such as racism, sexism and casteism, etcetera.

Consequently, the WCC's Faith and Order Commission, as part of its ongoing work on promoting Christian unity, undertook two studies: "Ethnicity, Nationalism and the Unity of the Churches" and "Theological Anthropology."[8] Another document, "Hospitality in a context of increasing plurality," was the focus of reflection of the plenary meeting of the Faith and Order Commission in Kuala Lumpur, Malaysia in 2005 as it met under the theme, "Receive one another as Christ has received you" (Rom.15:7).[9]

Migration was the theme of the Global Platform for Theological Reflection in 2007. Around 200 churches, specialised ministries, networks, and involved individuals participated in the process by sharing reports, papers, analysis, bible studies, and worship resources.[10] In view of the serious ecclesiological implications that migration has for churches—their identities, composition, relationships, theologies, mission—and consequently to the ecumenical movement itself, the migration desk became a part of the Just and Inclusive Communities programme. This programme, launched soon after the IX WCC Assembly in Porto Alegre in 2006, holds together the concerns of the marginalized within and outside the churches, with a view to draw on their contributions arising out of their experiences of discrimination and exclusion in the ongoing search for new expressions of ecumenism. The marginalized are those who are suffering on account of and struggling against racism and casteism, indigenous peoples, people living with disabilities, and vulnerable migrants. Against this backdrop, I will attempt to reflect on migration, not as a challenge, but more as an opportunity for the churches and the ecumenical movement to rediscover themselves afresh.

Re-membering the Othered and the Dismembered

Assertion of identities—national, religious, ethnic, or cultural—is perhaps one of the most serious causes of tensions between migrants and receiving communities. Sometimes the receiving communities resist or mistreat outsiders for the fear of what an intrusion of other identities could mean to their own identities, resources, and economic well-being. In other cases, some migrant communities assert their own identities in their desire to exist as distinct people. Religious and national identities have been the source of tensions and xenophobia in many contexts. Some right-wing groups aspiring to political power capitalize on these tensions by nurturing suspicion, hatred, and distance between and among communities. Some of them exert influence on political leaders who serve as mediators, promoting and enacting laws that block passage across national borders, or impeding migrants already within the host country from truly thriving. The other, the outsider, "the one who is different" is always seen as a problem, an unwanted intrusion, or a cheap commodity.

Most world religions, including Christianity, through their self-perpetuating missions, have played a major role in this process of "othering." Operating alongside nationalism, ethnicity, racism, patriarchy, and in my context, casteism, religions have always encouraged their members to develop self-aggrandizing notions of themselves and to belittle those who do not belong to their fold. In fact, this common but often ignored trait of 'othering' has been the source of most evils. Colonialism and neo-colonialism, slavery since ancient times and modern forms of slavery, violence against women, child labor, environmental exploitation and destruction, corruption and abuse of power—all have their roots in this dynamic of "othering." "I am more important than you; my needs and wants, my comforts and luxuries, my dreams and fantasies, my safety and security, my health and wealth are more important than yours, because I am special and even ontologically superior than you," is the attitude of neo-colonizers that devalues the humanity of everyone, especially those whom they seek to dominate.

Mathai Zachariah, an Indian ecumenical theologian, writes,

> Today's man's conscience is directed toward a small, parochial world; his family, his friends, his social group, his nation at the most. But there is no element of universality in his conscience formation. The world horizon is an unknown horizon in terms of conscience, morality and responsibility. Contemporary man is living in a planetary world with parochial conscience. The problem then is how to make his conscience contemporary.[11]

Ecumenism as an alternative vision of life in an excluding world is not merely fostering unity but inclusivity at all levels. Inclusivity is not merely co-opting but embracing the other, despite all the difference. Unity is oppressive when the weak and the vulnerable are forced to accept the identity and submit to the powerful. Unity is also deceptive when it is claimed alongside the presence of derisive notions of the other. Inclusivity, on the other hand, is more than a superficial expression of unity. It recognizes the rights and dignity of the other. It implies being respectful, affirming the dignity, and embracing the other even though he or she may be distinctly different. "Accept one another as Christ has accepted you for the glory of God," St. Paul writes to Romans (15:7). God's grace reaches out to us not because of our worthiness but because of God's generosity, which does not operate on the basis of the norms and standards set by the dominant, but by the sheer passion for life, especially of those for whom it is denied. Inclusivity, therefore, is a way of witnessing to the saving grace of God. To put it differently, attempts to exclude others on the basis of their identities and status run the risk of rejecting or abusing God's grace.

Inclusivity is not paternalistic compassion but a call for decisive moral and spiritual choices, to look at the other as being as important as yourself. As Jesus said, "You shall love...your neighbor as yourself" (Lk 10:27, NRSV). Such a moral choice, the gospel tradition points out, involves re-membering the dis-membered, that is, bringing into the fold those who are on the outskirts, expelled, and disenfranchised. "I have come to seek the last and the least" (Mt. 18:11; Lk. 19:10) and "the last shall be the first" (Mt. 20:16) are the sayings that echo through the gospels as the most important purposes of Christ's mission.

Unfortunately, Christian churches around the globe are in the grip of these exclusionary and oppressive social identities and their corresponding influences, so they are not able to present themselves as open and inclusive communities to those others with different identities. Unfortunately, the ecclesiastical preferences and expressions of the dominant churches, though local, are seen as normative globally, and others are encouraged or coerced to imitate or adopt.

However, migration offers an invitation and the possibility for churches to have new encounters. As Steven Bevans writes,

> This is an invitation that calls Christians constantly to open themselves to the mystery that reveals God as one who is always greater than we can imagine, who is most clearly found on the margins—in the desert, at the periphery, at the frontier—calling us beyond, calling us forward, outside our comfort zones to new and unexpected life.[12]

Therefore, the church by its own primary calling is expected to be a transformed community, transcending boundaries and embracing the richness of God's diversity among people, communities, and creation. Wati Longchar, a tribal theologian from India, writes,

> The goal of finding an integrated wholeness of relationships with God, nature and other persons reflects much that is deeply needed in the contemporary world... In the world of rationalization, mechanization,

objectification, and fragmentation, the vision of interrelatedness of all realities found in the tribal or indigenous traditions will help us.[13]

Ecumenism upholds the intricate web of life and is spirituality rooted in life and the corresponding interrelatedness and interdependence.

Hospitality as an Expression of Inclusiveness

An increased desire to accept the other has generated considerable reflection on hospitality as an important and timely Christian response in the context of migration. Whether hospitality or inclusivity, it raises a fundamental question: Who includes whom? It suggests that there is a center and margins, a mainstream and side streams, a host and guests, and the binary notion of "insider/outsider" with the "insider inviting the outsider" into the normative space. Someone is choosing to include someone else! It is possible to be hospitable for some—the familiar and those like us—but not to all. Hospitality in the context of migration is not just being polite to a guest but demands the courage to defy and resist the status quo and social privileges. The guest here is most often a despised and vulnerable stranger—an undocumented person (erroneously labelled as "illegal" or "alien")—and hence someone viewed as a criminal in the sight of the state, and for the local communities, an outsider who has come to take away opportunities that belonged to the locals.

In other words, hospitality is being guided not just by compassion and goodwill but by justice. Justice, in its essence, is about right relationships. The prophet Jeremiah reminds us that "to know God is to do justice" (22: 15, 16). Justice is neither an ideology nor a humanitarian gesture. It is a sign of spiritual maturity. It expresses itself in the ability to see the worth and dignity of every human being, especially of the vulnerable and the disempowered other. Swami Agnivesh, an outstanding Hindu leader, writes,

> Spirituality comprises the deeper core of religions. Justice is the essence of spirituality...Spiritually, justice calls for the creation of wholesome conditions of life and the affirmation of basic values whereby human beings are helped to attain fullness and find fulfilment in life. Spiritually, justice has a social foundation; for we are social creatures. Spirituality is not a matter of some formulae or dogmas. It is a dynamic phenomenon that expresses itself through an ongoing engagement with the human predicament.[14]

Perhaps incarnation in the figure of Jesus, can be viewed as the utmost expression of God's hospitality with humankind (Phil. 2: 5–11). Through the incarnation, Jesus showed a hospitality of obedience to God yet defiance to the world's norms and values. Jesus turned hostility into friendship as he went to places deemed unworthy or impure and invited himself into these environments filled with rejection. Hospitality, for him, was seeking "the lost and the least" (Mt.9:13); reaching out to provide opportunities for those who were denied them (Mt.20:1-16); celebrating the restoration of the dignity and humanity of the dispossessed (Lk. 15:11-32); levelling the playing field between the wealthy and the poor (Mk.10:17-22); and struggling *with* the marginalized and those striving for a dignified life (Mt. 25: 31-46). To create a world where the rejected are accepted, and especially where the poor are given opportunities to thrive, is to follow in the hospitable footsteps of Jesus.

While upholding the radical decision to imitate Christ and the radical call to solidarity with all people, Daniel Groody writes,

> No Christian is exempt from this option, not even the poor, and indeed our final salvation is integrally related to it... The face of Christ, in which we shall one day read our judgement, already mysteriously gazes on us from every human face, particularly those who suffer and are excluded.[15]

Peter Phan further elaborates this point to ground it in the incarnational event itself:

> Solidarity with the marginalized and the excluded corresponds to God's being and acting in history. The vulnerable human beings become, in a mysterious way, the sacramental presence of Christ in our midst. This sacramental presence of Christ becomes, for the first generations of Christian communities, the corner stone of hospitality, *philoxenia*, toward those needy people who do not have a place to rest, a virtue insisted upon by the apostle Paul (Romans 12:13).[16]

Thus hospitality is a deeply spiritual vocation via which migrant-strangers from diverse ethnic and economic backgrounds reshape the body-identity of Christ in their host countries. This incarnational love, also radically present beyond the church, disrupts socio-political structures based on exclusion.

The parables of the Kingdom that Jesus told call for repentance and conversion of the powerful and the privileged, who were admonished not to grumble and not to resist when the marginalized are given space and the opportunities to live well (Mt 20: 1–16; Lk 15. 11–32, etc). Inclusivity, consequently, is not a superficial coming together of the mighty and the weak; the wolf gives up its traits of aggression and of making a living by feeding on the weak and the powerless, and the weak lamb stops living with fear and submitting to aggression (Isaiah 65:24, 25, my paraphrase). It implies a radical transformation of situations in which the weak, the vulnerable, and the most disadvantaged as well as the aggressors have the possibility of living the way God intended all to live.

Inclusion combined with hospitality moves beyond mere acts of charity, thus breaking oppressive and dehumanizing practices intended to perpetually maintain the high status and power of the host—at times almost in their tyrannical expressions—over that of the incoming migrant. The representatives of the networks fighting marginalisation through the WCC's Just and Inclusive Communities Programme at their meeting in Nagpur, India in 2009 said,

> The intricate weaving of inclusion, hospitality and justice will lead to the emergence of communities, which are a tapestry of interdependence and human togetherness where human dignity is respected, celebrated and honoured; where liberation and freedom are a reality; and where oppressive power relationships are dismantled.[17]

Rather than a social-action rhetoric to the poor, hospitable inclusion is informed by a deeply evangelical vocation. Belief promotes just action, and not only words. The WCC's Just and Inclusive Communities Programme elaborated on its aspiration for justice: "The clamour of the excluded people for justice is often a clamour for acceptance and freedom to be. Justice is when every human person is aware that they have a right to sit down at the table without needing to be asked or to seek permission."[18]

Ecumenical vocation implies entering into human predicamentand working alongside people who are oppressed, marginalized and excluded, constantly making choices between the law of God and the law of the land. Migration increases the tension between obedience and defiance as well as challenges the churches to become more involved in the mission of God.

Migration: A Time to Celebrate Diversity!

Our world today is an increasingly diverse reality—of people, languages, creeds, living habits, cultures, identities, and ethnicities. Perhaps every part of the world is touched by this phenomenon of plurality. Migration, because of factors that cause people to be drawn to a foreign land or to flee from a particular location ("pull or push factors"), has been the main cause of this phenomenon. However, border-crossing has also caused tensions like harsh immigration and deportation laws, experiences of discrimination and exclusion in the job market, and the consequent violence and victimization of migrants, as in the lack of health benefits that are afforded to citizens who work in similar jobs. Some countries seem more reluctant to cope with the challenge of diversity for a variety of reasons. The rise of right-wing conservatism coupled with xenophobic attitudes, demonization of people with certain identities, human trafficking, and so forth have contributed to the rhetoric that views the migrant and migration as negative phenomena, and as a problem, while also detracting from addressing the root causes of migration, such as rampant economic inequality and unfair trade laws, and the harsh treatment given under the guise of retribution for having been sinned against by the transgression of borders.

Churches, if not attentive to the political and cultural climate within their own borders, can further fuel xenophobic attitudes. As communities of faith with a passion for justice and dignity for all, churches have the responsibility to reframe this discourse on migration, both in the church and the society. One way of doing this is create spaces to celebrate the diversity of God's creation as a way of understanding the mystery of life that God intended. To reiterate, migration needs to be seen not as a problem but as an opportunity for the churches to rediscover themselves afresh, to sharpen our capacity and skills as communities of love and compassion. Ecumenism is about affirming and celebrating God's creative wisdom expressed through the plural manifesations and complexities of life. In other words, when we affirm God as creator and the creation as God's self-expression, we also affirm the many, rather than the few. Therefore, we do not only seek unity amidst diversity as if it is a problem to overcome but to celebrate it. Through this celebration, the church affirms God's creative wisdom, and in the process,s becomes a sign of the world that God created in love and wants to re-create.

Perhaps it is time that we revisit the validity of the traditional Western concepts of *oikoumene* (the inhabited world) with their accents on Christian conciliar ecumenism (i.e., ecumenism created by means of councils). Visible unity does not necessarily mean overcoming denominational identities but embracing difference for the sake of a common goal and calling—mission. Theological formulations that attempt to overtly or tacitly undermine diversity, requiring submission to a centralized authority, need to be seriously questioned. A common identity and a political structure is not the answer for disunity but an ethic of respect, dignity, and justice is. Appreciation for difference, in fact, tests and enhances our capacity to love, forgive, be compassionate, considerate and just: in other words to be human. As leading Asian political analyst and thinker Chandra Muzaffar writes, "the unity of humankind transcends our particular religious identities but it does not negate them. By celebrating our religious identity we realize our common humanity—a humanity that embraces our natural environment and indeed the whole of the cosmos."[19]

At their meeting in Rio de Janiero in 2008, Just and Inclusive Communities, as part of their reflection on "Re-visioning Justice from the Margins," while attempting to reinterpret *Imago Dei* as different from notions of perfection and egoism, highlighted plurality, diversity, and connectivity. They said,

> it is not individuals who bear the image of God in them but that the Image of God can only be understood in terms of human community. Therefore, it is not 'I' who is made in the image of God but 'we' together are made in the image of God. No one individual is made in God's image but we together bear the image of God. When community is not complete then the image of God in humans is also not complete...Likewise the image of God can only be understood in terms of diversity, it cannot be contained in only one idea or connotation of what it means to be human but it is the whole human community together, with its variance and difference, with its multitude of skin colours and occupations, with its different talents, abilities and geographic locations that goes to make up together the image of God. If we believe that God is the source of all the diversity, then the image of God in humans does not look for singularity but plurality.[20]

If difference, then, is God's will and therefore to be celebrated, then migration needs to be seen and affirmed as a positive aspect of our lives, wherever it is. Ecumenical vocation in the context of migration means to reach out to the vulnerable migrant so that hope lives—through the many inclusive forms of being human in the world. This, too, would be justice. When the church becomes open, just, and inclusive, it becomes the microcosm of the world that God wants to create.

A New Opportunity for Relevant Forms of Ecclesial Life

As migrants move to new places, churches are caught in a complex situation. On the one hand, some churches are compelled to comply with the dominant public opinion or the position of the state and insulate themselves from the migrant populations, while other churches open themselves to them. Sometimes, those from outside opt to establish or seek their ecclesial existence as ethnic communities. Another phenomenon is the emergence of multicultural, multiethnic, and multidenominational congregations with new possibilities as well as risks and uncertainiites. Each of the above poses a number of challenges to churches.

A recent consultation organised by the WCC's Faith and Order, Mission and Evangelism, and Just and Inclusive Communities together with Ecumenical Network on Migration and Multicultural Churches (ENFORMM) in Utrecht, Holland in November 2010 emphasised the urgent need for World Council of Churches, in partnership with the Roman Catholic Church, the World Evangelical Alliance (WEA), Pentecostals, and other Church World Communions to begin constructive dialogue with member churches who "live" the reality of migration.[21] The consultation attempted to wrestle with questions such as:

1. How do Christian communities express theologically their self-identity / ecclesiology and mission each in their particular contextual reality, whether as a minority or majority community?
2. In the context of increasing multi-confessional reality of the church, how can mutuality be the basis of our ministry to the other?
3. How are the migrant churches living in the context of religious diversity? How can we promote interreligious dialogue and cooperation as a pastoral response?
4. What are the gifts and challenges of migration toward the unity of the Church?

The consultation noted that the migrant communities, continue to develop "migrant/multicultural" churches, especially in the Global North. The gifts and challenges that these migrant/multicultural churches bring demand a reimagining of mission, evangelism and being church. Highlighting two questions about Christian identity and migration, the consultation said,

> To the members of migrant communities, it means affirming who they are and what their internal, intra, and extra mission is in a new context. To the members of the local established communities, it means redefining Christian community beyond the limiting contours of nation, language, ethnicity, and status. It recalls the biblical language

of 1 Peter 2.11 in which we are all aliens and strangers. It necessitates a new paradigm for ecumenism that takes seriously the need to be inclusive and collaborative, taking into account inter/intra and extra approaches to mission, and that directly impact the life of people at the grassroots.[22]

Migration brings us together as a people on the journey of faith in search of how God's call is common to all of us, particularly as we address the challenges of injustice, human and environmental abuse, exploitation, discrimination, and so forth. It offers new possibilities for mutual learning and enriching.

While presenting what the migrants offer to the churches in the receiving countries, Castillo Guerra writes,

> The migrants are those who, starting with what is most basic—love for life—are unveiling one of the major factors of our time when they uncover the asymmetric and exclusive regulations that govern our world, and when they begin to judge the validity and objectivity of the values that guide the societies where they arrive: freedom, equality, and fraternity. In terms of human condition, the migrant offers a hermeneutic key to get to know how the world is, where it is going, and to what type of world we must aspire.[23]

Guerra adds, "From their human condition, from tragedy and hope, from their situation of grace and disgrace, the migrants make known the passing of God through our history..."[24]

To sum up, an excerpt from the Statement on Called to be the One Church from the WCC's IX Assembly in Porto Algre, Brazil in 2006 seems appropriate:[25]

> The relationship among churches is dynamically interactive. Each church is called to mutual giving and receiving gifts and to mutual accountability. Each church must become aware of all that is provisional in its life and have the courage to acknowledge this to other churches. Even today, when eucharistic sharing is not always possible, divided churches express mutual accountability and aspects of catholicity when they pray for one another, share resources, assist one another in times of need, make decisions together, work together for justice, reconciliation, and peace, hold one another accountable to the discipleship inherent in baptism, and maintain dialogue in the face of differences, refusing to say "I have no need of you" (1 Cor.12:21). Apart from one another we are impoverished.

Conclusion

Perhaps one last word needs to be said about the theologies arising out of the migrant's struggle for life. If we believe that the ecumenical movement is about the whole world, then our continued dependence on traditional theologies is not helpful. Most of these took shape and expression in predominantly Christian, socially, politically and economically powerful Western contexts. Their preoccupation has been the church and its place in the world. In the context of changed and changing social and ecclesial landscapes, the future of the ecumenical movement depends on its ability to reanchor itself in these contextual theologies everywhere, especially those arising out of multi-religious contexts and in the south. With their interaction with the movements for justice and life, they are articulating alternative visions, and redefining theology as an instrument of social change.

Craig Nessan, while upholding theologies from the south writes,

> Theology emerging from the new continent of post-Christendom is a theology that is engaged in social and political praxis in solidarity with the minjung of the earth...It is a theology that is by nature interreligious, conversant and creatively transformed...It is a theology in which the Christendom distinction between theology and ethics no longer holds. It is a theology that is already leading the Christian church toward "a new world order" and the urgently necessary global ethic that are [sic] a prolepsis of the kingdom itself.[26]

Christian faith and tradition are rooted in the narrative and story of the migrant. Jesus Christ himself was a refugee, and the early church was born in a multicultural and multi-religious context of mission and migration. In fact, the biblical story itself is a story of God's people on the move. As such, the Church ought to be the migrant body of Christ, *being* inclusive and hospitable to the marginalized bordercrosser. It must, in every context of time and space, discover itself afresh, negotiating possibilities and allegiances to be instruments of God's purposes in and for the world.

One of the distinct ways in which the churches have made positive differences in history is when they understood themselves as movements of people and when they were with the people in the way our Lord was. It was their ability to read the signs of the times, and to understand the purpose of their being in those contexts, that made them creative, life-affirming forces. We, as churches, need to be migrating partners, open to change, discerning change, in order that we may not only stay relevant but also play a creative part in shaping the world, in ways that make sense to the least and the last.

Notes

1. The International Missionary Conference in Edinburgh 1910 under the theme "Evangelisation of the World in this generation," which brought together many churches and mission organizations in Europe, North America, and a few other parts of the world, is often referred to as the beginning of the modern ecumenical movement.
2. André Jacques and Elizabeth Ferris, "Migration," *Dictionary of the Ecumenical Movement*, ed. Nicholas Losssky, et al., 2nd ed., 768–770 (Geneva, WCC, 2002).
3. Ibid.
4. "A Moment to Choose: Risking to be with Uprooted People: Statement Issued by the WCC Central Committee in 1995," World Council of Churches, http://www.oikoumene.org/en/resources/documents/wcc-commissions/international-affairs/human-rights-and-impunity/practising-hospitality-in-an-era-of-new-forms-of-migration, posted February 22, 2005.
5. Barney Pityana and Marilia Schuller, "Racism," *Dictionary of the Ecumenical Movement*, 953–955.
6. *Op.cit.*, http://www.wcc-coe.org/wcc/what/regional/uprooted/moment1.html, accessed January 28, 2014.
7. "Practising Hospitality in an Era of New Forms of Migration," World Council of Churches, http://www.oikoumene.org/en/resources/documents/wcc-commissions/international-affairs/human-rights-and-impunity/practising-hospitality-in-an-era-of-new-forms-of-migration, posted February 22, 2005.
8. *Participating in God's Mission of Reconciliation: A Resource for Churches in Situations of Conflict*, Faith and Order Paper No. 201 (Geneva: WCC, 2006); and *Christian Perspectives on Theological Anthropology: A Faith and Order Study Document*, Paper No.199 (Geneva: WCC, 2005).
9. *Faith and Order at the Crossroads: Kuala Lumpur 2004*, ed. Thomas F. Best, Faith and Order Paper No. 196 (Geneva: WCC, 2005).
10. "WCC Global Platform on theological reflection and analysis: Major learnings from the 2007 process." Accessed January 30, 2014, http://www.oikoumene.org/en/resources/documents/wcc-programmes/unity-mission-evangelism-and-spirituality/just-and-inclusive-communities/major-learnings-from-the-2007-global-platform-process/@@download/file/Major_Learnings_from_the_2007_Global_Platform_Process.pdf, posted January 10, 2008.
11. Mathai Zachariah, *Beyond Ecumenism: A Journey into Light* (Tiruvalla, Kerala, India: CSS, 2002), 23.

12. Steven Bevans, "Mission *among* Migrants, Mission *of* Migrants: Mission of the Church," in *A Promised Land, A Perilous Journey: Theological Perspectives on Migration*, eds. Daniel G. Groody and Giochchino Campese (Notre Dame: University of Notre Dame Press, 2009), 100–101. Bevans also highlights the expression of Gioacchino Campese that the Christian God is the "God of the Tent," to be found most fully on the road, crossing borders, and not confined "to special, holy buildings."
13. A. Wati Longchar, "An Emerging Tribal/Indigenous Theology: Prospect for Doing Asian Theology," *The Journal of Theologies and Cultures in Asia* 1 (February 2002), 13.
14. Swami Agnivesh, *Applied Spirituality for Justice Unlimited* (New Delhi: Dharma Pratisthan, 2005), 35.
15. Daniel Groody, *Globalization, Spirituality, and Justice* (Maryknoll, New York: Orbis Books, 2007), 255.
16. Peter Phan, "Migration in the Patristic Age," in *A Promised Land*, 35–61.
17. In exploring the theme of "Hospitality, Inclusion and Justice: A Theological reflection in response to old and new forms of discrimination and exclusion," the group was unanimous in affirming the importance of hospitality as a significant mark (identity) of Christian communities. It called on the member churches of the World Council of Churches to take seriously the biblical call to practice hospitality (as in *Deut 10:19; Lev. 19:33-34; Ex.23:9*) as they seek to live out their commitment in contexts challenged by discrimination, marginalization, and exclusion of several sections of people. Accessed January 28, 2014, http://www.oikoumene.org/en/resources/documents/wcc-programmes/unity-mission-evangelism-and-spirituality/just-and-inclusive-communities/theological-reflection-in-response-to-old-and-new-forms-of-discrimination/@@download/file/nagpur_report.pdf.
18. Ibid.
19. Chandra Muzaffar, "Religion in the Asia Pacific Region: The Challenge without and the Change within," in *Religion and Culture in Asia Pacific: Violence or Healing*, ed. Joseph A. Camilleri (Melbourne: Vista Publications, 2001), 38.
20. World Council of Churches, http://www.oikoumene.org/?id=7409.
21. Utrecht Consultation "Mission and Ecclesiology of the Migrant Churches" was the theme of this consultation. See World Council of Churches, http://www.oikoumene.org/en/resources/documents/wcc-programmes/unity-mission-evangelism-and-spirituality/just-and-inclusive-communities/migration/wcc-consultation-on-mission-and-ecclesiology-of-the-migrant-churches, posted January 1, 2011.
22. *Ibid.*

23. Jorge E. Castillo Guerra, "A Theology of Migration: Towards an Intercultural Methodology," in *A Promised Land*, 248–9.
24. Ibid., 250.
25. Luis N. Rivera-Pagan, ed., "God, in Your Grace: Official Report of the Ninth Assembly of the World Council of Churches," (Geneva: WCC, 2007), 257.
26. Craig L. Nessan, "Epilogue: Minjung Seen in the Fourth Eye: Theology from a New Covenant," in Paul S. Chung, et al., eds., *Asian Contextual Theology for the Third Millennium: Theology of Minjung in Fourth-Eye Formation* (Eugene, OR: Pickwick Publications, 2007), 353.

Chapter 9

Toward a Muslim Theology of Migration

Amir Hussain

This chapter is a starting point on the journey toward a Muslim theology of migration, a first word and certainly not anything like a last word. It is also important to point out at the outset that this chapter is a theological reflection on migration, not one concerned with the political realities (which are legion) of Muslim migrants. It is a chapter grounded in the teachings of my mentors, Muriel and Wilfred Cantwell Smith. When Wilfred finished his undergraduate degree at the University of Toronto, he wanted to learn more about Islam and Muslims. Since the Muslim population in Canada in the 1940s was small, he and Muriel moved to India, which before Partition in 1947 had the largest Muslim population in the world. In the first half of the last century, then, migration for Muslims often meant non-Muslims coming to them. In the second half of the last century and in our current one, migration for Muslims usually means moving to countries where the majority of the inhabitants are non-Muslim. From Wilfred and Muriel, I learned the distinction between "faith" and the "cumulative tradition." There is certainly a cumulative tradition from which individual Muslims draw the narratives of their lives. But it is those lives in connection with their individual communities that are of interest to me, those narratives that must be allowed to exist in the plural. In the epigraph to his magnificent novel about Toronto, *In the Skin of a Lion*, Michael Ondaatje uses the words of John Berger: "Never again will a single story be told as though it were the only one."[1] I tell only a very few stories in my chapter, mostly from my own experience. There are so many other stories to be told.

From the Smiths, I also learned the important idea that "religion" is best understood as the vital, living faith of individual persons.

This is how I understand this contested term. And what I attempt to describe in this chapter will be the different ways in which migration intersects with Muslim lives.[2] It also seems important to state, in the face of all of the cowardly conditionals in scholarly writing, that there is no religious tradition other than Islam that is so intimately linked in its origins to migration. As discussed below, Muslims begin their calendar with the event of the *hijra*, the migration of the Prophet Muhammad and the nascent Muslim community from Mecca to Medina in 622 CE. The chapters of the Qur'an, the scripture for Muslims, are usually indicated as belonging to Meccan or Medinan periods of revelation. So there are foundational as well as contemporary concerns about migration for Muslims. I begin with the historical context.

Historical Migrations

Muhammad was born in the city of Mecca in what is now Saudi Arabia in 570 CE. The city is not important to Muslims because Muhammad was born there, nor is it important because it was in Mecca that Muhammad received the first revelations from God in 610 CE. Mecca is important for Muslims because they believe that it is there that Abraham and his son Ishmael built the Ka'ba, the first place of monotheistic prayer to God. In other versions of the story, it is Adam, the first human being, who builds the Ka'ba, and Abraham and Ishmael who rebuild it.

When Muhammad began to get his first revelations from God, he understood them, with their focus on ethical monotheism, to be quite different from the polytheistic, tribal society of Mecca, with all of its social inequalities. Much like the case with early Christianity, some of the early converts to Islam were poor and marginalized, for in a society where slavery was common, to be told that all were slaves to God had some understandable appeal. However, there were wealthy converts as well, as there were in the early Christian context. As the community began to grow, some of the less powerful converts were susceptible to persecution from the polytheistic Meccans. It was in the fifth year of the revelation (615 CE) that Muhammad arranged for the first migration, or *hijra*. However, this was not the famous one seven years later to Medina, but a relatively understudied one to Abyssinia (modern Ethiopia).

While there is some discrepancy in the numbers (the historian Al-Tabari gives 82 adults, while the biographer Ibn Sa'd puts the number at 116),[3] the story is that Muhammad sent some of his followers who were most susceptible to persecution to Abyssinia. What is striking here is that the reason that Muhammad sent them to Abyssinia was because he knew that it was a Christian kingdom, headed by a Christian king, the Negus. He told his followers that the Negus would understand that what they believed as Muslims would be much closer to what he believed as a Christian than it was to the polytheistic traditions in Mecca. In traditional accounts, when the Muslims arrived in Abyssinia, and the Negus questioned them about their beliefs, the following verses of the Qur'an from the Chapter of Mary were recited:

> And mention Mary in the Book, when she withdrew from her family to an eastern place; and she took a curtain (*hijab*) in seclusion from them. Then We sent to her Our Spirit, and he represented himself to her as a well-proportioned man. She said, "Surely, I seek refuge in the All Merciful from you, if you should be God-aware." He said, "I am only the messenger of your Lord to give you a pure boy." She said, "How can I have a boy while no man has touched me and I have not been unchaste?" He said: "Even so; your Lord says: 'It is easy for Me: and We will make him a sign for people and a mercy from Us, and it is a matter which has been decreed'" (Qur'an 19:16–21).[4]

Upon hearing these words, the Muslim tradition holds that the Negus gave his protection to the Muslims who sought asylum in his country, and did not turn them over to the Meccan emissary who asked for their return.

This incident is crucial, as it represents the first encounter between the Muslim community (the Prophet had earlier encounters with individual Christians) and the Christian tradition. What is particularly instructive is that Muslims were a minority, in a position of weakness, while Christians were in a position of strength. The Ethiopian Christians, one of the oldest Christian communities in the world, when asked, gave their help and support to Muslims. The incident speaks volumes both for interfaith dialogue and the respect and debt that Muslims owe to Christians. When Muslims first migrated, it was Christians who helped them.

The second *hijra* is the more famous one. In 622 CE, Muhammad accepted an invitation to move his community north from Mecca to the city of Medina. Medina had a number of Arab tribes, several smaller Jewish tribes, and a growing Muslim population. The migration to Medina was crucial for the survival of the Muslim community. The persecutions in Mecca had increased following the death in 619 CE of Muhammad's uncle, Abu Talib. While Abu Talib never converted to Islam, he provided protection for Muhammad from the hostilities of his tribe, the Quraysh. After Abu Talib's death, another uncle, Abu Lahab, became the head of the Quraysh. He did not continue Abu Talib's protection, and so the persecutions increased against both the Muslim community in general and Muhammad in particular. For this and other reasons, Abu Lahab is the only human being condemned by name in the Qur'an (in Chapter 111, the Chapter of the Palm-Fibre).

It was in Medina that the Muslim community could exist as a community, openly and without fear of persecution. Muhammad established a mosque there inside his home, allowing people to worship together and creating a community space. It is for this reason that the *hijra* was chosen as the starting date for the Islamic calendar, not the birth of Muhammad, nor the occasion of the first revelations. In most printed Qur'ans, if one looks at the chapter title, one sees a heading indicated if the verses were first revealed in Mecca or in Medina. So the sacred text for Muslims, what they consider to be the Very Word of God, is marked with the distinguishing mark of the emigration.

It was in Medina that the Muslims who emigrated from Mecca became known by that very title: emigrants, or *muhajirun*. Those who assisted them in Medina became known as the helpers, or *ansar*. Clearly there is a parallel here for contemporary migrants who are often assisted by people from their tribe, or country of origin, or coreligionists. What is interesting is not only the guest/host dichotomy introduced here, but the other ancient dichotomy (at least since the time of Cain and Abel) of the city and the country. The Meccans were city people, used to the refinements of the city, and the commerce and trade that made the city possible. But Medina was an oasis town, known in particular for its date palm trees. So the Muslim emigrants had to deal not only with being guests in a new land, but also being city folk in a much more rural setting. Again, there are connections here to recent migrations, where refugees from the city may be settled in the country, a physical geography that would be strange enough to them in their countries of origin.

Contemporary Migrations

The roots of the contemporary situations for Muslim migrants are to be found in the Qur'anic text and Islamic tradition in the story of Hagar, the mother of Ishmael. Her story is described in the hadith, the oral traditions of Islam, in the most authoritative sound collection of Al-Bukhari (*Volume 4, Book 55, Number 583*). Ibn Abbas narrates:[5]

> Abraham brought Ishmael's mother and her son Ishmael while she was suckling him, to a place near the Ka'ba under a tree on the spot of Zam-zam, at the highest place in the mosque. During those days there was nobody in Mecca, nor was there any water. So he made them sit over there and placed near them a leather bag containing some dates, and a small water-skin containing some water, and set out homeward. Ishmael's mother followed him saying, "O Abraham! Where are you going, leaving us in this valley where there is no person whose company we may enjoy, nor is there anything (to enjoy)?" She repeated that to him many times, but he did not look back at her. Then she asked him, "Has God ordered you to do so?" He said, "Yes." She said, "Then God will not neglect us," and returned while Abraham proceeded onwards, and on reaching Thaniya where they could not see him, he faced the Ka'ba, and raising both hands, invoked God saying the following prayers (Qur'an 14:37):
>
> "O our Lord! I have made some of my offspring dwell in a valley without cultivation, by Your Sacred House [the Ka'ba] in order, O our Lord, that they may offer prayer perfectly. Fill the hearts of people with love toward them, and provide them with fruits, so that they may give thanks" [end of Qur'anic verse].
>
> Ishmael's mother went on suckling Ishmael and drinking from the water (she had). When the water in the water-skin had all been used up, she became thirsty and her child also became thirsty. She started looking at Ishmael tossing in agony. She left him, for she could not endure looking at him, and found that the mountain of Safa was the nearest mountain to her on that land. She stood on it and started looking at the valley keenly so that she might see somebody, but she could not see anybody. Then she descended from Safa, and when she reached the valley, she tucked up her robe and ran in the valley like a person in distress and trouble, 'til she crossed the valley and reached the Marwa mountain where she stood and started looking, expecting to see somebody, but she could not see anybody. She repeated that (running between Safa and Marwa) seven times.
>
> The Prophet said, "This is the source of the tradition of the walking of people between Safa and Marwa. When she reached the Marwa mountain (for the last time) she heard a voice and she asked herself to be quiet and listened attentively. She heard the voice again and said, 'O, (whoever you may be)! You have made me hear your voice; have you got something to help me? And behold! She saw an angel at the

place of Zam-zam, digging the earth with his heel (or his wing), till water flowed from that place.

Of this portrayal, Muslim scholar Riffat Hassan writes that Hagar is "a woman of exceptional faith, love, fortitude, resolution and strength of character. Once she hears from Abraham that God commands her and her infant son to be left in the desert, she shows no hesitation whatever in accepting her extremely difficult situation. She does not wail or rage or beg Abraham not to abandon her and Ishmael. Instead, surrendering spontaneously and totally to what she believes to be God's will, she says that she is 'satisfied with God,' who will never neglect her. She lets Abraham go, without any words of recrimination or sorrow, and returns to her infant son."[6]

It is also important to mention that Hagar is understood to be a Black slave, and thereby has to deal with a triple threat of racial, class and gender bias. And it is instructive for Muslims to remember this heritage, as the Prophet Muhammad claimed descent from Ishmael and his mother. He comes not from a lineage of princes and kings, but from the quiet dignity of a slave. Thomas Michel, a Jesuit who, among Jesuits, has done the most interfaith work with Muslims, sees Hagar as our "Mother in Faith," and writes,

> I believe that Hagar is a key religious figure and that meditation on her story can enrich the understanding of Jews, Christians, and Muslims concerning the nature of the God whom we worship and what it means to do God's will in contemporary societies. The image of Hagar and her child in the desert is part of today's reality. The low-born, hard-working domestic laborer, used and misused and cast out by her employers, the single mother abandoned by the father of her child, the foreigner and the refugee far from her native land, desperately trying to survive, frantic in her maternal concern for the safety of her child –this Hagar I have met many times.[7]

The account of Al-Bukhari continues in the hadith literature:

> Ishmael brought the stones and Abraham was building, and when the walls became high, Ishmael brought this stone and put it for Abraham who stood over it and carried on building, while Ishmael was handing him the stones, and both of them were saying, "O our Lord! Accept (this service) from us, Truly, You are the All-Hearing, the All-Knowing."
>
> The Prophet added, "Then both of them went on building and going round the Ka'ba saying: O our Lord! Accept (this service) from

us, Truly, You are the All-Hearing, the All-Knowing." [The verse is from the Qur'an, 2:127]

For Muslims, these are also crucial elements in the story of this family. The well revealed to save Hagar and Ishmael is the well of Zamzam, the well that to this day still waters the pilgrims that come to Mecca. Part of the pilgrimage ritual is running between the hills of Safa and Marwa, remembering the frantic search of Hagar. And then the rebuilding of the Ka'ba, the first place of monotheistic prayer, by Abraham and Ishmael. So Hagar and Ismael's migrations are crucial as well for Muslim practices, informing the pillar of *hajj* or pilgrimage.

In the contemporary world, so many Muslims are migrants, refugees, émigrés, or exiles. It was this beginning to Hans Magnus Enzensberger's magisterial 1992 essay that made me first think seriously about issues of migration, especially how migrants are received by their hosts:

> Two passengers in a railway compartment. They have commandeered the little tables, clothes-hooks and baggage-racks: made themselves at home. Newspapers, coats and handbags lie around the empty seats. The door opens, and two new travellers enter. Their arrival is not welcomed. The original passengers, even if they do not know one another at all, behave with a remarkable degree of solidarity. There is a distinct reluctance to clear the free seats and let the newcomers share them. The compartment has become their territory to make available, and they regard each new person who comes in as an intruder. This behaviour cannot be rationally justified; it is more deeply rooted.[8]

That metaphor, of passengers in a train compartment, has always stayed with me. It is an apt metaphor for the ways in which Muslim migrants, such as Turkish "guest workers" are viewed in majority non-Muslim societies like Germany, which Enzensberger was writing about. However, it also works for the case of Muslim migrants from India or Bangladesh to Muslim majority settings such as the United Arab Emirates. Clearly, there is much work to be done here on the ways in which Muslim migrants are living out their lives.

Let me shift the discussion of Muslim migrants to the context of contemporary North America. In trying to understand recent events, I was reminded once again about the relationship between "narrative" and "history." I am aware that the Latin and Greek roots, respectively, of both words have to do with the telling of stories. The knowledge of established historical facts may disappear quickly, but the narratives that are constructed from that history develop great force and help to shape our lives. Let me give my own example of what I mean by this. Almost a decade ago, in 2004, I watched with great interest the state funeral for former President Ronald Reagan. The Reagan Presidential Library was very near where I was living at the time; so many of the events were quite literally close to home.

Reagan was the first US president during my adult life. As such, I remember well certain incidents about his presidency. The ones that remain most vivid in my mind are his handling of the air traffic controllers strike; the policy that for the purpose of school lunches, "ketchup is a vegetable"; the social implications of the closing of mental institutions when he was California's governor; and the Iran-Contra scandal. Reagan also helped to arm the Afghanis in their war against the Soviet invasion, and spoke of the mujahideen as "freedom fighters." That, for me, was the Reagan of history.

But in watching the funeral, I was amazed to hear pundits talking about him as "the greatest president of the twentieth century." That was the Reagan of narrative, the one that some people remember. They spoke of his single-handedly ending the Cold War, as if Mikhail Gorbachev never existed. His state funeral was replete with military honours (21 gun salutes, horse and caisson, military pallbearers, etc.), even though he did not serve in World War II (I understand, of course, that one of his titles as president was 'commander in chief,' but it was still odd to see a head of state who wasn't a military man given full military honors). There was no talk of events from his presidency coming back to the modern world. No reference to the Book of Hosea, about sowing the wind and reaping the whirlwind, when it came to our present-day conflicts with Afghanistan or Iraq.

Mahmood Mamdani has an excellent book on this topic.[9] In that book, Mamdani writes about how Reagan and the Cold Warriors of his administration helped to arm and train the mujahideen in what was the largest covert operation in the history of the CIA. Jihadists were recruited from much of the Muslim world, and trained in camps across Pakistan and Afghanistan to fight against the Soviets. It was this policy of bringing together, training, and arming Muslim radicals that would lead to the Taliban, and indirectly, 9/11. There seems to be a collective amnesia about these events among some Americans, including those in positions of authority. The next time I teach my religion and film course, I will show my students *Rambo III* and see how they interpret it some twenty-five years later. For those readers unfamiliar with the Rambo oeuvre, that one was set in Afghanistan, with Rambo being recruited to help the mujahideen in their fight against the Soviets.

With regard to the power of narrative, people are, by now, familiar with the phrase, "the clash of civilizations." It was brought into current usage in a very influential article by a political scientist at Harvard University, Samuel P. Huntington.[10] He later expanded his article into a book, *The Clash of Civilizations and the Remaking of the World Order*.[11] Most recently, he has updated the thesis. In that new version, *Who Are We? The Challenges to America's National Identity*, the clash is not between White American Protestants of European descent in the United States and Brown Muslims.[12] Instead, it is between White American Protestants of European descent in the United States and Brown (mostly Catholic) Latino/as. For Huntington, there is always an "other" to White Protestant America, and whether that "other" is Muslim or Catholic is not important to his argument or rhetoric.

The best refutation of Huntington's thesis is by another Harvard professor, the historian Roy P. Mottahedeh.[13] Mottahedeh is best known for his magisterial book, *The Mantle of the Prophet: Religion and Politics in Iran*,[14] which I consider to be the best one-volume introduction to contemporary Iranian history. Mottahedeh wrote that book while at Princeton University, and he describes how he came to write it, after a visit to Princeton by an Iranian religious scholar (a mullah) who had been educated in the traditional way at a seminary in the city of Qom:

> I asked my friend about his early education: How did one study to become a mullah? He told me that in the Shiah seminaries such as those in Qom a student began by studying grammar, rhetoric, and logic. From that moment I knew I wanted to write this book.
>
> Grammar, rhetoric, and logic comprise the *trivium*, the first three of the seven liberal arts as they were defined in the late classical world, after which they continued to constitute the foundation of the scholastic curriculum as it was taught in many parts of medieval and Renaissance Europe. So basic were the subjects of the trivium that people who had passed on to more advanced levels of learning considered an elementary knowledge of all three commonplace and therefore of little importance; hence our word 'trivial.' I realized (and subsequent study confirmed) that my friend and a handful of similarly educated people were the last true scholastics alive on earth, people who had experienced the education to which Princeton's patrons and planners felt they should pay tribute through their strangely assorted but congenial architectural reminiscences of the medieval and Tudor buildings of Oxford and Cambridge.[15]

That quote gives the lie to the simple dichotomy of "Islam" and "the West," and the simplistic worldview of the "clash of civilizations." It is mullahs in Iran who are getting the traditional liberal arts education, not undergraduates in Princeton. It is those mullahs, moreover, who are reading Aristotle, and thereby weakening the case for distinct, pure "civilizations."

In debunking Huntington's thesis, Mottahedeh made a comparison between the ways Catholics were viewed in America in the past, and the ways in which Muslims are viewed in the present:

> In America, the distrust of Catholicism seems only to have died with the election of John F. Kennedy as president in 1960. In 1944 the most distinguished American Protestant theologian of his time, Reinhold Niebuhr, lamented the chasm 'between the presuppositions of a free society and the inflexible authoritarianism of the Catholic religion.' To distrust the ability of sincere Catholics to be true democrats seems as quaint and fanciful to us at the end of the twentieth century as will seem, in a generation, our present distrust of the ability of sincere Muslims to be true democrats.[16]

A newer phrase in contrast to the "clash" is the "dialogue of civilizations," which President Khatami of Iran proposed. In 2001, the United Nations adopted the metaphor of "dialogue of civilizations" for worldwide discussions during that year. In addition to the metaphors of "clash" and "dialogue," there are also (as noted above) the metaphors of "Islam" and "the West." I do not like the metaphorical contrast of "Islam and the West." To me, this is unhelpful, and presents "Islam" and "the West" as mutually incompatible. Instead, I prefer the phrase "Islam in the West." First, this phrase acknowledges the reality of Muslims living in the West. Islam is, of course, a "Western" religion, more deeply connected with Judaism and Christianity than with "Eastern" religions such as Hinduism or Daoism. Muslims are also a strong presence in "the West." Islam is the second-largest religion in Canada, Britain, and France, and may well be the second-largest religion in the United States. Secondly, the phrase "Islam in the West" recognizes the entwined heritage of Islam and the West. The West as we know it would not be what it is without the contribution of Muslims (as well as the contributions of many other peoples, to be sure). The danger of presenting Islam as "Islam and the West" (within a clash or a dialogue) is the generalization and subsequent obfuscation of what is actually a complicated, multicultural social and historical dynamic.

One aspect of Muslim contributions to the construction of the West is in literature. The late María Rosa Menocal published a groundbreaking book in 1987, *The Arabic Role in Medieval Literary*

History. In that book, she talked about a derivation for the English word "troubadour" (in Provençal *trobar*) from the Arabic word *taraba*, meaning "to sing": "'*Taraba*' meant 'to sing' and sing poetry; *tarab* meant 'song,' and in the spoken Arabic of the Iberian peninsula it would have come to be pronounced *trob*; the formation of the Romance verb through addition of the -*ar* suffix would have been standard."[17]

So the tradition of troubadours, playing guitar and singing love poetry, which is a hallmark of mediaeval European society, has deep roots in the Islamic world. In the contemporary world, one of the best modern troubadours is Richard Thompson, a British convert to Islam now living in the United States.[18] That challenges our easy assumptions, our simple dichotomy between "Islam" and "the West," when we consider that one of the best guitar players in the world is a Muslim. In all seriousness, for me Richard Thompson playing the Fender Stratocaster guitar is one of the proofs for the existence of God. Of spirituality in music, Richard has said in an interview on his web page: "Music is spiritual stuff, and even musicians who clearly worship money, or fame, or ego, cannot help but express a better part of themselves sometimes when performing, so great is the gift of music, and so connected to our higher selves. What we believe informs everything we do, and music is no exception."

I often play my students a recording of his song, "Shoot Out the Lights." The particular version that I play is a live recording with Richard on guitar and Danny Thompson (no relation despite the common surname), another British Muslim convert on bass. The song, which most people take to be about a relationship gone wrong, was actually written about the Soviet invasion of Afghanistan.

Let me conclude my chapter with these thoughts. María Menocal described another important connection between Islam and the West:

> In the destruction of the whole of the magnificent National Library and other major collections in Sarajevo several years ago, in 1992, it now appears one very significant book was rescued, the famous manuscript called the Sarajevo Haggada...the book that inscribes the story of the exile from Egypt, was carried out of Spain by members of the exiled Sephardic community in 1492...But the manuscript had to be rescued once again, during World War II, and it was when a Muslim curator in Sarajevo saved that Spanish Haggada from Nazi butchers.
>
> Surely, the morals of the story are perfectly clear: to understand the richness of our heritage we must be the guardians of the

> Haggada—the Muslim librarian who was not an Arab, of course, but who in saving the manuscript was fulfilling the best of the promises of Islamic Spain and Europe...We must, in other words, reject the falsehoods of nations in our work, and reveal, with the exquisite Ibn 'Arabi, the virtues of what he more simply calls love. 'My heart can take on any form,' he tells us, and then he simply names those temples at which he prays, the temples that inhabit him: the gazelle's meadow, the monks' cloister, the Torah, the Ka'ba. These are the temples whose priests we need to be, if we are to understand what any of this history is about. [19]

This is the virtue of exile, the great good that secularism brings. Remember, however, that "secular" does not mean without religion. When we say, for example, that America is a secular society, we do not mean that it is a non-religious society. Indeed, by any measure, America is one of the most religious countries in the world, certainly much more "religious" in terms of observance than most European nations. Instead, what we mean by secular is that there is no official state religion in America.

It is in secular North America where I work, a Muslim scholar of Islam. It is here where Muslims are trying to live out the poetry of their ordinary lives in all of the splendid diversity that those lives are lived. It is here, we hope, that we can be seen as full participants in our societies and not as threats to the common good. Again, this does not mean that we are naïve or silent about the problems in our communities. We cannot see ourselves as innocent victims, and shift the blame for our internal problems to outsiders. We need to deal with the social and ideological problems such as hunger, abuse, discrimination, and so on, that are part of any society. We need to address the alarming conservatism among some Muslims, whose ahistorical and non-contextual readings of Islam allow for misogyny and violence against Muslims and non-Muslims. We as scholars can provide different alternatives, different narratives to give meaning to our lives and allow us all to be fully human.

Migration and the metaphor of exile deepen my compassion and clarify my work. With his usual brilliance, Edward Said wrote this about the condition of exile: "Most people are principally aware of one culture, one setting, one home; exiles are aware of at least two, and this plurality of vision gives rise to an awareness of simultaneous dimensions, an awareness that—to borrow a phrase from music—is contrapuntal."[20] Perhaps this is the best descriptor for those of us who are Muslim migrants: We live contrapuntal lives.

Notes

1. Michael Ondaatje, *In the Skin of a Lion* (Toronto: Vintage, 1997 [1987]), 2.
2. Of the many tributes to Wilfred Cantwell Smith following his death, one of the most powerful was by William Graham of Harvard University. In that tribute, published in the *Harvard Divinity Bulletin* 29, no. 2 (Summer, 2000): 6–7, Graham wrote: "Wilfred was no friend of the growing academic focus on the strictly theoretical aspects of the study of religion, literature, or history: he always maintained that one should in the first instance study subjects, not 'methods,' 'theories,' or 'disciplines.'"
3. Muhammad al-Faruque, "Emigration," in *Encyclopaedia of the Qur'an*, ed. Jane McAuliffe, 2:18–23 (Leiden: Brill, 2002).
4. The translation from the Qur'an, as with all others in this chapter, is my own. I should confess here, as a Muslim, the power I find in the Qur'an's description of Jesus as a sign for people and a mercy from the All Merciful.
5. Accessed February 6, 2014, http://www.sultan.org/books/bukhari/055.htm.
6. Riffat Hassan, "Islamic Hagar and Her Family", in *Hagar, Sarah, and Their Children: Jewish, Christian, and Muslim Perspectives*, eds. Phyllis Trible and Letty M. Russell (Louisville: Westminster John Knox, 2006), 154.
7. "Hagar: Biblical and Islamic Perspectives", in *A Christian View of Islam: Essays on Dialogue by Thomas F. Michel, SJ*, ed. Irfan Omar (Maryknoll: Orbis Books, 2010), 87.
8. Hans Magnus Enzensberger, "The Great Migration," *Granta* 42 (Winter 1992): 17.
9. Mahmood Mamdani, *Good Muslim, Bad Muslim: America, the Cold War, and the Roots of Terror* (New York: Pantheon Books, 2004).
10. Samuel Huntington, "The Clash of Civilizations", *Foreign Affairs* 72, no. 3 (1993): 22–49.
11. Samuel Huntington, *The Clash of Civilizations and the Remaking of the World Order* (New York: Simon & Schuster, 1996).
12. Samuel Huntington, *Who Are We? The Challenges to America's National Identity* (New York: Simon & Schuster, 2004).
13. Roy P. Mottahedeh, "The Clash of Civilizations: An Islamicist's Critique" in *The New Crusades: Constructing the Muslim Enemy*, eds. Emran Qureshi and Michael A. Sells, 131–151 (New York: Columbia University Press, 2003).
14. Roy P. Mottahedeh, *The Mantle of the Prophet: Religion and Politics in Iran*, new ed. (Oxford: Oneworld, 2000).
15. *Ibid.*, 8.
16. Mottahedeh, *The New Crusades*, 140.

17. María Rosa Menocal, *The Arabic Role in Medieval Literary History: A Forgotten Heritage* (Philadelphia: University of Pennsylvania Press, 2004 [1987]), xi.
18. For more information, see his web page, accessed February 6, 2014, http://www.richardthompson-music.com/.
19. María Rosa Menocal, *The New Crusades*, 269–270.
20. Edward W. Said, *Reflections on Exile and Other Essays* (Cambridge: Harvard University Press, 2002), 186.

Chapter 10

Challenges of Diversity and Migration in Islamic Political Theory and Theology

Charles Amjad-Ali

I

Islam is often viewed in the West as monolithic, when in fact it is a highly diverse global religion. Muslims constitute about 23 percent of the world's population. According to a 2009 Pew Report, "there are 1.57 billion Muslims living in the world today" and they are "found on all five inhabited continents."[1] Fifty-seven states throughout the world are full members of the Organization of Islamic Cooperation (OIC).[2] While for many the term "Muslim" is synonymous with Arab, actually the 23 or so Arabic Islamic countries (including Sudan, despite its huge Christian Dinka population) constitute only around 20 percent of all Muslims. The largest Islamic country, Indonesia, has a Muslim population larger than that of the whole Arabian Peninsula.[3] Further, there is also a contentious divide between Sunnis and Shi'as (roughly 86–14%), which has deep religious, historical, and ethnic roots.

In the contemporary context, Islam is facing a series of new challenges. More than 20 percent of all Muslims live as minorities in largely Hindu, secular, Christian, and other dominant social constructions. The 2009 Pew Report found that "more than 300 million Muslims, or one-fifth of the world's Muslim population live in countries where Islam is not the majority religion."[4] India, for example, has the third largest Muslim population, and is not an Islamic state; rather, Muslims there have faced rising threats from the Hindutva ideology since 1989.

The question that arises for Muslims living as minorities is what theological sources and historical paradigms are relevant for their faith praxes? Should they continue to use the orthodox approach of an exclusively Medinese paradigm, as having sole universal and atemporal application? This obviously has limited validity outside those political situations in which Islam is exercised as the *de facto* or *de jure* state religion. It overlooks the Meccan period (610–622), which after all is the founding moment of Islam. Muslims were not only a persecuted minority there; some even had to seek refuge in Abyssinia (615). Further, even within Medina there are two distinct periods: one from 627–661 (including the 29 years of the authoritative Caliphs, the Khulafa-ur-Rashidun) when Muslims were the controlling majority; and the other earlier period, when they were a minority in the first few years after the migration to Medina (622–624 or 627). In these contexts Islam was also dealing with multiple levels of diversity which affected their identity.

There is clear need for a new paradigm, hermeneutics, and contextual application of the foundational sources and the larger historical experience of the Islamic community as a minority when Muslims were not in control of the state structures and the overall society. This becomes especially significant because it poses a challenge for the character of the political theory and orthopraxis in Islam for the contemporary situation, which has much in common with the plurality and diversity of early Islamic history.[5]

II

Judaism, Christianity and Islam all have a significant place for migration in their respective sacred texts and historical traditions. Thus, multicultural and multiethnic plurality and related diversity is ontologically present within these monotheistic religions. Such plurality, however, is not always given a significant place in their cultic and theo-ethical religiosity and their related discourses. Their orthodoxies when emphasizing the sacredness of their respective monotheism, and cultural and tribal particularity, look at these diversities and pluralities as problematic at best. They even see them as serious syncretizing threats, which relativizes their faith and makes it merely one among many and thus of "lesser significance." At times, the recognition of these pluralities is even viewed as blasphemous against their self-perceived sacred communities, which are generated by God's direct intervention in their history. Thus, their respective orthodoxies always emphasize and seek an authentic, almost transcendent, religious monovalent community. Therefore, these religions do not always pay attention to the various pluralistic tendencies that are also core values of their traditions and resources.

Unlike Christianity, whose particular migration story has still not developed into a major theological theme, both Judaism and Islam have a very strong theology of migration. All migration stories have a deeply inherent plurality and multivalency as a core element, and this is certainly the case with the migration narratives of Judaism and Islam. While these migration narratives hold very central places in their respective theologies and political theories, the concomitant plurality and multivalency is often not given much substantial value, especially by their respective orthodoxies. All three religions accept the centrality of the dwelling in the lands of others and under their hospitality, grace, and patronage, and they go on to make clear adjustments to their own proclaimed monocultural, monoethnic, monoreligious heritages and see it as a part of the gracious and miraculous blessings of God.

By way of demonstrating that all three of these monotheistic traditions contain a common element of significant migrations, with their implicit pluralities, consider the following cases, which are critical for the self-definition of these religions:

1. Abraham's migration to Canaan, and from there to Egypt and back to Canaan, initiates the migratory heritage of the monotheistic traditions and is thus of critical importance to all three religions. While Abraham's obedience to God and right to other's lands and property takes center stage, the hospitality shown to Abraham in both Canaan and Egypt is given little theological significance.
2. The Exodus migration of the Hebrews with Moses from Egypt across the Sinai to the "promised land" is of major importance in Jewish history, theological and political discourse, as well as in the other monotheistic traditions.[6] This migration provides major theological symbols, such as the Passover, God choosing sides, the character of covenant, God's privileged people, and God's accompaniment, etc.
3. The Babylonian captivity under Nebuchadnezzar, though not a voluntary migration, entailed a massive enforced movement of the Jewish people. This was followed by their return under the patronage of the Persian king, Cyrus.[7] This provides the context for understanding the destruction of the First Temple and the construction of the Second Temple—two very significant events in Jewish history. Unlike the exodus of the Hebrews from Egypt in the face of oppressive opposition by Pharaoh, the Jews returned from Persia at the instigation, and even persuasion, of foreign kings. Further, this Persian intervention is based on Cyrus' vision

from God and thus his mandate for the construction of the Second Temple (a Gentile getting a vision for the building of the exclusive holy central symbol of Jewish faith) makes for an interesting theological issue. In the case of the Exodus, Pharaoh sees the "immigrant community," even after 200+ years, as a threat, but instead of kicking them out of Egypt, he harshly blocks their return in order to keep his now enslaved cheap labor. This clearly makes for an interesting contrast with the Persians and their kings, who, on a human historical level, are the real *raison d'être* behind the return migration of the Jews and the construction of the Second Temple.[8]

4. The last of the significant migrations in the Bible is the migration of the Holy Family to Egypt because of the threat of Herod. While in the case of Exodus, the first Jewish sons are protected by the Passover mark, and the Egyptian sons die without this protection, in the case of the migration of the Holy Family, all Jewish boys under two in the region are murdered by Herod (i.e., a Jewish king killed Jewish children in order to the protect his power). According to the narrative, Jesus is the only one who escapes.[9] This is a significant contrast. This major sacrifice of Jewish young boys under Jewish monarchical oppression because of Jesus is seldom discussed as part of Christian incarnation and salvation theologies. At the same time, for at least 1,700 years, Jews were classified by the epithet of being "Christ killers" because of the death narratives of Jesus; they are never seen as "Christ saviors" as in the birth narrative. This migration is rarely a focus in Christian theological discourse, though there is a liturgical feast for the "Massacre of the Innocents" in different Christian traditions.

There are other migration narratives of critical importance in Jewish history. One of the most important and devastating post-biblical migrations is the expulsion of the Jews from Palestine after the destruction of the Second Temple in 70 CE by the Romans. After this, the Jews were scattered in global diaspora. The fate of the early Christian community was partly similar, but ends with the Edict of Milan in 313 CE, through the "conversion" of Constantine, and is finalized in the Edict of Thessalonica (380 CE), when Christianity becomes the state religion. After this, previously persecuted Christianity sees all plurality (especially Jewish plurality), as problematic; thus begins the sustained Christian persecution of the Jews, among others, which lasts until the end of the Second World War.

III

The narratives I have highlighted are an important part of Islamic history and theology. Islam, however, has a very critical and highly significant migration history of its own, which substantially informs its own self-understanding. A Muslim scholar asserts that "The Qur'an speaks of the migration experiences of many prophets prior to Islam, such as Adam, Abraham, Lot, Jonah, Jacob, and Moses. Since Adam, the father of humanity, migrated from heaven to earth, the tradition of Islam considers all human beings as immigrants."[10] Thus, plurality, diversity, and other multivalencies should be central to Islamic theological and political anthropology. Further, although Islam draws largely upon the earlier monotheistic history, it has its own unique hermeneutics and theology of these events and God's intervention in history. This provides Islam a theology of continuity and change, commonality and abrogation of revelation, and ultimately, the necessity of the finality of Islam.

Islam's own major distinctive migration (*hijra*) occurred in 622 CE, when the Prophet Muhammad and his followers left Mecca for Medina. This hijra takes place at the height of the persecution of the early Islamic community in Mecca by the Quraysh, the Prophet's own tribe. The Prophet had been under the responsible protection (*dhimma*) of his uncle Abu Talib (a critical figure among the Quraysh), and his wife, Khadija (an important and respected Quraysh business leader, and the Prophet's only employer). Abu Talib and Khadija both died in 619 CE, and consequently the Prophet and his followers became open targets in Mecca, which would never have happened in the deceased leaders' lifetime.[11]

There is, however, another earlier hijra/migration that is also of critical importance in Islamic history: that is, the migration of the early Muslim community from Mecca to Abyssinia, in 615–616. Though this migration is regarded as being of lesser importance in Islamic history than the migration to Medina, I believe it has major paradigmatic value for the contemporary global Islamic context, and for the development of theology and political theory that focuses on the issues of diversity and plurality in Islam.

This earlier migration also took place because of the persecution of the Muslims in Mecca. Ibn Ishaq, before introducing "The First Migration to Abyssinia,"[12] describes this persecution in great detail, saying the Muslims were shunned, isolated and even beaten:[13]

> When the apostle saw the affliction of his companions and that though he escaped it because of his standing with Allah and his uncle

Abu Talib, he could not protect them, he said to them: 'If you were to go to Abyssinia (it would be better for you), for the king will not tolerate injustice and it is a friendly country, until such time as Allah shall relieve you from your distress.' Thereupon his companions went to Abyssinia, being afraid of apostasy and fleeing to God with their religion. This was the first hijra in Islam.[14]

According to Muslim sources, the Christian king of Abyssinia (the Negus) not only provided the refugees hospitality, but also protected them against the Quraysh, telling the Muslims three times in front of the representatives of Mecca, who had come to Abyssinia to take them back by force, "'He who curses you will be fined. Not for a mountain of gold would I allow a man of you to be hurt.'"[15] Then the chapter on the Abyssinian migration ends with a personal witness of one of the Prophet's close companions: "We lived in happiest conditions [in Abyssinia] until we came to the apostle of God in Mecca."[16] This early experience of the Muslims living as minorities under the instruction of the Prophet could provide critical guidance for the piety of living as a Muslim in a non-Muslim context.

Coming back to the second migration of 622, the background is that during the last years of the Prophet in Mecca, a delegation representing the 12 major clans of Yathrib (the original name of the city, which was later called *Medinat-un-Nabi*—the city of the Prophet, and then simply Medina) appealed to the Prophet to be the arbiter and conciliator to end the clash between their two major tribes (viz., Aws and Khazraj, and their respective clans). These two tribes had been feuding for about 120 years with no end in sight. In addition, a very serious attempt on the Prophet's life by the representatives of the major Quraysh clans had taken place, which he escaped miraculously.[17]

These two factors made it imperative for the Prophet to leave Mecca, and migrate to Medina. In terms of sheer numbers and distance, this is a lesser migration: whereas 83 Muslims migrated to Abyssinia,[18] a large transcontinental distance from Asia to Africa,[19] only some 70 Muslims went to Medina,[20] merely a distance of some 200 to 230 miles. However, in terms of its significance for Islamic history, theology, and politics, the migration to Medina is clearly much more important, and holds a very high place in Muslim self-understanding. It is of such high significance that it constitutes the starting point of the Islamic calendar.

After a daring flight from Mecca, the Prophet finally arrived in Medina with his comrade Abu Bakr (the first Caliph after the prophet's death).[21] Once in Medina, the Prophet is hosted by the *ansar* (the local Medinese, mostly Muslim, "helpers" or hosts) who therefore take the dhimma for the Prophet and his companions. According to Saritoprak,

> After arriving at the city of Medina, which was a multicultural and multi-religious city, the first thing he did was to establish foundations for an interconnected society where people could live peacefully with one another. Muslims made up only fifteen percent of Medina's population when Prophet Muhammad migrated to the city. The population was otherwise made up of Arab idol worshippers, members of Jewish tribes, and a few others. Successfully, he brought a peaceful life to the conflicting tribes through an important document that he developed, the Constitution of Medina or the Medina Charter, in which equality between all members of society, regardless of religion, was established. There is no doubt that the Muslims who migrated from Mecca were financially weak because they had to leave everything behind in Mecca. They were unable to carry their possessions with them.[22]

Interestingly, this story illustrates that the Muslims were a small minority in the largely non-Muslim community of Medina; the majority were not only their hosts but selected the Prophet to be the head of this city state. This gives a clear impression that Muhammad was a person of good repute and moral standing, especially in the context of the fractious and revengeful nature of Medina at the time. Further, he wrote a constitution that proposed one united *ummah* (community) out of the plurality and diversity of Medina, whose population was mostly idol worshippers, with a large contingent of Jews and at least a few Christians.

This famous Constitution of Medina is a formal agreement between Muhammad and his Muslim companions and the full diversity and plurality of those dwelling in Medina at the time—the significant tribes, clans, and multiple religious groups. There was clearly a need for some code of conduct for this plurality to live together irenically, end the old feuds amicably, and face together the new threats that were bound to come from the Quraysh of Mecca. The constitution thus addressed the religious, tribal, and clannish diversity and the difficulties that this plurality engendered. At the same time, this document generated a peace initiative, and spurred conflict resolution and reconciliation, which were the main reasons the Prophet was invited to Medina. Consequently the various caliphates, as well as the post independent nation states in Islam, have all looked to this document as a significant source for their respective contemporaneous politics.

The most significant and comprehensive contribution of the constitution, however, is the notion of *ummah* (community). Ummah here is not based on the exclusivity of Islam (the later restrictive interpretation which is applied to it today) but on the inclusivity of the plurality and diversity of religions, tribes, and clans that lived in Medina at the time. The document states:

> This is a document from Muhammad the prophet [governing the relations] between the believers and Muslims of Quraysh and Yathrib, and *those who followed* them and joined them and laboured with them. They are one community (*umma*) to the exclusion of all men.... Believers are friends one to another to the exclusion of outsiders. To *the Jew who follows us* belong help and equality. He shall not be wronged nor shall his enemies be aided. The peace of the believers is indivisible.... The God-fearing believers enjoy the best and most upright guidance. The Jews... are one community with the believers (the Jews have their religion and the Muslims have theirs), the freedmen and their persons except those who behave unjustly and sinfully, for they hurt but themselves and their families... The close friends of the Jews are as themselves... Yathrib shall be a sanctuary for the people of this document... If any dispute or controversy likely to cause trouble should arise it must be referred to God and to Muhammad the apostle of God.... The contracting parties are bound to help one another against any attacks on Yathrib.... God is the protector of the good and God-fearing men...[23]

Muhammad thus declares not only a new community but also that Medina will be a *haram*, a sacred enclave or sanctuary, where there will be trust, responsibility, and peaceful coexistence. Ruven Firestone rightly argues that the "major, and indeed revolutionary, contribution of the agreement is that it begins the process of creating a single community out of disparate kinship and religious groups," creating "a 'supertribe,' in which a new determinant of relationship was to replace the old kinship ties.... the agreement established a single, common, political community made up of Muslims, Jews, and idolaters."[24] Further he argues that this community was "under the authority or supervision of Muhammad.... it became the basis for the powerful institution of the Muslim Ummah... an extremely effective and powerful religious, political, and military force."[25]

So while we have the creation of one transcendent ummah from the plurality present in Medina at the time, there is to be no duress to give up their other organic identities. Instead, these distinct identities were to be honored. F.E. Peters, describing this new community, remarks that

> the contracting parties did not embrace Islam: They did agree to recognize the authority of Muhammad, to accept him as the community leader, and to abide by his political judgment. In so doing they were acknowledging, as was the Prophet himself, that they were one community, or *ummah*, under God, Muhammad's God, not yet uniquely composed of Muslims, but committed to defend its own joint interests, or what was now defined to be the common good.[26]

Following this, the Prophet established what Ishaq describes as a "brotherhood" between "his fellow immigrants [*muhajjirs*] and the helpers [*ansars*]."[27] This can easily be seen as the caring responsibility—the *dhimma*—of the resident Medinese (mostly Muslim) ansars for the immigrant Meccan muhajjirs. The latter had few, if any, possessions, having escaped from Mecca, and were dependent on the hospitality and generosity of the Medinese ansars.

IV

The term *dhimmi* (a derivative from dhimma, which I explained above) is of critical importance for Islamic theology, political theory, *shariah* and *fiqh* (law and jurisprudence), especially as it deals with the plurality in the Islamic context. In Islam it has been largely applied to religious minorities living under Muslim rule, who are given a different political status depending on the political and legal context. It has had and continues to have a largely negative impact on such citizens, which is not always evaluated honestly by Muslim scholars. In Western scholarship, it has become a critically important issue when dealing with Islamic political, theological, and legal structures, and so forth. The evolving democratic concerns after WWII, the "Cold War," the emerging independent states in the post-colonial period, the collapse of the Soviet Union, and the expanding understanding of rights as well as political anthropology, have all led to a rather negative evaluation of Islam and its attitude toward dhimmis. Much has been written on this, and some Western scholars have used it for polemical purposes to vilify Islam.[28]

What is of special significance here is that most global normatives are now grounded in "universal" principles (deontological or meta-ethical) based on some transcendent *a priori* rationality. Being a product of Western developments, this rationality is not accepted as universal by many Muslim societies and thinkers. They see it as yet another imposition of Western hegemony, and thus clearly a pseudo-universal which should be challenged rather than blindly followed as normative. This does not mean that there is no discourse among Muslim scholars on these issues, only that they are not always willing to take Western approaches as authoritative vis-à-vis the issues of rights, responsibilities, and privileges of minorities living under Muslim rule.

Taken generically, dhimma simply means to live under someone's protective responsibility (*adh-dhimmah*). It is a kind of accountability for a dependent person, with no negative implications as such, except that an adult person lives under someone else's protective responsibility, and therefore does not have the full freedom to exercise their rights themselves. Legally and historically, however, this concept has provided the parameters for Muslim attitudes toward other religious minority communities, who get classified as *dhimmis*. In orthodox Islamic theology and political theory, dhimma is applied directly on minorities living under Muslim rule who are therefore regarded as non-citizens, not full citizens, or as citizens with "different rights," in some combination or even all three at the same time, to some degree or another.[29] For example, a dhimmi may not be classified as a citizen of the state, such as in Saudi Arabia, or may have the right to exercise full adult franchise, but not have the right to build places of worship or marry a non-dhimmi citizen. This depends on the school of religious jurisprudence (*fiqh*) which is adhered to in that state.[30]

It is imperative to acknowledge the fact that the Prophet himself on several occasions generically speaking experienced the status of being a *dhimmi*, and indeed survived persecution and lived because of it. In Mecca, he lived under the protection of his uncle and his wife and he was invited to Medina as a *dhimmi* and as a leader of that community. His early followers, upon his instruction, sought the protection of the Christian Negus in Abyssinia, and his closest companions also shared the Prophet's status of being *dhimmi* in Medina.

If a political theory and theology of true diversity and multivalency in an Islamic society is to be developed in fresh ways, to meet the contemporary challenges facing Islam, it is imperative that the concept of dhimmi be reconfigured. A more critical hermeneutic of the primary sources, as well as of the historical documents and their record, must be developed in order to search for a more just, equitable, and participatory understanding of this concept, which should be central for Islamic political theory and its religious piety toward its non-Muslim citizens. After all, the concern for *adl* and *insaf* (both words meaning "justice") are central imperatives for Islamic theology and polity.[31] Such a hermeneutical shift would also help develop new ways of approaching Muslim piety and faithfulness in contexts where Muslims are in the minority with no hope of ever controlling the overall polity.

This is especially critical because in Islam, the exclusive sources for the development of Islamic political theory, shariah, fiqh and theology, are the Qur'an, the hadith (the sayings of the Prophet), and the sunna (the practices of the Prophet). The Qur'an, being the actual word of God, and the mother of all the revealed texts (the *Umm al-Kitab*[32]), is most valid, such that even the hadith and sunna of the Prophet should be subjected to its criterion. In the hierarchy of broader resources, everything else is subservient to these three sources, and if any other ideals clash with them, the latter must be rejected.

However, the concept of dhimmi, as exclusively applicable on non-Muslim minorities, is not actually grounded on these foundational sources. They are rather a construct of political contingencies which evolved during the rule of the *al-Khulafa ur-Rashidun*,[33] especially under the Covenant of Umar.[34] The concept evolved from this in subsequent Islamic polities in the eighth and ninth centuries, and thus becomes normative for shariah, fiqh, Islamic political theory, and theology.

V

There are a few other references in the early period of Islam that are relevant to the issues of religious plurality and diversity in Islam:

The Treaty with the Najrani Christians (631). Ibn Ishaq writes about a deputation of Christians from Najran who came to Muhammad in Medina "to the apostle's mosque as he prayed the afternoon prayer... The time of their prayers having come they stood up and prayed in the apostle's mosque and he said that they were to be left to do so."[35]

It is very significant that first they were allowed into the Prophet's mosque (i.e., *al-masjid al-nabawi*, the second most holy site in Islam) and even allowed to pray there. Later they engaged in an inconclusive religious discussion, and then signed a treaty with Muhammad, in which they agreed upon certain tributes in return for which "they were indemnified against any attack on their persons, property or religion. Bishops and priests would not be removed from their sees, or monks from their monasteries."[36]

This tradition is often confused with a much more comprehensive treaty that the Prophet Muhammad is said to have made in 628 with the oldest Christian monastery, St. Catherine's, in Sinai, which gives assurance of freedom of religion and profession of Christianity. If anybody were to break this treaty, they would be violating God's covenant and disobeying the Prophet. A part of this treaty reads as follows: "Their Churches are to be respected. They are neither to be prevented from repairing them nor the sacredness of their covenants. No one of the nation (of Muslims) is to disobey this covenant till the Last Day (end of the world)."[37]

Negotiations between the Patriarch of Jerusalem and Caliph Umar (637). After the conquest of Jerusalem in 637 by Caliph Umar, Jews were given the freedom to practice their religion in Jerusalem, just eight years after their massacre by Byzantium in 629, and nearly 500 years after their expulsion from Palestine by the Roman Empire. Umar signed a covenant with the residents of Jerusalem which gave guarantees of civil and religious liberties to Christians in exchange for a poll tax (*jizya*). The Pact or Covenant of Umar outlined the rights as well as the restrictions and limitations of Jews and Christians—the *ahl al-kitab* (the People of the Book)—as dhimmis. This is considered by orthodox Islamic scholars to be a foundational moment for the classification of dhimmis and their treatment in an Islamic state.

The Ottoman Millat System (1299–1924). The other critical element is the *millat* system initiated by the Seljuk Turks and then fully developed by the Ottomans. The Turks had more or less taken over the helm of the Islamic ummah by the 10th century but became fully established under the Ottomans in the 13th century. They took the dhimmi system and gave it a contemporary, and less restrictive, expression under the millat system, which was based on the early traditions and sources in Islam but applying a more moderate hermeneutics.

The term "millat" comes from the Arabic word *milah* and literally means "nations" (Greek *ethnos*), as in our contemporary "nation state." The concept was originally based on ethnicity, but in the context of the Ottoman Empire, it referred to the religious and confessional communities of the old dhimmi system. Just as Islam had overcome multiple ethnicities under one ummah, the same process was applied for a transcendent identification of Jews and Christians. Millat also covered the separate courts and laws governing personal and family matters of different religious communities using their own systems, and it granted them a great deal of autonomy to set their own laws and to collect and distribute their own taxes. It was seen as one of the best early examples of a pre-modern religiously pluralistic political order. So the Muslims were under the shariah, the Jews under the *halakhah*, and the Christians under canon law. All these different millats, however, had to demonstrate loyalty to the Ottoman Empire. If one millat group caused injury or violation to another, the laws of the victim were applied on the aggressor, and the shariah was only applied where these laws did not function.[38] With the rise of nineteenth century nationalism, this millat system was substantially altered. The Armenian genocide (1915–1923) was part of this change and has remained an enduring mark of shame on the millat system and the Ottoman Empire.

The Jews of Medina and Muslim Exclusivity. In spite of highly laudable ideals, and long practiced policies of tolerance during most Islamic rule, there were a series of deeply regrettable events in the Prophet's own lifetime which mar this record. These are the expulsion of the two Jewish tribes of Banu Qaynuqa in 624 and Banu al-Nadir in 625, and finally the killing of men and enslavement of women and children of the Jewish Banu Qurayza tribe, in 627. These highly immoral acts took place ostensibly because these Jewish tribes betrayed the Muslims with whom they had made a covenant through the Constitution of Medina. Up to this point, the Muslims were a minority in Medina, definitely up to the expulsion of these two Jewish tribes in 624, 625, and possibly as late as 627.

These are clearly deeply shameful aspects for any history, but they are especially egregious when they happen in the name of religion. Yet very unfortunately, such events are part of the history of every civilization, whether carried out in the name of religion, culture, race, reason, or whatever are seen as the defining symbols by the ruling status quo. In the case of Islam, however, these acts are often used to stigmatize Islam itself as ontologically morally deficient. In the last 500 years, there have been several deeply shameful episodes in the West's history: 1. the horrific tragedy of the Holocaust (*shoah*) during the Second World War and the systematic killing of six million Jews; 2. the enslavement and mass deaths of the African slaves to serve the needs of the European American migrant Christian community; and 3. the massive genocide of the Native American population in North America, numbering in the tens of millions. All these are horrific events that cannot be justified and took place much more recently than the events of Medina, yet they are not seen as ontologically defining Christianity, the West, or its rationality and secularity.

If a deontological ethics is to be applied, then we are as guilty, if not more so, of an inability to deal with plurality and diversity. We should not be allowed to get away with applying a deontological ethics to others, whom we do not like, while allowing justification for ourselves through some situational, contextual, or relativized ethical norms for our own similar, if not worse, deeds. One is reminded of the biblical demand of taking the beam out of our own eyes before pointing to the straw in our neighbors'.

VI

In order to fully grasp the current diversity, plurality, and complexity of Islam it is also important to understand some of its history. During its heyday, Islam controlled Spain, parts of Eastern and Byzantine Europe, the whole of the Middle East, large parts of Africa, almost all of South Asia, and as far as Philippines, Malaysia, and Indonesia. The first real defeat it faced after its inception in the early seventh century was when the Mongols defeated the Abbasid Caliphate and sacked Baghdad in 1258. Even there, the victors soon converted to the religion of the vanquished and became Muslims. And when Islam was finally pushed out of Spain in 1492 as part of the *Reconquista*, after some 800 years, it had already begun to expand in the eastern part of Europe. It had taken Constantinople (the capital of Rome, which Muslims knew simply as *Rum*) in 1453, and then the Balkans and the Caucasus right up to Chechnya.[39] Well into the eighteenth century Islam was building major empires and centers of learning and undertaking great architectural feats.

Then in the last 250 years or so, everything began to collapse, and Muslims faced defeat, colonization, humiliation, and dislocation. Their lands were taken, and they were divided, both by internal strife and by external manipulation. So wherever they turned, they faced defeat. A religion that for centuries had met success in every endeavor was now reduced to being represented by petty sycophantic leadership in the service of, and at the behest of, colonial and post-colonial Western masters.

After the anti-colonial struggle, and post-independence euphoria of the mid-twentieth century, the new rulers who emerged in these post-independent states were found wanting. They neither provided fair distribution of goods and services, nor of economic and political power, and they suppressed the freedoms and rights of their own people. Their failure was all the more egregious because they were local Muslims and not colonial Western rulers.

Within the Sunni-dominated states, this led to a revival of conservative *Salafi* fundamentalism, which saw the orthodoxy of the first three generations of Muslims as being normative, authoritative, and ideal for all Muslims at all times and in all places. This fundamentalist movement blamed all the problems in these new states on the continuation of the secular common law traditions, the colonially trained leadership, and their colonially inspired governance and statecraft, which betrayed Islamic orthodoxy. The fundamentalists who had denounced colonial power as being infidel now turned their ire upon the new local leaders, condemning them of "Westtoxification."

They claimed that Islam was absolutely valid for legal and legislative purposes as well as for the moral and righteous functioning of the state. They needed to produce learned Muslims, and they tried to convert and control the hearts and minds of the people. In large measure, these steps failed to gain ground *per se*. However, with the expansion of the Cold War, and the clear alliance between the West and Saudi Arabia, things began to change. At the same time, there also emerged a socialist call in Islamic countries through people like Sukarno of Indonesia, Nasser of Egypt, Bhutto of Pakistan, (three of the largest Muslim countries), as well as the Baathist parties of Syria and Iraq. During the later part of the Cold War period, the "fundamentalists" were given free reign to control the locus for socialism such as universities, trade unions, etcetera. The West and its feudal Arab partners began to mobilize and finance these fundamentalists against communist and socialist movements. Because of this relationship, they kept their critique of the West mostly as a sophistic rhetorical device for recruitment.

With the end of the Cold War in 1989, this privileged position was taken away. The fundamentalist leaders felt betrayed, viewing the West's earlier alliance with them as Machiavellian utilitarianism, and as a clear indication of their overall immorality, which had to be kept in check through harsh draconian measures, otherwise their own societies would undergo moral and religious corrosion. They were now being condemned as fundamentalists, an epithet thrown at them from outside and not the classification they had chosen for themselves. Similarly, the *Mujahidin* (freedom fighters) went from being lauded as heroes, fighting against godless communism for the freedom of the people on the path of God, to now being negatively classified as terrorists: two opposite labels for the same acts, praised when committed against the Soviets and vilified when committed against the West and their allies. Now the Mujahidin were without privilege or status and were deprived of all their natural habitats. So they moved toward a more radical jihadist Islam with *Salafi* roots and a strong emphasis on shariah, ummah, and jihad. This aspect of Islam has confronted the West most specifically since September 11, 2001, and through the wars in Afghanistan and Iraq, and against terrorism.

VII

In the West, there is nearly always a very facile equating of Islam, almost exclusively, with the Middle East, Near East, or Arab world. This practice perhaps dates back to the period of the meteoric rise of Islam in the seventh century in the Arabian Peninsula. It expanded rapidly around the region, capturing most of the Asian and African parts of the Mediterranean, and then most of southern Europe, especially Spain. So what the Arab world does is very quickly projected as being true of the whole Islamic world, not taking into consideration the massive plurality that exists in it.

When it is convenient, the Arab world is quickly extended to include the countries surrounding the region, even when such an extension and inclusion is patently false. Such is the case, for example, with Iran, Afghanistan, and Pakistan. None of these countries are part of the Middle East, nor are they Arabic speaking at all. In fact at least 80 percent of the world's Muslims are *not* Arabic speaking, as stated earlier. Therefore, to use Arab Islam and its practices as either paradigmatic or normative for judging all Muslims is not only blatantly wrong, it produces a whole set of epistemological fallacies which, consciously or unconsciously, substantially distort everything else and do serious injustice to the diversity and plurality of the Islamic world.

The political, cultural, social, historical, and particularly colonial, experiences of Muslims outside of the Arabic-speaking states, which are substantially different from the experiences of Arab countries, are not given any real status when discussing the character of Islam and its struggle with and for democracy, plurality, and diversity. In short, an exclusively Arab-centered reading of Islam conveniently overlooks and ignores the experiences and struggles of the majority of the Islamic world and *de facto*, if not *de jure*, denies them any relevance in this context.

The forced Arabization of Islam is justified on the grounds that Islam's *lingua sacra* (religious or sacred language) is Arabic, at least scripturally and liturgically, and therefore such a connection can and should be made. This argument does not acknowledge that there has been and continues to be a division between the *lingua franca* (common language) and the lingua sacra in almost all religions of the world. The sixteenth century Reformation was the first widespread successful attempt to combine these two languages by the vernacularization of the sacred texts and liturgy. Some 450 years later, the Roman church followed this Reformation move after Vatican II (1962–65), and replaced Latin as the lingua sacra with the various contextual linguae francae. They were both part of Latin Christianity, but in other Christian traditions, this is still not the case, and not the case at all with other religions.[40]

In the best tradition of Eurocentricity, the more orthodox and conservative sides of European societies expect all religions to practice their faith in the same way the West does, which means, among other things, to have no separate linguae sacrae, if they are "civilized," "rational," "modern," and so forth. The continuing maintenance of a lingua sacra by anyone after the European experience of Reformation and "Enlightenment" is a clear sign of their backwardness. This patronizing assumption is made despite the fact that it is the European experience that is clearly the exception. This Enlightenment-based challenge to the continuing use of a lingua sacra is most vociferously and negatively applied when it comes to dealing with Islam and Arabic. This bias against the continued use of a lingua sacra affects the Muslim world in two main ways: first, it is yet another way in which Islam is characterized as "barbaric," and second, it leads to the contraction of the categories of Arab and Muslim, resulting in the invisibility of the 80 percent of Muslims who speak other languages, and live outside the "Middle East." This gross distortion of reality complicates efforts to get beyond the current hostilities between Islam and the West.

VIII

Many of the recent events in the Islamic world have brought the issue of Islam strongly back into Western consciousness, in a way that has revived old Islamophobic feelings in spades. We must be aware of the issues we have discussed above as we attempt to engage in genuine dialogue between Islam and other monotheistic faiths.

General Western perceptions of Islam and Muslims in recent years have been negative, but some saner voices have asked for a deeper analysis of Islamic history, politics, law, theology, etcetera. Even here, however, the non-Arab, non-Middle Eastern Islamic societies are rarely, if ever, taken into consideration, and thus the genuine plurality and diversity of Islam is not duly considered for epistemological purposes.[41]

The presence of Islam in Europe, through immigrants from ex-colonies since the Second World War, is now causing serious problems and consternation. Most of the early immigrants were invited from the colonies for the purposes of the reconstruction of European infrastructure, industries, and economies that were destroyed during the war. Those countries that did not have large colonial bases, like Germany, imported labor from their old allies, such as Turkey, as *gastarbeiter* (guest workers). Today, most of these immigrants are third generation European- born, with this being their predominant identity, and only a romantic link to the countries of their origin. In the aftermath of September 11, they have experienced highly prejudiced, vilifying sophistry and attacks on their heritage, race, status, and most critically, their religion: Islam. This growing European chauvinism and antipathy toward Islam has raised the ire of these Muslim immigrants, so some are hitting back against it with their own unquestioned religious chauvinism and narrowmindedness. Some are retaliating by increasingly joining more conservative (even underground) Islamic groups that have used these events and gestures as occasion to recruit disaffected Muslim youth.

In the last few years, these expanding hostilities have died down a little, but given Europe's economic woes, tensions can always escalate against immigrants in general and Muslim immigrants quite vehemently. On the one side are growing conservative, right-wing European groups, who can no longer invoke their own religion due to Western Europe's secular ideology, but hype their nationalism and some romantic notion of "Europeanness." Paradoxically, they emphasize the historically exclusive Christian identity of Europe and the West and its longstanding hostility against Islam. On the other side are the conservative Muslims groups in Europe who draw upon jihadist groups in Islamic countries for generating paradigmatic values and shaping their actions and goals.

Europeans tend to regard their own religion, Christianity, as an antiquated and benighted part of their history, so now, finding among its own population people who not only have another faith and seriously practice it, is seen as harmful to the society and a superstitious anachronism. Ironically, they are reviving some of the old hostilities that Europe generated from the eleventh to the fifteenth centuries during the Crusades, and again from the sixteenth century in the Reformation struggles and the expansion of the Turkish Empire. While earlier this antipathy was generated in a religious context and as a religious concern, now it is articulated in the name of modernity, secularity, and rationality.

In this context, Muslim scholars like Tariq Ramadan and others have begun to develop new political theories and theologies of plurality and diversity, and in some cases, even to reexamine Islamic doctrines within a contemporary context. Thus, migration is once again generating not only a diversity and plurality of location but these pluralities as causally linked with new hermeneutics, new political theory, and political anthropology, as well as for the purposes of a critical theo-ethical Islam.

We may not see the full political implications of these developments in the near future, but I sincerely believe that these new trends auger well for a common cause on major religious and ethical issues of rights and democracy, justice and participation, and sustainability of human communities in their fullest diversity and plurality.

Notes

1. *Mapping the Global Muslim Population: A Report on the Size and Distribution of the World's Muslim Population* (Washington D.C.: Pew Forum on Religion & Public Life, October 2009), 1.
2. See list of states in the Organization of Islamic Cooperation, http://www.oic-oci.org/oicv2/states/, accessed on June 28, 2013.
3. "China has more Muslims than Syria, while Russia has more than Jordan and Libya combined." See Pew's *Mapping the Global Muslim Population*, 1.
4. Ibid.
5. Here it is important to point out that Islam has a doctrine of abrogation, where the later text is given more value than the earlier ones. However, there is never a loss of value in the earlier texts and imperatives, especially those in the Qur'an, thus our appeal.
6. Over the last century, the Exodus has acquired major significance as Christian theologians have challenged the Greek notion of the impassibility of the unmoved mover, instead viewing the God of the Hebrews as the one who responds to the cries of the victims (*vox victimarum vox dei*). This theme has also been developed further by liberation theologians. See, Jose Severino Croatto, *Exodus: A Hermeneutics of Freedom* (Maryknoll, N.Y.: Orbis Books, 1981).
7. This migration has nuances similar to African-American migration and the Atlantic slave trade, whereas the Exodus from Egypt to the Promised Land is claimed to be similar to the migration from Europe. The latter, according to this reading, was against the oppressive feudal domination of the serfs and was an exodus from Europe to the freedom of the land God provided. In this European migration narrative, the native people were irrelevant in the divine plan.

8. This Zoroastrian link could also be seen as the foundational plurality in the very beginning of the Christian incarnation story at the manger, wherein the magis (Greek *magoi,* Zoroastrian priests) come bearing gifts and travel a long distance from the East. Interestingly, there is no record of their ever being or becoming Jewish or Christian.
9. Three of these significant migration narratives entail substantial movement between Asia and Africa, as does the first migration in Islam, from Mecca to Abyssinia. So not only were these two continents joined together, but religiously, they are of critical significance. From a Eurocentric perspective, this is not epistemologically recognized, nor is the fact that almost all the ante-Nicene fathers were from southern Mediterranean (i.e., Africa and Asia).
10. Zeki Saritoprak, "The Qur'anic Perspective on Immigrants: Prophet Muhammad's Migration and Its Implications in Our Modern Society" *The [E]Journal of Scriptural Reasoning* 10, no.1 (Aug 2011). See http://jsr.lib.virginia.edu/vol-10-no-1-august-2011-people-and-places/the-quranic-perspective-on-immigrants/, accessed on June 26, 2013.
11. This shift in status is clearly reflected in Ibn Ishaq's *Sirat Rasul Allah* (or "Life of the Prophet of Allah," which is considered one of the earliest authentic biographies of Muhammad. See, Alfred Guillaume, *The Life of Muhammad: A Translation of Ibn Ishaq's Sirat Rasul Allah* (Karachi, Pakistan: Oxford University Press, 1982). There is a section entitled "The Death of Abu Talib and Khadija" in which Ishaq states that "Khadija and Abu Talib died in the same year, and with Khadija's death troubles followed fast on each other's heels, for she had been a faithful support to him in Islam...With the death of Abu Talib [Muhammad] lost a strength and stay in his personal life and a defense and protection against his tribe. Abu Talib died some three years before [Muhammad] migrated to Medina," and it was then that Quraysh began to treat him in an offensive way which they would not have dared to follow in his uncle's lifetime" (191).
12. *Ishaq,* 146–155.
13. Ibid., 143–145.
14. Ibid., 146.
15. Ibid., 152–3.
16. Ibid., 153.
17. "Each clan should provide a young, powerful, well-born, aristocratic warrior" and "each of them should strike a blow at him and kill him," thus ensuring the implication of all the clans and their leadership in this murder, so that no blood feud could be carried out against a particular clan by the followers of Muhammad. *Ishaq,* 221–223, esp. 222; see also Qur'an 8:30.
18. *Ishaq,* 148.
19. See my footnote 7 on this point.

20. Montgomery Watt, *Muhammad: Prophet and Statesman* (London: Oxford University Press, 1961), 90.
21. Ironically, the first person to witness Muhammad's arrival in Medina was a Jew, *Ishaq*, 227.
22. Saritoprak, 2011.
23. *Ishaq*, 231–33.
24. Ruven Firestone, *Jihad: The Origin of Holy War in Islam* (New York: Oxford University Press, 1999), 118.
25. Firestone, 118.
26. F. E. Peters, *Muhammad and the Origins of Islam* (Albany: SUNY Press, 1994), 199. See also, Qur'an, 2:256 (a Medinese sura).
27. *Ishaq*, 234.
28. The best example of this is Bat Ye'or, *The Dhimmi: Jews and Christians under Islam* (Cranbury, NJ: Fairleigh Dickinson University Press/ Associated University Presses, 1985). For a more sympathetic read, see Mahmoud Ayoub, "Dhimma in the Qur'an and Hadith," *Islamic Studies Quarterly* 5 (1983): 172–82; C.E. Bosworth, "The 'Protected Peoples' (Christians and Jews) in Medieval Egypt and Syria," *Bulletin of the John Rylands University Library of Manchester* 62 (1979): 11–36, and his "The Concept of *dhimma* in Early Islam," in *Christians and Jews in the Ottoman Empire: the Functioning of a Plural Society*, 2 vols., eds. B. Braude and B. Lewis, 1:37–51 (New York: Holmes and Meier, 1982).
29. Sometimes this has been classified as "second class citizen" status, because of the highly restricted rights of the dhimmis. In this context, the political theory question is, Is one a citizen or not? The acceptance of a second class status for certain citizens is to acknowledge that they do not have equal rights with those who claim to be full citizens. This then raises questions about the character of justice, equality, participation, and the breadth of democratic dispensations in a given society.
30. The four schools (*madahabs*) of law in the Sunni traditions, ranging from moderate to conservative are:
    1. The ***Hanafi*** school, followed in places like Turkey, parts of larger Syria (Fertile Crescent), lower Egypt and India.
    2. The ***Maliki*** school, followed in the *Maghrib* (i.e., North African countries).
    3. The ***Shafi'i*** school, followed in Lower Egypt, Syria, India and Indonesia.
    4. The ***Hanbali*** school, the most conservative of the four, had declined in influence until the eighteenth century, when it was revived through *Wahabism* in Saudi Arabia and those influenced by it and by the conservative *salafi* Islam.

Among the Shi'as, there are also a number of schools, but the ***Ja'fari*** school of law predominates.

31. One of the classical examples of this justice is Qur'an 4:135: "O believers, be upholders of justice, witnesses for Allah, even if it be against yourselves, your parents or kinsmen. Whether rich or poor, Allah takes better care of both. Do not follow your desire to refrain from justice. If you twist [your testimony] or turn away, Allah is Fully Aware of what you do."
32. Qur'an 3:7; 13:39; 43:4.
33. The four rightly guided caliphs are Abu Bakr (632–634); Umar (634–644); Uthman (644–656); and 'Ali (656–661).
34. Though now quite dated, A. S. Tritton has a comprehensive discussion in *The Caliphs and Their Non-Muslim Subjects: A Critical Study of the Covenant of 'Umar* (London: Oxford University Press, 1930). See also Yohanan Friedmann, *Tolerance and Coercion in Islam: Interfaith Relations in Muslim Tradition* (Cambridge: Cambridge University Press, 2003).
35. *Ishaq*, 270–271.
36. Maxime Rodinson, *Muhammad* (New York: Pantheon Books, 1980), 271.
37. As quoted by Maryam Sakeenah in *Us Versus Them and Beyond* (Kuala Lumpur, Malaysia: The Other Press, 2010), 41.
38. Abdulaziz Abdulhussein Sachedina, *The Islamic Roots of Democratic Pluralism* (New York: Oxford University Press, 2001).
39. It is important to acknowledge that Islam has historically very significant roots in Europe, which is not always recognized or admitted, and European history is seen as exclusively Christian, and then secular.
40. Almost all other religions retain their lingua sacra: Hinduism uses Sanskrit; Buddhism, Pali; Zoroastrianism, Farsi; Sikhism, Gurmukhi; and Judaism uses Hebrew. Even within the context of Christianity, all its expressions outside of the Western denominations continue to use a lingua sacra: *cf.,* Greek Orthodox and Greek; Ethiopian Orthodox and Ge'ez; Syrian Orthodox and Syriac, etcetera.
41. Iran in recent decades has been given honorary Middle Eastern and Arab status, as the Ottoman Turks were earlier. However, present-day Turkey is ignored, and the Islamic communities in Eastern Europe are not even acknowledged.

Chapter 11

Signs of Wonder: Journeying Plurally into the Divine Disclosure

Elaine Padilla

> Up above the stars call out
> Inviting us to awaken, to evolve
>   to venture forth into the cosmos.
> Engendered they by pressure and heat.
>   Like merry boulevards lit up
>   or towns seen by night from a plane.
>   Love: which lit up the stars...[1]

As these lines of the poetry by the Nicaraguan priest-mystic Ernesto Cardenal imply, love beckons us to migrate into the boulevards of the cosmos, to be transformed continuously and interconnectedly through our inner journeys. Spiritually, Cardenal implies, migration transforms inner worlds by moving all beings beyond themselves to partake of the surrounding newness of other selves bodily, and by returning them to the one who bore the cosmos: love. Moment by moment, the inner cosmos becomes one with outer universes by continuously participating in this process. Inwardly and planetarily, the inner being migrates, oscillating between permanence and newness, energy and form, evolution.

    With reference to those who call themselves religious, particularly the mystics—the focus of this chapter—migration widens their inner worlds so that they can carry within their small suitcase-like spaces experiences of sacred universes. Whatever geographical frontiers they might cross, their remembrance of that love who bore their cosmos, their faith, if not merely the ancestral memory of religious convictions, travels along with them, transforming the religious landscapes of their host countries.[2] And because believers also carefully pack and carry the migrants' religious symbols, relics, language, and scriptures among their belongings, their most sacred places also become reformed, even if only sluggishly. Seemingly lost fragments gradually reconstitute within, in shapes not previously imagined, when love takes on shapes unlike the self, when the new breathes into the old.

This discourse of evolutionary transformation that occurs through the experiences of migration calls therefore for another element: contemplation. For some mystics of the three Abrahamic faiths, the journeying "into" and "out of" the self undergirds the migrant's life-sustaining beliefs and practices, and their daily living and involvement in both private and public spheres. The beauty of the macrocosm (outer world) shines through for the divine ineffability to sensuously entice the microcosm (inner world) of wayfarers, and with a vision of the unknowable mysteriously embedded in the known, to dynamically reconfigure new worlds. The worlds outside and inside disclose the divine mystery that embraces the mystic believer. Entrance through a series of mirror-like dimensions harmonizes the outer worlds or macrocosms with inner or smaller worlds: the self with others, the cosmos, and God.

By means of rituals such as prayer, the self sharpens its capacity to gain insight into the meaning of signs displayed in the cosmos and the soul. Importance is given to what the vestiges of God are saying in the eternal present. As with Bonaventure, are these images, whether material, spiritual, temporal, or everlasting, inside or outside the self, conducive for contemplating what is most significant?[3] To be in tune with God through both the miniature and giant cosmos carries the potential for finding oneself bodily and spiritually in the world and in relationship with others.

Implied in the harmonizing of inner and outer worlds is the awakening of the planetary self. Even as many negative outcomes have resulted from the movement of religious beliefs across frontiers, a divine love perceived in the plurality of the divine in the cosmos can awaken a memory of loving interconnection as ancient as the consciousness of the religious self. In seeking to follow these divine traces, and in the act of rearranging inner worlds, selves internally can subvert structures aiming at the institutionalization of the mystery and the isolation of bodies. The outer world can become reconfigured within the inner world (already imbued with a freeing mystery) so that metanarratives turned into history and fate can be emancipated to transform futures. A caring passion for co-creating worlds intended for the flourishing of each thing can be fueled by fragile and complex harmonies. Such can be the influence of the metaphors and poetic words described in the migratory spirituality of the mystics in this chapter.

The Migratory Process of the Mystic

Typical of the imagery of migratory spirituality is the element of mystery that accompanies the religious wayfarer. This notion of mystery means that God, while ultimately unknown and unnameable, limits the divine self for the sake of the believer, making God's love recognizable by means of signs being displayed along her arduous journeying. The signs of divine accompaniment declare that God desires to be perceived. They entice the mystical seeker to start her journey with God, who is all things and in all things. The wonder of the created order evoked in the self signifies a darkened glory in order to draw all things toward God by means of all things. Like an alluring *theotokos,* or God-bearer, each creaturely thing calls out in the streets, inviting the mystic to dwell where God dwells and to partake of the manifold banquet of the divine beauty that the cosmos hosts.

Islamic Mysticism: Creatureliness In Islam, this principle of migration imbued with the divine life can be understood through the doctrine of *tawḥīd,* which, according to Muslim scholar William C. Chittick, refers to how "everything comes from the Mystery, everything is sustained by it moment by moment, and everything returns to it in the end."[4] The sacredness of reality or the natural order is such that the cosmos is bidirectional, moving from and toward it, centrifugal and centripedal. The path of *tawḥīd,* of greater awareness of this migratory mystery, for some Islamic mystics like Ibn al-'Arabī resembles "stations (*maqāmat*) or waystations (*manazil*), both of which designate the halting places of a caravan."[5] Increasing awareness of God, the self, and the cosmos at each station creates a dwelling, a home, or sacred space for worship that has as its goal to arrive at the "Station of No Station" where the whole can be set free from circumscribing definitions.[6]

The initial migratory movement starts within God: the divine love. As with other mystics, so for Ibn al-'Arabī: God births the universe and gives it life out of love for it, and out of love, God, while ultimately unmanifest, discloses the divine loving self through signs and creatures.[7] God's love effectuates a limitation in God, so that the cosmos and each thing in it can become a signpost of that other whom God loves. Everything is a beloved. Consequently, "there are nothing but loved ones (IV 424.21),"[8] intimate companions displaying the divine love. The cosmos and every created being are signs of divine companionship, of the journey not being of the self alone, rather of a path taken along with the mystery.[9]

This principle of the whole universe serving as a point of reference of the unmanifest being intimately knitted in love to it means two things. First, God will never withdraw "from the forms of the Cosmos in any fundamental sense, since the Cosmos, in its reality, is [necessarily] in the definition of the Divinity."[10] So intricately intertwined are God and cosmos that being in the cosmos is the same as being with God, if not also in God. Second, the cosmos is the uttered word of God, the *tasbih* that speaks of the divine accompaniment. As one turns one's face, wherever it is turned, there one sees God (the divine face), Ibn al-'Arabī affirms.[11] The divine self-disclosure of all forms being beautiful, and through them God being God, as all things are in God proclaims the divine accompaniment, the divine presence, as all things can be present to all things. As all things are, so God is present in their midst, and as God is present, so all things are.

Even though forms of removal from earthly affairs are often also part and parcel of the migratory path of many mystics, the above principles mean that the mystical journey is typically one to be taken in the world and with the world in mind. For instance, female Sufi Rābi'a practiced asceticism until the end of her life. She understood that casting aside all that belonged to this world led to paradise, which is reached only when, in the state of contemplation, one beholds solely the face of God.[12] Nonetheless, what is also evident is that as for Rābi'a, so for many other Sufi mystics: the cosmos offers many ways to God. Because there are many created things, a way to God can be found "through every creature," Margaret Smith explains.[13] Every creature being a path is possible because, as Ibn al-'Arabī puts it, "the Reality is manifest in every created being and in every concept."[14] Each thing can lead the wayfarer to God since "the cosmos as a whole is in the divine form" (IV 231.5).[15]

Qur'anically, the universe being a "source of knowledge" about itself and a receptacle or locus for the divine disclosure would mean that an aim in the journey of the mystic is to see evidence of the mystery in the whole of life.[16] Chittick describes it as the cosmos being "the sum total of the words of God articulated within the Breath of the All-Merciful. Hence each thing in the cosmos is...also a letter or a word spoken by God," with an "ultimate meaning" being God in respect to the divine names and attributes.[17] Each encounter with a thing, each event and moment, has the potential for wonder since each is a letter, a theophany, a trace of the divine self-disclosure. Inasmuch as *wujūd* (the pursued divine presence) is present to all things, there are traces of the divine names in the universe. Even if a thing appears to be bad, it possesses some good, "since the Mercy of God inheres in both the good and the bad,"[18] argues Ibn al-'Arabī.

Jewish Mysticism: Dwelling In the Jewish Kabbalah of Moses de León, the allegorical aspects to the migratory journey vividly tell a tale of departures and returns intertwined with the inner being of God, who discloses the divine self by means of ten names, rungs, or *Sefirot*.[19] The start and end of the journey is similarly God's. God migrates from and returns to the divine self, paralleling the migration of the soul-breath from God and the points of return upon union of the soul-breath with God. Migration begins with Adam having caused a disruption within the inner being of God that resulted in driving out or exiling God's *Shekhinah* or tenth *Sefirah: Et*.

> Moses de León describes it as,
> "'He drove out et.'
> *Et*, precisely!
> And who drove out *Et*?
> 'Adam'
> Adam drove out *Et*!"[20]

Along with Et or Shekhinah, so was the soul-breath separated from God, and are beckoned to return. As the soul-breath enters into God, one loves (union as in lovemaking), and broken relations are mended on earth, so does Shekhinah migrate to the deepest or highest rungs of the Sefirot. Particularly regarding the path of contemplation, according to de León, only by the *neshamah*, or soul-breath, ascending from the lowest rungs to the highest can the believer be directed, trained, and guided into the straight path of returning to where it has been carved, "the bedrock of the Throne of Glory."[21] The soul, with its holy body, seeks to return to its homeland, place of birth, its dwelling, and place of bliss.[22]

But here is no mere effort of the soul-breath alone. Enticement comes most vividly via God's longing for intimate dwelling. God places the divine *mishkan* (God's place, tabernacle, or dwelling) in their midst and offers them a *mashkon*, which is the pledge of the gift of God's dwelling or indwelling presence.[23] None other than the very divine accompanying-dwelling, Shekhinah, offers herself as promise and guarantee: "Since My Dwelling is with you, you can be certain that I will go with you,"[24] and "So wherever Israel goes in exile, *Shekhinah* is with them."[25] Ultimately, the return of the soul-breath to its place of birth resembles the union of Shekhinah with her spouse *Ti'feret*, and her reconstitution (and healing union within

God) from before she was driven out becomes the reconstitution of God within.

In a manner that resonates with Islamic mysticism, the migrating Jewish mystic, even when exiled, is assured in her spiritual journey by a sense of divine intimacy, of encounters here on earth that have a touch of the heavens, of paths taken whose turns and ends can be gently wooed by the divine embrace. Signs shown to those spiritually journeying make manifest the divine company, so that they, too, can dwell where God dwells. God brings God's bed, so that they can intimately join God.[26] Viewed through this interpretative lens, one such physical sign was the burning bush out of which the angel appeared to the prophet Moses. Another example is the tabernacle offered as a divine pledge during their pilgrimage in the desert at the time of the exodus from Egypt. For a mystic like de León, these signs entice the seeker to happily dwell "in the palace!"[27] that is the seventh *Sefirah* or *Binah*, drawing all rungs within God by means of union of the souls with God. Like the prophet Moses who delighted in the All while in the cloud,[28] seekers can perceive the All that encompasses the cosmos.

Rabbi Tirzah Firestone explains that according to Jewish female mystic Beruriah, since the heavenly abode and earthly plane indwell each other, and male and female join together at the point of mystical union,[29] this path to the divine palace would not be merely upward. Because the whole of the self, including the moist and sensual aspects of the human body, can be "doorways" to the path toward God,[30] there is also a downward pull to the sensual and embodied life, God being found also in "the wisdom of the earth, the power of the present moment, the life force that fills our bodies when we breathe in the fragrant earthly air."[31] Ecstasy, thus, can also be about sexuality, physical bodies, the senses—"the holiness of the earth...sanctity in what our senses would have us enjoy."[32] *Shekinah* draws us bodily. In this ecstatically sensuous expression of planetary love, God dwells.

Christian Mysticism: Beauty In the Christian view of Bonaventure, the journey also commences with God enticing or drawing all things by means of the signs of the divine love displayed in the cosmos. Among its first steps is the one in which the migrating mystic passes through the cosmic mirror. For Bonaventure, "*From the greatness and beauty of created things, their Creator can be seen and known* (Wisd. 13:5)."[33] Through this mirror reflecting the vestiges of God, "we are led to contemplate God in all creatures."[34] The world or divine macrocosm then enters the soul or divine microcosm, through the doors of the senses, for by means of apprehension one can also see God.

Here is how Bonaventure describes this movement:

> "...all the creatures of the sense world
> lead the mind
> of the contemplative and wise man
> to the eternal God"[35]

The migrating wonderer witnesses infinity daringly limiting itself via shapes and forms. Even if most familiar, they become altogether beautiful, for by way of representation each form can lead to God as a partial prophetic prefiguration.[36] Being universally perceptible by all, even by the most untrained self, the traces of God in the earthen cosmos call out all things to the eternal in the now and the sublime in the common. To those journeying toward union with God, the cosmos in its titillating beauty becomes a wooing companion.

A subsequent aim in the migrating journey of the mystic is to discover the truth of the interconnected life-giving quality of the cosmos. For instance, Hildegard of Bingen in her many visions describes the concept of the sacredness of life as an egg-like wheel or wheel-like egg shaped by concentric circles and passageways in which all things partake of the process of breathing-in-and-out through layers of purification. The divine breath and the breath of the soul join the planetary breath. The eggs' winds strengthen all things, their stars illumine them, and without them nothing can survive.[37] All the circles provide the cosmos with its "greening freshness of life" and "the fertility that it needs."[38] Here lies another revelatory aspect of the cosmos: it offers itself as a ground of love. While it is not ultimate, the whole of reality can nonetheless purify itself there, reaching out to God while breathing there together.

* * *

For these mystics, therefore, the wayfarer is drawn and sustained by the divine love, which is the guarantee that the spiritual wayfarer will be physically traveling with company—of the divine presence in the cosmos, of many beloveds accompanying her, and of her being intimately drawn near to God. Certainly neither spiritual path is the same as the other, even though there are points of resemblance. Each journey is unique to these mystics, as it is to each spiritual wayfarer within each of the traditions. Furthermore, these paths are messier and countertraditional, including details that could also turn them in opposite directions, multiple twists and turns that I cannot bring forth in this chapter for the sake of space. Still, placing the views of these few mystics side by side, one can infer, shows that the divine accompaniment by means of signs is generously offered to others with other journeys of their own, religious others (and non-religious) who are likewise loved. The cosmos shows how plural the divine love is! It offers itself as a sign of this divine design, as wayfarers in themselves are and can continue to become signs of wonder before one another.

A cosmologically inspired ethic of love can emerge when we perceive archetypical forms of accompaniment in the journey via signs. The Kabbalah of de León suggests that the cosmos offers a message of divine love in the sense of God not only being "Master of the world!" but called "Compassionate and Gracious," one who feels compassion for the world, and one who arouses compassion so that everyone might know that the foundations of the world are established "solely on love."[39] For the "world is built by love" and love is that which "sustains the world!"[40] Without the divine love, and without deeds of love, the world would collapse.[41] There is great comfort when, in a journey, the divine love continues to ground planetary existence with its various interconnections. A *shared* wisdom deriving from deciphering cosmic signs and mirroring the wayfarer's processes of migration and movement can then disclose the divine mystery in the enactment of planetary love—love beyond the self.[42] For the purposes of this chapter, divine love being disclosed can be by means of the self migrating through the cosmos and into the self toward God, and it can also be disclosed by translating this migration tangibly as care.

Developing a Cosmic View

In much of the twentieth century, divine revelation had to find itself in history so that humans could free history from oppressive structures, and as historical beings, responsibly enact new histories that might reveal freedom.[43] A similar need arises in the twenty-first century, but in line with cosmology, as a way to further expand the geo-religious limits in which history finds itself confined. The expansive and pluralizing instrumentality of the cosmos partly evinced above can help paint a religious landscape that can perhaps more amply offer itself as a ground for multiple views to coexist.

If we perceive migration universally via signs of the divine love, we note that it contains elements of care for the created order and those in it. In the words of the mystics of the three Abrahamic faiths voiced in this chapter are traces of a longing and yearning that is perhaps intended to energize contemplative selves to caringly migrate toward "the other." This human and nonhuman other can remind religious participants of the possibility to overcome their prejudices. Nonetheless, to think of care is to wrestle with a crude vision of cosmic reality deriving from observable evolutionary processes. Living things have an innate tendency to vanquish the weak, especially when resources are scarce, and humans specifically reimagine things according to their own desires. Furthermore, humans tend to ossify interpretations of signs to protect their own kind when perceiving danger, and so tend to abstain from caring for others for the sake of their preservation.

When considering the cosmic character of shared wisdom being posited in this chapter, a reason for the difficulty in making care more tangible at a full planetary scale can be that any collective that chooses to communicate its version of the divine message does so from the perspective of its own set of universals. Each collective comes to understand itself, first and foremost, by its *a priori* significations, and so draws from its own wells not as *tabula rasa*, but as already having been irrigated by its own long past history of interpretations. The mystics being discussed in this chapter are no exception. As these mystics searched for words to describe the signs each of them perceived to be embedded in the created order, they were limited by the space they occupied in their time. The accompanying nearness of the divine mystery they made exclusive. In each interpretation, their provincial lens colored the meanings of their spiritual migration.

For instance, in Hildegard of Bingen we see that instrumental to returning to God through signs displayed in the cosmos—in addition to being consumed with longing for the love of God—is the delight that one takes in the contemplative faith and holy scripture.[44] The human figure of Jesus as Son of God also plays a climatic role in leading humanity back to God, for he is a sign of the divine highest love and providence.[45] Similarly for Bonaventure, the visions he describes of seraphs with their six levels of illumination are a representation of the visions St. Francis had when contemplating the crucified Christ.[46] The path forged is "through the burning love of the Crucified, a love which so transformed Paul into Christ when he *was carried up to the third heaven* (2 Cor. 12:2) that he could say: *With Christ I am nailed to the cross.*"[47] When seeking to see God as through a mirror, what glows upon the face of the contemplative mind is "the image of the most blessed Trinity."[48] And while each creature compares to "a kind of effigy and likeness of the eternal Wisdom," one especially, the scripture, prefigures spiritual things. In this regard, for these two Christian mystics, the self specifically signifies a Christian self.

The goal, at least for Bonaventure, is to transform the embodied self according to the flesh of the Crucified, to be like St. Francis, bearing the marks of "the sacred stigmata of the passion,"[49] and to become a living sign of the Trinity and of a Christian view of scripture.

We can see a similar tendency to interpret signs from within a particular religious framework in Islam and Judaism. For Ibn al-'Arabī, of utmost importance is that Muhammad is the primary messenger of God. Even though there are other messengers, Muhammad most perfectly takes on the form of the message of God to humanity.[50] In addition, the Qur'an, as the cosmos does, displays the divine verses, and quite poignantly is a special knowledge that can be given by God so that the divine signs can be read.[51] Likewise, through the Qu'ran and *Sunnah*, God guides people back to God to ensure their permanent happiness, balance, and harmony with God and with the self and society.[52] Not surprisingly, for de León the Name is found within the Torah. All the paths of Torah are of peace.[53] Knowing and following the divine paths occurs "by striving for Torah day and night!"[54] Therefore, even as signs displayed can be universal or cosmic in nature, there can be an interpretation of them that is particular to each faith, evoking feelings nourished by their divinely inspired but individual and humanly built beliefs and structures of faith. Socially constructed orders evoke a complex web of symbolic growth as designations and meanings are given to these feelings.[55]

Yet stimuli coming from the physical realm, while evoking feelings that produce habits or patterns, simultaneously instill a kind of *longing* for the new. Everything in the cosmos has the potential for change, for transformation in continuity with its ecosystems of feelings. According to Charles Peirce, this potential is inexhaustible since "no multitude of individuals can exhaust"[56] the possibilities of determination that exist in the true continuum. For me, an example of this "true continuum" is the cosmos. The cosmos, in being continuous, offers countless relationships that continue to multiply the chances for other possibilities, for uncertainty and indeterminacy. Meanings of signs can evolve from past to present and future and through space. As the earthly sphere *spaces* or breathes in and out (Hildegard), meanings spread their wings and migrate from one collective to another. Especially if we draw from a Peircian model of planetary evolution to recast the concept of spiritual migration, we can add another level of *sharing* since sets of interpretations of signs are passed down and rephrased.

A good illustration of this process of evolutionary migration of signs can be the borrowing of symbolic language that took place in

Spain. There Christians, Jews, and Muslims (or Moors) found themselves enjoying the peninsular territory from the time of the Middle Ages to the early Modern Era (and still in the present time). Migration of Christians and Jews into Spain began at the time of the Roman Empire, and for Muslims during the eighth century. Moving between periods of peace, upon the defeat of the Visigoths at the hands of the Muslims, and intolerable religious persecution, with the collapse of the unified Muslim Spain and the spirit of the Christian *Reconquista*, hopes for peace among these three dominant religious streams grew faint. The formal expulsion of Jews and Moors after 1492 led many to external migrations in search of more tolerable territories. For many who remained, however, internal migration took on the form of conversion, even if it was forced, and their true sentiments and beliefs therefore cloaked.[57]

In the midst of these struggles, one finds evidence of meanings traveling among Moorish, Jewish, and Christian communities of mystics in Spain, spreading from one ethnic group to another, leaving an indelible trace on key concepts such as the migrations of the soul toward God. In particular, I am interested in traces of the imageries of twelfth- and thirteenth-century Spanish mystics Ibn al-'Arabī and de León that were left upon the metaphoric language of St. Teresa of Ávila, a sixteenth-century Spanish Christian mystic of presumed Jewish *converso* stock. Any form of influence or sharing, of course, would not have been explicitly conveyed, due to the intolerant religious climate of the day. Still, despite the fact that linguistic borrowing cannot be scientifically proven, the resemblance among their texts is worth highlighting. Particularly, I think the seventh mansion of her "Interior Castle" resembles "a single diamond or a very clear crystal"[58] that contains many inner dwellings shaped in concentric circles, rungs, or layers similar to the other two traditions. The possibility for this influence increases when we consider that much of medieval cosmology viewed space as sacred, and represented it in drawings by spheres or concentric layers, hence the common trope of ascent or descent into the soul through seven to ten spheres to reach the heavenly throne.[59]

As with the imageries above, St. Teresa de Ávila describes the soul as "spacious, ample and lofty (*a palace*),"[60] calls it "home" that has a "Host Who will put all good things into its possession."[61] She compares it to a paradise in which God takes delight,[62] and to an *Oriental* pearl. This interior castle is planted in the living waters of life—"namely in God."[63] These waters that overflow it with love enlarge the castle. At its very center is the cellar of wine, "the room or *palace* occupied by the King,"[64] the abiding place of God, and "a second Heaven."[65] And since the castle mirrors the divine dwelling, the divine self is this beautiful mansion or palace.[66]

In considering this concept of the castle or palace (as divine dwelling), Catherine Swietlicki notes how Teresa's voyage to the *siete moradas* (seven dwellings) up to the innermost chamber of God where her marriage is consummated resembles the Jewish mystic's journeys of the soul through the *Moradas* of Kabbalah and into the depths of God as well as the marriage of Shekhinah to Ti'feret. In the Zohar, whose author for the most part is thirteenth-century Jewish mystic de León, also from Ávila, Spain, prayers serve to elevate the mystic into "the seven Palaces, to wit, the Palaces of the King" (4.202a-b) and contrition into "the secret and hidden place" (5.203a), a place reserved for the worthy known as "the Palace of Love" (3.97a).[67]

It is especially *Binah*, "one of the three uppermost divine emanations" (the other two being *Keter* and *Hokhmah*) that is known as the divine Palace "through which the whole world is created and transformed into being from nothing."[68] It is through Binah that the light emanates to the lower rungs of the divine embodied expression. Ascending toward Binah is by means of the Sefirot, which, like moradas, would turn the inward *aposentos* of the castle of Teresa de Ávila into openings that lead to other openings, granting access to the beyond of the beyond level. In both mystical strands, God dwells both in the uppermost heavenly palaces and in the deepest palaces of the soul, the soul resembling the dwellings of the heavens: that is, God's being.

Similarly, Luce López-Baralt finds commonality between St. Teresa's path into her interior castle and her fellow twelfth-century Spanish mystic Ibn al-'Arabī's slow ascent through a multitude of rooms and doors that one goes through as the contemplative soul advances spiritually in mystical knowledge, as described in his *al-Futūḥāt al-Makkiyya* (II, 768–774).[69] The soul has many layers, and the seventh is called the blood of the heart and is the mine from which all the illuminating lights emerge in the *Tohfa* (7, 8).[70] Likewise, in his *Libro del Nocturno Viaje hacia la majestad del más generoso*, Ibn al-'Arabī uses as his point of departure the seven heavens or mansions of the soul's castles.[71] As with St. Teresa, in Ibn al-'Arabī's view of the sacred dwelling, God also draws all things to God's abode.

I suggest that by these mystics making use of similar symbolic terms to describe the most sacred places, a liminal space gapes open.[72] Religiously, the concept of sacred space would not be restricted to their own kind of godly people at the exclusion of others. Moreover, politically, we find a subaltern reality almost mockingly mimicking the imperial Spain being represented in these palaces or castles. In the seventh mansion, rather than finding the royals of Spain Fernando and Isabel, we find the home of divine love. The human inward being mirrors the divine dimensions that layer the soul and transform it into a palace or a castle ornamented with precious stones, yet fit for divine habitation. Perhaps rather than a Spanish Empire bent on using the sword and conversion, or a castle's walls built for war, this castle symbolizes something more enduring: the merciful and porous boundaries of God. This spiritual castle overturns the imperial tendencies of its time, not only with regard to the Church and its inquisitorial power, but also politically, with regard to the migrant traveler finding her way into a compassionate and merciful God. Instead of being a space that opens for the inbreeding of religious violent conquests, quite subversively the seventh mansion offers a vision of humble surrenders. Likewise, the religious community and state of today can be turned into an abode free of selfish pursuits and violence, and instead of being places of power, become places of self-abnegation.

The images also serve as signs with the capacity to stand for something that exceeds them in terms of meaning, the *moreness* of the appearance that can also free particular interpretations from grasping for ultimacy, hence from objectifying the accompanying mystery. So close and intimate, yet also quite ungraspable is the mystery of divine dwelling in motion. For Teresa de Ávila, in the seventh mansion dwells "some kind of darkness,"[73] "a cloud of the greatest brightness"[74] where she and her beloved become one.

In the Islamic mysticism of Ibn al-'Arabī, because God is the All-Encompassing (*al-muḥīṭ*),[75] and because the divine entity, as it is with all entities, makes itself manifest by its form, the whole and each of its forms also make absent the divine presence.[76] For instance, revelation of God through the cosmos would entail re-veiling or curtaining,[77] or perceiving God through the cosmic forms, for the Real, according to Ibn al-'Arabī, can never be known. Subsequently, the spiritual steps taken to know God then paradoxically lead the seeker through paths of unknowing—"the Station of No Station." Chittick explains that, "Once the servants find themselves in the luminous clarity of *wujūd*, the perfect among them are guided to another kind of darkness which, in fact, is the highest stage of knowledge."[78] This stage compares to a sense of "bewilderment," to knowing that one knows nothing, and understanding that God is exalted beyond all creatures (signifiers).

Likewise, in the Jewish mysticism of de León, as the soul-breath enters through the Sefirah, whose first opening is Shekhinah, in order that the Blessed Holy One can become known,[79] it must arduously continue on to the inner depths of God Sefirah by Sefirah, rung by rung, continuously longing for the Infinite or *Ein Sof.* As with the prophet Moses entering the cloud, Shekhinah entices as she reveals herself by resting upon the mountain covered with thick darkness.[80]

Similarly in the mysticism of the thirteenth-century Italian thinker Bonaventure, the migratory path of the self entails negation. The heart ascends *"in the valley of tears"* by steps toward the mountain, as for the prophet Moses. [81] Borrowing from a medieval cosmology, *six days* the Lord called the prophet Moses "from the midst of the cloud," thus six steps are required before one might encounter full peace, the Sabbath, or rest (Exod. 24:16), which is the seventh and last one of the steps into the depths of God. First the beauty of the cosmos, then the illuminating rays of God draw the mystic, who soon encounters a most sublime light. The enkindled heart groans "by an outcry of prayer," as the soul turns the innermost parts of the self "directly and intently toward the rays of light,"[82] a light which is "the superluminous darkness of a silence," a teaching in obscurity that is "supermanifest," "a darkness which is super-resplendent," an "overflowing" of the intellect "with the splendors of invisible goods that surpass all good."[83] The ecstatic entrance into the "superessential ray of the divine darkness."[84] When one is in prayer for the ecstatic unctions and affections for God, therefore, the request for grace accompanies that for a flame of darkness. Such passion seeks an abundance or excess of God's being that overflows all preconceived forms of knowing, of perceiving, of naming the divine mystery.

Given that our best metaphors or linguistic signs must in the end endure the utter divine darkness, this journeying into a seeming absence, while it can lead to distorted recognitions of self, cosmos, others, and God, might also provoke one to wonder. Indeed, it can be quite humbling to accept that the spiritual migration into the deepest parts of the divine mystery by means of indwelling signs of divine love is one shrouded by the unmanifest. The wanderer knows and yet does not comprehend or grasp the full meaning of who God is and what things are. The mystery is clothed in layers or rungs, partly reached by steps or waystations, through which the mystic can come to know—but never fully. The layered depths reveal as much as they hide, for the nearness and the magnitude of the mystery in all things that accompanies the wayfarer overflow the spiritual senses. In such overflow, its higher ethic can be evident. An awareness of these veiling and revealing effects of signs has the potential to free the wayfaring dwellers from loving only their tribe and people, and from erecting idols out of these signs, while affirming the relevance of the particular interpretations of each for good living.

Therefore, the peripatetic quality of moving across religious boundaries holds creative possibilities, even when sometimes such movement can be restrained by the institutions that safeguard these belief systems. The welcoming of the new in language that dynamically partakes of the excessiveness of the sign, the *moreness* that reaches beyond each collective, cannot be exhausted. Symbolic language can welcome new meanings that more lovingly reimagine the self, religious others, and God, through a reconfigured stock of shared images. Could it be that souls and bodies—any of them willing to do so—can be offerings of divine indwelling, an accompanying love for any human, as is implied in the above cosmic views?

Perhaps the value of divine indwelling in humans and human indwelling in the divine can help restore the basis for developing habits of care toward each other during times of great intolerance and persecution. And while there is no evidence of this shared wisdom having impeded the inhuman ideology and harshest impacts of the *Reconquista*, which ultimately resulted in the forced migrations of many non-Christians, many pseudo- or cryptic Jews and underground Moorish communities survived, possibly due to such interreligious acts of care. "Feelings" must have been grounded centuries earlier as a result of the cosmic visions prevalent in mysticism, their impact on Spanish Christian thought, and the mutual sharing of symbolic language and meaning among all three faiths, at least at a popular level or by intermarriage.[85] In humility, I recognize direct positive effects can be difficult to discern, and that one can only hope and continue witnessing their unfolding more fully day by day into the future.[86]

Planetary Love

In the spiritual journey, signs encountered along the way can spark a memory in the being of the mystic wayfarer. Something more immemorial, like the love of God illustrated in the work of these mystics, can generate new feelings that can lead to acts of care across all kinds of boundaries. Paradoxically, for the migrant mystic, the awakening to that divine love that interconnects all things (a form of bordercrossing) comes by means of the individual soul migrating into the self and seeking to expansively interpret the signs of the cosmos, as if entering through a series of mirrors.

Since humans were also created in the image of the cosmos—that is, God also chose to shape human form "according to the bulwark of the cosmic system and the universe," as Hildegard of Bingen affirms[87]—therefore the human migratory movement through the cosmos parallels its journeying into the self toward God. More broadly, as if moving through concentric circles, or Sefirot, or moradas, or mansions, the migratory journey through the mirrors of the cosmos corresponds to the deepening of the self into itself, the knowing of itself, and through it knowing each thing as it is. The side-by-side movement is a planetary one, since each human being is part of the mystery of the earth and of each cosmic element.

Love signified in the cosmos awakens the mystic's memory, the deepest membranes of the soul toward love of self in loving God and others, a loving memory that for some mystics requires polishing the mirror of the soul. For Bonaventure, so that one is lifted up in wonder and partakes in God, one polishes one's inner mirror in order to discover the divine impression in the cosmos reflected on one's inner being. This type of mirror-journeying into one's self is the path toward presence of self in relation to God and the cosmos.[88] Once the mirror of the soul of the one who loves the divine wisdom and who delights in savoring God "has been cleansed and polished," the self can faithfully disclose the divine desire or love displayed in the cosmos.[89] To migrate or enter into oneself means one's soul loving itself most fervently,[90] knowing itself, and remembering itself.

Remembrance (*dhikr*) by way of polishing the mirror, likewise leads to the ability to see with the eye of God,[91] which in following Ibn al-'Arabī's thoughts, entails fuller awareness of who one is, which for him means a greater awareness of God, and the relation that all things hold to their creator and one another. In Islam, the sin of Adam was to forget God,[92] hence to forget who he was, and disassociate himself from the created order. Indeed, in remembering he was forgiven, no residue of his sin was passed down, and his relationality was restored. It is the same with others. According to Ibn al-'Arabī, through remembrance, the human unites in herself the entire cosmos and the Real, her two hands.[93]

We also find in the Islamic mysticism of Ibn al-'Arabī that in remembering, the mystic develops an anthropocosmic vision that tunes the heart to the caring desire for healing toward God, creation, and society.[94] This act of remembrance is the aim of the journey, "to discover the ultimate truths of the universe within the depths of one's soul, the only place where truth can be found," argues Chittick.[95] The "organismic" character of the whole becomes evident. As he argues, "The truth and reality of God and the universe – their *haqq* – can be known; the rights of God, people and other creatures – their *huqúq* – can be discerned; and the appropriate and worthy response to truth can be put into practice."[96] We must know what the world signifies to us in order to act properly in the world and love out of a sense of our embodiment. Chittick summarizes this truth as, "The goal of human life is to harmonize oneself with heaven and earth and to return to the transcendent source of both humans and the world."[97]

The Kabbalah adopts a similar principle of aligning divine signs with seeking social wholeness. It refers to *tikkun*, or the act of mending the fragments within God caused by the sin of Adam, and of healing the separation or broken ties between all living things that resulted. Entering the divine palace, or *Binah*, returning to "the bedrock of the Throne of Glory" in the human union with God through prayer, could potentially spill over into the social sphere. God and *Shekhinah* unite for "the broken to be repaired, for that which is lost to find its way home, and for the grace of the Spirit to bring renewing love to wounded hearts,"[98] argues Jewish feminist Lynn Gottlieb. *Tikkun* interconnects or mends relational brokenness (internally and externally). For the exiled Jewish kabbalists, Adam expelling the *Shekhinah* (hence the shattering of the vessels) had to be made whole; God had to be reconstituted in unison with human relations being co-constituted. That is why for Gershom Scholem, the Jewish exile was a call to recreate a broken world by each one occupying space in different worlds, mending wounded relationships and easing separation.[99]

Hence the mirror correspondence between the cosmos, soul, and God awakens in the self a memory of the power of *affect*—feelings. As Hildegard of Bingen suggests, each soul holds a certain "greening" power that I interpret as healing care. Everything divine done in the soul migrates, extending itself beyond the body, and has the possibility of permeating the universe, an act that for Hildegard consists of the human being reaching out to *"the entire globe."*[100] Such an image of interconnectivity can illustrate how intimacy carries the potential for actions of care *affecting* the many, provoking the feelings of others toward love. Being in "simplicity of heart" and longing for God,[101] the self inhales the healing powers of the cosmic elements needed for life, breathes them in, while the cosmos also breathes in the powers of the souled self. Upon being flooded with the longing of the cosmos, the self climbs "from virtue to virtue," and begins to feel "a greening power."[102] Likewise, good deeds have a ripening effect that extends to the whole in all sweetness and gentleness.[103]

For some of the reasons above, one can live up to the fullness of one's humanity by understanding the cosmos and all things as they are.[104] The signs contained in the cosmos declare the divine message, or become the messengers of God declaring that to each thing its *haqq* or realness must be given.[105] To do otherwise is to forget one's self, hence to cause our own self-impoverishment. Since soul and cosmos are dimensions of the same reality, the more the impoverished view of the cosmos and other beings one holds, as with Chittick, the more flattened the view of one's being in this world will be.[106] Having contempt for the cosmos and others would be the same as having contempt for one's self and the creator.[107]

Hence the migratory journeying into the soul can be as entering a cave, a site of redefinition or deconstruction, where things living become divinely gifted, things temporal become signs of the eternal, and where presence extends to all times by means of a memory that spreads interspatially. Memory retains and represents not only present, corporeal, or temporal things but also successive, simple, and eternal things. "For the memory retains the past by remembrance, the present by reception and the future by foresight," argues Bonaventure.[108] Memory is remembering how things really are interconnected and also bringing them into a newness of life in-breathed by loving care.

Subsequently, forms of collective remembrance or memory, even if evoked by feelings arising from each particular religious community, have the potential for love across boundaries. Signs of love displayed in the cosmos, even for those who would not adopt a religious view, can become discernible in the ardent desire to witness the fulfillment of "another's highest impulse."[109] They signify how the cosmos is capable of greater evolution through love, of making the whole of life more lovely. As Peirce puts it, "Love, recognizing germs of loveliness in the hateful, gradually warms it into life, and makes it lovely."[110] Rather than the sole individual's good being the Darwinian struggle for existence (every individual for himself), love is.[111] In the most repressive and closed regimes, or free capitalist forms of global exchange, habits of love for the whole, including a religious other, can be developed.

This evolutionary love that is enacted bodily, and interconnectedly in collectives, could be an expression of sympathy acquired in the continuity of memory. In the continuum that religious spaces inhabit, and by means of time enabling newness, feelings can enact care in unison with that something that is as immemorial as the divine love. Hearts, divine, human, and nonhuman can healingly touch one another. In the continuum resides a "greening" power for collectives to affect one another intimately, as sympathy is developed among overlapping ecosystems. Attraction can grow within, even prior to consciousness, because of a remembrance of a self that locates itself in a cosmos saturated with love. In this, the cosmos is a sign of migrating passion (desire and longing), a reality and existence that loves as existent things dwell in shared environments. As in the greening power of healing, there is an appeal for a God of love, a universal organ that loves all, and for a border-crossing care to be actualized in the enactment of that shared love.

Towards Ecosystems of Care

How can we tangibly create ecosystems of care mindful of the plurality of religious interpretations of signs? For one, as already surmised, in these mystics a divine message of loving care was already primary. They perceived an unknown and mysterious expanse where the cosmos rests and that draws all things toward a source of love. Even as each particular view distinctly defined it through a set of symbols, collectively, that universal Compassion and Mercy accompanied the wayfarers. For these mystics, a desire beyond all desire rested in the divine love, a movement beyond the divine self, seeking to draw all things toward itself in terms of care. For the purposes of this study, its wooing and enabling force can quicken a desire to co-create ecosystems of care for the possible cosmic transformation needed for the nurturing of multiple worlds interrelating, for *mindfulness* of the vulnerable, so that all life can teem in its diverse plurality.

Much remains to be done. Among humans, one vulnerable population is women. With regard to migration, while there are many instances in which the quality of life of women improves with relocation into areas where resources abound, the opposite can also hold true. Women, particularly the very young, single mothers, and widows can fall prey to forms of violence, deprivation, sex-trafficking and the sex-industry, low wages, and poverty. Communities of faith in all three traditions need to continue to intensely labor toward minimizing these negative effects by offering a home and relief, and getting involved in bringing reform. Furthermore, without advocating for a totalitarian *sameness* when considering equality, the Abrahamic faiths would need to continue collaborating to confront the negative impact of androcentricism in the overall well-being of women. Having male primacy in all spheres, particularly the religious, limits the co-caring "response-ability" that can come as a result of the divine-human encounter.

For Jewish feminist Ellen Unsmansky, the repairing of the world (*tikkun olam*) that ultimately unifies all Sefirah within God cannot occur unless there is partnership at all levels: religiously, personally, and politically.[112] Similarly, as Muslim feminist Riffat Hassan points out, "Islamization" needs to be reexamined. She lists some of the ways Islamization has been used as an instrument of oppression against women: high levels of illiteracy among women in many Muslim countries, especially in rural areas; the "facelessness" Muslim women endure through segregation; and issues of forced procreation and childbearing without sexual pleasure that some of them endure.[113]

Christianity, even in the progressive West,[114] likewise needs to reexamine its rhetoric of "natural," or God-prescribed, inequality that results not only in many of the above mentioned, but also in creating structures that prevent women from ordination, or from attaining the level of pulpit ministry in large and successful congregations, or from having their work published and equally engaged in academia.

Nonhuman communities at the brink of disappearing from the globe are another sign of divine distress. Indeed, the dying species are too many to list here. Among them, the Mexican gray wolves are on the verge of extinction, in great part due to their need for free roaming and migration to and from the territories of the Grand Canyon (areas of northern Arizona and southern Utah), northern New Mexico, and southern Colorado.[115] Without the free movement across these boundary lines, the wolves cannot benefit from the genetic diversity needed to build their immune system and to fight certain diseases. Their survival, moreover, ensures the well-being of their ecosystems, which depend on their predatory role to keep low the overpopulations of other species.

Likewise in other parts of the world, endangered species are in need of healing care across international lines. Their stories could have more thriving endings if cross-communal efforts, even interreligious ones, can be made to ensure their survival—as was done for the snow leopard in the rugged mountains of Pakistan, Afghanistan, Tajikistan, and China.[116] An increased awareness of their endangerment and a desire to safeguard their fragile ecosystems can result in setting aside political views often guided by religious feelings evoked from within each distinct community. Cooperation can lead to the co-creation of ecosystems for the thriving of vulnerable populations among the nonhuman as well.

In this regard, together with Charles Peirce, I am cautiously optimistic, since human beings are "intensely individualistic," and so mostly draw wisdom from their "racial" base, that is, the human race.[117] Admittedly, in all three traditions, humans are the apex of the divine self-disclosure. As with Islam, humans—like no other created thing—make manifest the full splendor of the *wujūd* of God. Nonetheless, modern day thought aiming at bringing greater awareness of the intimate relation between the cosmos, the self, and God continues to offer a call for the "greening" of theology in all three traditions. Another collaborative effort worth mentioning is Green Faith Interfaith Partners for the Environment in the United States, an organization seeking to promote mindfulness on behalf of the nonhuman and to train religious leaders of all faiths and their communities to become better stewards of the created order.[118]

Regarding mysticism, an integrative vision can be born together with the migratory journeying into the depths of a polished mirror of cosmos and divine self-imaging. A practical wisdom for daily living can be drawn from the vision of the universe that is gained, as G. William Barnard points out, when one participates in a universe "in which each one of us is seen as integrally connected to wider, deeper dimensions of a dynamic, multileveled, and open-ended reality, experiences, choices, and behavior."[119]

Looking Ahead

In conclusion, the cosmos offers itself as passage, the space for erotic journeying into the divine depths that can make coexistence more ecologically *whole*some. The whole cosmos is an active participant of healing care in history. The divine impulse toward shared goodness and migratory love can also become our impulse, either through mimicry or inward disposition. In agreement with the affirmations of de León: for God has loved, one loves one's neighbor (for me, human and nonhuman), and God, as one loves oneself.[120]

Being religiously, if not "interreligiously,"[121] could mean that the cosmos shares an ancient wisdom of loving care with the human self. Freeing interpretations of religious signs can result in fuller expressions of the well-being of the planetary coexistence. There is an ethic to understanding that there is no privileged vantage point and that no representation can fully grasp the divine dimensions. In humility, there can be dialog and co-creation.

Even in the particularity of rituals, the caring heart of things divine can be enacted. Rituals as vehicles of memory and ideals, though cemented, though doctrinal and habitual, can yet contain the potential for new breath. Being capable of noticing the newness *actualizing* the divine love in other communities of faith (internally and across religions) points to migration away from self-centeredness. The interpretation of signs availed to us can aid in interpreting *salvation* universally. Such have been the living examples of people like Azizah Y. al-Hibri, Abraham Joshua Heschel, and César Chávez.[122] In seeking to enact collaboratively the free act of solidarity and movement toward doing away with oppressive systems, communities of faith can also participate in bringing about salvation to ecosystems in distress.

Might cosmic truths bearing traces of the divine (plurally and multiply) be shared by all living things and take root in social life more fully so that ecosystems of care can be nurtured! Might these cosmic proverbs be collectively enacted so that better actions can ensue in history! The soul that is enticed by the love of God displayed in the cosmos and that enters the self to better discern this divine love in all its nearness, excess, and manifoldness can better understand itself as a relational being in history. Encountering bliss and happiness in God through the cosmic self can mean that the enjoyment that ensues from love is humanly communal and universally planetary.

Notes

I want to thank the students of my mysticism seminar, taught at New York Theological Seminary in the spring of 2012—Kris Watson, Jabez Springer, Lori Hartman, and Bushawn Akhbar McMillan-El—for having inspired me to develop this topic on the plural journeys of the soul toward God. I'm also grateful for the insights that Imam Askia Muhammad, the faculty of New York Theological Seminary, and Leo D. Lefebure of Georgetown University shared with me on earlier stages of this chapter.

1. Ernesto Cardenal, *Cosmic Canticle*, translated by John Lyons (Willimantic, CT: Curbstone Press, 1993), 60. For an understanding of Cardenal's mysticism and activism in Nicaragua, see Georgia Frances Cooper, *Mysticism and Revolution: Conversations with Ernesto Cardenal* (Claremont: School of Theology, 1981).
2. Note, for instance, how as a result of the migration of Sufis and the spread of their devotional traditions and practices into areas like Asia, many devotees assemble annually at the graves of Sufis on their death anniversary to celebrate "when they migrated to heaven through *urs*, or 'wedding,' with Allah." See Michael H. Fisher, *Migration: A World History* (Oxford and New York: Oxford University Press, 2014), 33.
3. Bonaventure, *The Soul's Journey into God*, in *Bonaventure*, trans. and intr. Ewert Cousins (Mahwah, NJ: Paulist Press, 1978), 60.
4. William C. Chittick, "Ibn al-'Arabi on Participating in the Mystery," in *The Participatory Turn: Spirituality, Mysticism, and Religious Studies*, ed. Jorge N. Ferrer and Jacob H. Sherman (Albany, NY: State University of New York Press, 2008), 258.
5. Chittick, "Ibn al-'Arabi," 258.

6. William C. Chittick, *The Self-Disclosure of God: Principles of Ibn al-'Arabi's Cosmology* (Albany: The State University of New York Press, 1998), 56.
7. Syafaatun Almirzanah, *When Mystic Masters Meet: Towards a New Matrix of Christian-Muslim Dialogue* (New York: Blue Dome), 211.
8. Ibn al-'Arabī, *al-Futūḥāt al-Makkiyya* (Cairo, 1911), Vol. IV, Part 6, Ch. 559, 424.21; quoted in Chittick, *The Self-Disclosure of God*, 6.
9. Ibn Al 'Arabi, *The Bezels of Wisdom*, trans. and intr. R. W. J. Austin (Mahwah, NJ: Paulist Press, 1980), 73.
10. Ibid., 74.
11. Ibn al-'Arabī interpreting from the Qu'ran 2:115; see Chittick, *The Self-Disclosure of God*, 90.
12. Margaret Smith, *Muslim Women Mystics: The Life and Work of Rābi'a and Other Women Mystics in Islam* (Oxford, England: Oneworld Publications, 2001), 94.
13. Ibid., 74.
14. Ibn Al 'Arabi, *The Bezels of Wisdom*, 73.
15. Ibn al-'Arabī, *al-Futūḥāt al-Makkiyya*, Vol. IV, Part 6, Ch. 558, 231.5; quoted in Chittick, *The Self-Disclosure of God*, 28.
16. For a similar understanding of the cosmos as both source and signpost, see Chittick, *The Self-Disclosure of God*, 3.
17. Chittick, *The Self-Disclosure of God*, 5.
18. Ibn Al 'Arabi, *Bezels of Wisdom*, 279.
19. In the Kabbalah, the Infinite of *Ein Sof* reveals itself by means of ten emanations (*Sefirot*) with which the Infinite also continuously creates the world. The *Sefirot* is male and female and can be represented through enduring qualities such as justice and beauty, the human body with its various parts, and levels of consciousness. The sense one gains when gazing at the various visual models of the *Sefirot* is one of balance between the different aspects of God (for example, understanding and wisdom, power and love).
20. Moses de Leon, *Zohar: The Book of Enlightenment*, trans. and intr. Daniel Chanan Matt (Mahwah, NJ: Paulist Press, 1983), 54.
21. Ibid., p. 60.
22. Ibid., p. 61.
23. Ibid., p. 154.
24. Ibid., p. 155.
25. Ibid., p. 156.
26. Ibid., p. 155.
27. Ibid., p. 118.
28. Ibid., p. 123.
29. Rabbi Tirzah Firestone, *The Receiving: Reclaiming Jewish Women's Wisdom* (New York: HarperSanFrancisco, 1999), 53.
30. Ibid., p. 43. For her, also, all human, and particularly all female, parts that have been compartmentalized or fragmented by the world (into

categories such as mother, scholar, female) are healed and unified when Shekinah joins Ti'feret.
31. Ibid., p. 55.
32. Ibid.
33. Bonaventure, *The Soul's Journey into God*, 63.
34. Ibid., p. 69.
35. Ibid., p. 76.
36. Ibid., pp. 76–77.
37. Hildegard of Bingen, *Book of Divine Works: With Letters and Songs*, ed. Matthew Fox (Santa Fe, NM: Bear & Company, Inc., 1987), 26.
38. Ibid., p. 33.
39. Moses de Leon, *Zohar*, 69.
40. Ibid.
41. See Daniel Chanan Matt's notes on Moses de Leon, *Zohar*, 223.
42. The term "planetary loves" was the the driving theme of one of the Transdisciplinary Theological Colloquia at Drew Theological School. During this particular year, as I was completing my doctoral work, I served as its coordinator. While the meaning being used in this chapter may be distinct from that of the colloquium, the term "planetary love" itself has remained with me since then. For more on this theme, see the book that emerged from the essays presented there: Steven D. Moore and Mayra Rivera, eds., *Planetary Loves: Planetary Loves: Spivak, Postcoloniality, and Theology* (New York: Fordham University Press, 2010).
43. See Karl Rahner, *The Hearer of the Word: Laying Down the Foundation for a Philosophy of Religion* (New York, NY: Continuum, 1994).
44. Hildegard of Bingen, *Book of Divine Works*, 111.
45. Ibid., p. 12.
46. Here Bonaventure refers to when St. Francis, in seeking solitude in La Verna, Italy, at the entrance of a cave had a vision of a suspended Christ with open arms as if nailed on a cross. A bright light and six long-winged creatures were encircling the extended body. Finding himself in an ecstatic state, St. Francis saw the marks of Christ's corporeal punishments being transferred onto his flesh (stigmata).
47. Bonaventure, *The Soul's Journey into God*, 54–55.
48. Ibid., p. 79.
49. Ibid., p. 55.
50. It is important to note that the Qu'ran states, "We make no distinction between one and another of the Messengers" (2:285).
51. William C. Chittick, *Science and the Cosmos, Science of the Soul: The Pertinence of Islamic Cosmology in the Modern World* (Oxford: Oneworld Publications, 2007), 5.
52. Ibid., p. 7. For a history of the institutionalization of the spiritual path in Muslim mysticism like Sufism, see Nile Green, *Sufism: A Global History* (Malden and Oxford: Wiley-Blackwell, 2012), esp. 71–124.

53. Bonaventure, *Zohar*, 87.
54. Ibid., p. 84.
55. See Charles Pierce, *Philosophical Writings of Peirce* (New York: Dover Publications, 2011), 115. In this chapter, I turn to Peirce, for whom the physical laws of the cosmos acquire the character of having some predictability, uniformity, and universality alongside its unpredictable and surprising offshoots of creative evolution. I see in his work a cosmic tendency toward the habitual that leads to evolution, a form he also calls *disobedience*, or the idea of the universe constantly evolving by means of slight departures from the laws (323). The more certain a law is, the more chances there are to find irregularities that can be explained away by chance. For Peirce, "there is an approximate regularity" (333). And while every event is influenced by this regularity, there is also diversity that can lead to, "[i]nexhaustible multitudinous variety of the world" (335). Another important aspect I see in his views is that of habits being formed via excitation of feelings (320–321), a relationship between the physical and psychical that I cannot utilize more fully yet employ to speak of the concepts of memory and habits of care I find embedded in mystical imagery.
56. Peirce, *Philosophical Writings*, 354.
57. See Dale T. Irvin and Scott W. Sunquist, *History of the World Christian Movement, Vol. I: Earliest Christianity to 1453* (Maryknoll, NY: Orbis Books, 2001), Parts V and VI; and *History of the World Christian Movement, Vol. II: Modern Christianity from 1454–1800* (Maryknoll, NY: Orbis Books, 2012), Part I.
58. St. Teresa de Avila, *Interior Castle*, in *The Complete Works of St. Teresa de Avila*, trans. and ed. E. Allison Peers, vol. 2 (London and New York: Burns & Oates, 2002), 201.
59. See Catherine Swietlicki, *Spanish Christian Cabala: The Works of Luis De Leon, Santa Teresa De Jesus, and San Juan De LA Cruz* (Missouri: University of Missouri Press, 1987); and Luce López-Baralt, *Huellas del Islam en la literatura española: De Juan Ruiz a Juan Goytisolo* (Madrid, España: Hiperion, 1985).
60. St. Teresa de Avila, *Interior Castle*, 208. Emphasis is mine.
61. Ibid., p. 215.
62. Ibid., p. 201.
63. Ibid., p. 205.
64. Ibid., p. 207. Emphasis is mine.
65. Ibid., p. 330.
66. Ibid., p. 322.
67. Swietlicki, *Spanish Christian Cabala*, 54.
68. Ibid., p. 56. One must keep in mind that the concept of "nothing" most likely refers to *Ein Sof* or the Infinite, out of which all things emanate.
69. López-Baralt, *Huellas del Islam*, 85.
70. Ibid., p. 86–87.

71. Ibid., p. 87.
72. Victor Turner used the term "liminality" to speak of an in-between space suitable for anti-structure, where meaning can become unfamiliar and be recombined creatively with cultural elements. Victor Turner, *The Ritual Process; Structure and Anti-Structure* (New York: Aldine De Gruyter, 1995).
73. St. Teresa de Avila, *Interior Castle*, 330.
74. Ibid., p. 331.
75. Chittick, *The Self-Disclosure of God*, 12. Chittick is interpreting a variety of passages from Ibn al-'Arabi's *al-Futūḥāt al-Makkiyya*.
76. Ibid., p. 27.
77. Ibid., p. 104.
78. Ibid., p. 132.
79. Moses de Leon, *Zohar*, 66.
80. Ibid., p. 118.
81. Bonaventure, *The Soul's Journey into God*, 59.
82. Ibid., p. 55.
83. Ibid., p. 114.
84. Ibid., p. 115.
85. Swietlicki highlights the folk tradition of Kabbalah in Spain. Middle- and lower-class Jews were attracted to Abulafia's mysticism and the interpretations of de León of the Hebrew scriptures. Folk beliefs also absorbed some of the kabbalistic views on "the Messiah, the transmigration of souls, and demonology" (*Spanish Christian Cabala*, 45). She also argues that most likely Kabbalah and Sufi religious imagery interacted at least at the popular level. Intermarriage may have also been a means of sharing beliefs. Prayers would be taught and passed down from one generation to the next. Shephardic converts, for example, developed syncretistic beliefs that combined both Jewish and Christian elements. Certainly, St. Teresa, even if not too overtly, would have felt free to follow in the footsteps of various other Christian thinkers who likewise borrowed from thinkers of others faiths, as evinced in the writings of St. Thomas Aquinas, who cites from Aveccina, Averröes, and Maimonides. Muslim influence on Christianity continued, leaving its trace even on the American continents. See Vincent Barletta, *Covert Gestures: Crypto-Islamic Literature as Cultural Practice in Early Modern Spain* (Minneapolis: University Of Minnesota Press, 2005); and Carina L. Johnson, *Cultural Hierarchy in Sixteenth-Century Europe: The Ottomans and Mexicans* (Cambridge: Cambridge University Press, 2011). Certainly, the opposite can also hold true. When Spaniards arrived in what is now known as Central and Latin America, the palaces and temples of Incas, Aztecs, and Mayans resembled those of the moors, a symbolic identification (among others) that fueled violence, as Luis N. Rivera describes in *A Violent Evangelism: The Political and Religious Conquest of the Americas* (Louisville, NY: Westminster/John Knox Press, 1992), esp. 42–62.

86. An example of a continuous unfolding of care in history could be the Spanish government's recent bill offering citizenship to Sephardic Jews. As reported in an article in the *New York Times*, on February 7, 2014, the Spanish government, "as a conciliatory gesture," will be granting citizenship to those whose ancestry can be traced (with proper documentation) to the expelled Jews of 1492. See Isabel Keshner and Raphael Minder, "Prospect of Spanish Citizenship Appeals to Descendants of Jews Expelled in 1492," in *New York Times*, February 16, 2014, A 16.
87. Hildegard of Bingen, *Book of Divine Works*, 121.
88. Bonaventure, *The Soul's Journey into God*, 80–81.
89. Ibid., p. 56.
90. Ibid., p. 79.
91. Almirzanah, *When Mystic Masters Meet*, 184.
92. See it in terms of responsibility being put forth by Chittick, *Science of the Cosmos, Science of the Soul*, 43
93. Ibn Al 'Arabi, *Bezels of Wisdom*, 56.
94. Chittick, *Science of the Cosmos, Science of the Soul*, 46.
95. Ibid., p. 61.
96. Ibid., p. 65.
97. Ibid., p. 109.
98. Lynn Gottlieb, *She Who Dwells Within: A Feminist Vision of a Renewed Judaism* (New York: HarperSanFrancisco, 1995), 35.
99. Gershom Gerhard Scholem, *Major Trends in Jewish Mysticism* (New York: Schocken Books, 1954), 284.
100. Hildegard of Bingen, *Book of Divine Works*, 35–36.
101. Ibid., p. 113.
102. Ibid.
103. Ibid., p. 108.
104. Chittick, *Science of the Cosmos, Science of the Soul*, 110.
105. Chittick, *The Self-Disclosure of God*, 96.
106. Chittick, *Science of the Cosmos, Science of the Soul*, 132.
107. Chittick, *The Self-Disclosure of God*, 10.
108. Bonaventure, *The Soul's Journey into God*, 80.
109. Peirce, *Philosophical Writings*, 362.
110. Ibid., p. 363.
111. Ibid. In this regard, it will be evolution by creative love. This evolutionary process, which he labels as "genuine agapasm," would take place "by virtue of a positive sympathy among the created springing from continuity of mind" (365).
112. Ellen M. Unmansky, "Feminism in Judaism," in *Feminism and World Religions*, edited by Arvind Sharma and Katherine K. Young, 179–213 (Albany, NY: State University of New York Press, 1999).
113. Riffat Hassan, "Feminism in Islam," *in Feminism in World Religions*, 248–278.

114. See also Rosemary Radford Ruether, "Feminism in World Christianity," in *Feminism in World Religions*, 214–247.
115. Courtney Sexton, "Lobos in Limbo: FWS Proposal Would further Stall Mexican Gray Wolf Recovery," *Defenders* (Fall 2013): 8–9. *Defenders* is a periodical of Defenders of Wildlife, an organization committed to saving endangered species around the globe. More information on Defenders of Wildlife can be accessed through its website: http://www.defenders.org.
116. Peter Zahler and George Schaller, "Saving More Than Just Snow Leopards," in *The New York Times*, February 2, 2014, SR 4.
117. Pierce, *Philosophical Writings*, 73.
118. More information on Green Faith can be accessed through its website: http://greenfaith.org.
119. G. William Barnard, "Pulsating with Life: The Paradoxical Intuitions of Henri Bergson," in *The Participatory Turn*, 321.
120. de Leon, *Zohar*, 165.
121. See Peter C. Phan, *Being Religious Interreligiously: Asian Perspectives on Interfaith Dialogue* (Maryknoll, NY: Orbis Books, 2004).
122. Azizah Y. al-Hibri, professor at the T. C. Williams School of Law, University of Richmond in Virginia, was the founding editor of *Hypatia: A Journal of Feminist Philosophy*, and founding president of KARAMAH: Muslim Women Lawyers for Human Rights. Firmly believing in the positive role Islam and the teachings of the Qu'ran can play in the public sphere, particularly in the betterment of the woman-condition, al-Hibri finds inspiration in the Sufi interpretation of the Qu'ranic principle of *shahadah* (principle of unity) in which the world is a manifestation of the divine unity and the miraculous, and reasons that particularly Islam can be instrumental in speaking about fairness and equality, spiritually enlightened leadership, and a democratic spiritual society. See Azizah Y. al-Hibri, "Faith and the Attorney-Client Relationship: A Muslim Perspective," *Fordham Law Review* 66, no. 4 (1998): 1131–1140. In Judaism, the prophetic and mystical words of Shoah survivor, Polish refugee, and rabbi, Abraham J. Heschel, continue to resound in our world. Viewing Kabbalah as interwoven in the fabric of Judaism rather than peripheral to it, and as "permeating its ways of thinking and living," Heschel's views on ethics and involvement in the civil rights movement and his persistent protest against the Vietnam war can only be understood in relation to "the inner roots of his devotion to God, Torah, faith, prayer, and the life of radical amazement—his mysticism." See Byron L. Sherwin, *Kabbalah: An Introduction to Jewish Mysticism* (Lanham, etc.: Rowman & Littlefield Publishers, Inc., 2006), xxiii; and John C. Merkle, *Abraham Joshua Heschel: Exploring His Life and Thought* (London: Collier Macmillan Publishers, 1985), 125. Lastly, the

work of Chicano and Catholic activist César Chávez with the farmworkers in California, on immigration and land reform also finds its roots in his "encounters with God during his extended fasts." The organization he founded, the United Farmworkers of America, has become known for linking "environmental with social justice" in their concerns with labor rights. See Stephen R. Lloyd-Moffett, "The Mysticism and Social Action of César Chávez," in *Latino Religions and Civic Activism in the United States*, eds. Gastón Espinosa, Virgilio Elizondo, and Jesse Miranda, 35–51 (New York: Oxford University Press, 2005), 35; and Devon Peña, *Tierra y Vida: Mexican-Americans and the Environment* (Tucson: The University of Arizona Press, 2005), 103.

Selected Bibliography

Mapping the Global Muslim Population: A Report on the Size and Distribution of the World's Muslim Population. Washington, DC: Pew Forum on Religion & Public Life, October 2009.
Sourozh: A Journal of Orthodox Life and Thought, no. 80 (May 2000).
Adler, Leonore Loch, and Uwe P. Giellen, eds. *Migration, Immigration and Emigration in International Perspective.* Wesport, CT: Praeger, 2003.
Agnivesh, Swami. *Applied Spirituality for Justice Unlimited.* New Delhi: Dharma Pratisthan, 2005.
Alexander, Philip. "The King Messiah in Rabbinic Judaism." In *King and Messiah in Israel and the Ancient Near East*, ed. John Day, 456–473. Sheffield: Sheffield Academic Press, 1998.
Almirzanah, Syafaatun. *When Mystic Masters Meet: Towards a New Matrix of Christian-Muslim Dialogue.* New York: Blue Dome.
Amishai-Maisels, Ziva. *Depiction and Interpretation: The Influence of the Holocaust on Visual Arts.* Oxford: Pergamon Press, 1993.
Anderson, Allan. *An Introduction to Pentecostalism: Global Charismatic Christianity.* Cambridge: Cambridge University Press, 2004.
Anderson, Allan. *Spreading Fires: The Missionary Nature of Early Pentecostalism.* London: SCM Press, 2007.
Aviv, Caryn, and David Shneer. *New Jews: The End of the Jewish Diaspora.* New York: New York University Press, 2005.
Ayoub, Mahmoud. "Dhimma in the Qur'an and Hadith." *Islamic Studies Quarterly* 5 (1983): 172–82.
Baggio, Fabio, and Agnes Brazal, eds. *Faith on the Move: Toward a Theology of Migration in Asia.* Quezon City, Philippines: Ateneo de Manila University Press, 2008.
Bakhtin, Mikhail M. *Speech Genres and Other Late Essays*, trans. Vern W. McGee. Austin, TX: University of Texas Press, 1986.
Barletta, Vincent. *Covert Gestures: Crypto-Islamic Literature as Cultural Practice in Early Modern Spain.* Minneapolis: University Of Minnesota Press, 2005.
Batnitzky, Leora. *Idolatry and Representation: The Philosophy of Franz Rosenzweig Reconsidered.* Princeton, NJ: Princeton University Press, 2000.

Battistella, Graziano, ed. *Migrazioni: Dizionario Socio-Pastorale*. Chinisello Balsamo, Milano: Edizione San Paolo, 2010.
Berkovits, Eliezer. *With God in Hell: Judaism in the Ghettos and Deathcamps*. New York and London, Sanhedrin, 1979.
Bhabha, Homi K. *The Location of Culture*. London and New York: Routledge, 1994.
Bonaventure. *The Soul's Journey into God*. In *Bonaventure*, trans. and intr. Ewert Cousins (Mahwah, NJ: Paulist Press, 1978), 60.
Bonifacio, Glenda Tibe, and Vivienne S. M. Angeles, eds. *Gender, Religion, and Migration: Pathways of Integration*. Lanham, MD: Lexington Books, 2011.
Bosworth, C.E. "The 'Protected Peoples' (Christians and Jews) in Medieval Egypt and Syria." *Bulletin of the John Rylands University Library of Manchester* 62 (1979): 11–36.
Bosworth, C.E. "The Concept of *dhimma* in Early Islam." In *Christians and Jews in the Ottoman Empire: The Functioning of a Plural Society*, 2 vols, eds. B. Braude and B. Lewis, 1:37–51. New York: Holmes and Meier, 1982.
Boyarin, Daniel, and Jonathan Boyarin. "Diaspora: Generation and the Ground of Jewish Identity." *Critical Inquiry* 19, no. 4 (Summer, 1993): 693–725.
Braiterman, Zachary. *The Shape of Revelation: Aesthetics and Modern Jewish Thought*. Stanford, CA: Stanford University Press, 2007.
Brettell, Caroline B., and James F. Hollifield, eds. *Migration Theory: Talking across Disciplines*, 2nd ed. New York: Routledge, 2007.
Bryan, Christopher. *Render to Caesar: Jesus, the Early Church, and the Roman Superpower*. Oxford: Oxford University Press, 2005.
Bundy, David D. *Visions of Apostolic Mission: Scandinavian Pentecostal Mission to 1935*. Uppsala: Uppsala University Library, 2009.
Campese, Gioacchino, and Pietro Ciallella, eds. *Migration, Religious Experience, and Globalization*. Staten Island: Center for Migration Studies, 2003.
Campese, Gioacchino. "Mission and Migration." In *A Century of Catholic Mission: Roman Catholic Missiology 1910 to the Present*, ed. Stephen Bevans, 247–260. Oxford: Regnum Publications, 2013.
Campese, Gioacchino. "The Irruption of Migrants: Theology of Migration in the 21st Century." *Theological Studies* 73 (32012), 3–32.
Campese, Giocchino. "La théologie et les migrations: La redécouverte d'une dimension structurelle de la foi chrétienne." *Dossier: :es catholiques et les migrations*, 139 (2012), 135–155.
Cardenal, Ernesto. *Cosmic Canticle*, trans. John Lyons. Willimantic, CT: Curbstone Press, 1993.
Carroll R., M. Daniel. *Christians at the Border: Immigration, the Church, and the Bible*. Grand Rapids, MI: Baker Academic, 2008.
Carter, Warren. *The Roman Empire and the New Testament: An Essential Guide*. Nashville: Abingdon, 2006.

SELECTED BIBLIOGRAPHY

Castles, Stephen, Hein de Hass, and Mark J. Miller. *The Age of Migration: International Population Movements in the Modern World*, 5th ed. New York: Guilford Press, 2013.
Chittick, William C. *Science and the Cosmos, Science of the Soul: The Pertinence of Islamic Cosmology in the Modern World*. Oxford: Oneworld Publications, 2007.
Chittick, William C. *The Self-Disclosure of God: Principles of Ibn al-'Arabi's Cosmology*. Albany: The State University of New York Press, 1998.
Cohen, Arthur A., and Paul Mendes-Flohr, eds. *20th Century Jewish Religious Thought: Original Essays on Critical Concepts, Movements, and Beliefs*. New York: Charles Scribner's Sons, 1987 [reprinted Philadelphia: Jewish Publication Society, 2009].
Cohen, Aryeh. "Reading Exile and Redemption: A Meditation on the Talmudic Project." *The Reconstructionist* 61, no. 2 (Fall 1996): 34–35.
Coleman, Simon. *The Globalization of Charismatic Christianity: Spreading the Gospel of Prosperity*. Cambridge: Cambridge University Press, 2000.
Collier, Paul. *Exodus: How Migration Is Changing Our World*. Oxford: Oxford University Press, 2013.
Cox, Harvey G. *Fire from Heaven: The Rise of Pentecostal Spirituality and the Reshaping of Religion in the 21st Century*. Reading, MA: Addison-Wesley, 1995.
Croatto, Jose Severino. *Exodus: A Hermeneutics of Freedom*. Maryknoll, NY: Orbis Books, 1981.
Cruz, Gemma Tulud. *An Intercultural Theology of Migration: Pilgrims in the Wilderness*. Studies in Systematic Theology 5. Leiden: Brill, 2010.
Dempster, Murray W., Byron D. Klaus, and Douglas Petersen, eds. *The Globalization of Pentecostalism: A Religion Made to Travel*. Oxford, UK, and Irvine, CA: Regnum Books, 1999.
Eck, Diana. *A New Religious America: How a 'Christian Country' Has Become the World's Most Religiously Diverse Nation*. San Francisco: HarperSanFrancisco, 2002.
Eickelman, Dale F., and James Piscatori, eds., *Muslim Travellers: Pilgrimage, Migration, and the Religious Imagination*. Berkeley: University of California Press, 1990.
Eisen, Arnold. "Exile." In *Contemporary Jewish Religious Thought*, eds. Arthur A. Cohen and Paul Mendes-Flohr, 219–225. New York: Simon and Schuster, 1987.
Ferrer, Jorge N., and Jacob H. Sherman, eds. *The Participatory Turn: Spirituality, Mysticism, and Religious Studies*. Albany, NY: State University of New York Press, 2008.
Finger, Reta Halteman. *Of Widows and Meals: Communal Meals in the Book of Acts*. Grand Rapids and Cambridge, UK: Eerdmans, 2007.
Firestone, Rabbi Tirzah. *The Receiving: Reclaiming Jewish Women Wisdom*. New York: HarperSanFrancisco, 1999.
Firestone, Ruven. *Jihad: The Origin of Holy War in Islam*. New York: Oxford University Press, 1999.

Fishbane, Michael. *Biblical Myth and Rabbinic Mythmaking.* Oxford: Oxford University Press, 2003.
Foley, Michael W., and Dean R. Hoge. *Religion and the New Immigrants: How Faith Communities Form Our Newest Citizens.* New York: Oxford University Press, 2007.
Fox, M., ed. *Western Spirituality: Historical Roots and Ecumenical Routes.* Santa Fe, NM: Bear & Company 1981.
Friedmann, Yohanan. *Tolerance and Coercion in Islam: Interfaith Relations in Muslim Tradition.* Cambridge: Cambridge University Press, 2003.
Gafni, Isaiah. "Babylonian Rabbinic Culture." In *Cultures of the Jews: A New History*, vol. 1, ed. David Biale. New York: Random House, 2002.
George, K.M. *The Silent Roots: Orthodox Perspectives on Christian Spirituality.* Geneva: WCC Publications. 1994.
Gilman, Sander. *Jewish Self-Hatred.* Baltimore: John Hopkins University Press, 1986.
Goff, James R., Jr. *Fields White unto Harvest: Charles Fox Parham and the Missionary Origins of Pentecostalism.* Fayetteville, Ark.: University of Arkansas Press, 1987.
Gottlieb, Lynn. *She Who Dwells Within: A Feminist Vision of a Renewed Judaism.* New York: HarperSanFrancisco, 1995.
Green, Nile. *Sufism: A Global History.* Malden and Oxford: Wiley-Blackwell, 2012.
Gregorios, Paulos, et al., eds. *Does Chalcedon Divide or Unite? Towards Convergence in Orthodox Christology.* Geneva: WCC Publications, 1981.
Groody, Daniel. *Border of Death, Valley of Life: An Immigrant Journey of Heart and Spirit.* Lanham: Rowman & Littlefield, 2002.
———. *Globalization, Spirituality, and Justice.* Maryknoll, New York: Orbis Books, 2007.
Groody, Daniel and Gioacchino Campese, eds. *A Promised Land, A Perilous Journey.* Notre Dame: Notre Dame University Press, 2008.
Guillaume, Alfred. *The Life of Muhammad: A Translation of Ibn Ishaq's Sirat Rasul Allah.* Karachi, Pakistan: Oxford University Press, 1982.
Hanciles, Jehu H. *Beyond Christendom: Globalization, African Migration, and the Transformation of the West.* Maryknoll, NY: Orbis Books, 2008.
Harrell, David Edwin, Jr. *Pat Robertson: A Life and Legacy.* Grand Rapids, MI: William B. Eerdmans Publishing Company, 2010.
Hassad, Yvonne Yazbeck, Jane L. Smith, and John L. Esposito, eds. *Religion and Immigration: Christian, Jewish, and Muslim Experiences in the United States.* New York: Rowman & Littlefield, 2003.
Hildegard of Bingen. *Book of Divine Works: With Letters and Songs*, ed. Matthew Fox. Santa Fe, NM: Bear & Company, Inc., 1987.
Hollenweger, Walter J. *Pentecostalism: Origins and Development Worldwide.* Peabody, MA: Hendrickson, 1997.
Hunter, Harold D., and Peter Hocken, eds. *All Together in One Place: Theological Papers from the Brighton Conference on World Evangelization.* Sheffield, England: Sheffield Academic Press, 1993.

Hussain, Amir. *Oil and Water: Two Faiths, One God.* Kelowna: Wood Lake Books, 2006.
Ibn Al 'Arabi. *The Bezels of Wisdom*, trans. and intr. R. W. J. Austin. Mahwah, NJ: Paulist Press, 1980.
Irvin, Dale T., and Scott W. Sunquist. *History of the World Christian Movement, Vol. I: Earliest Christianity to 1453.* Maryknoll, NY: Orbis Books, 2001.
———. *History of the World Christian Movement, Vol. II: Modern Christianity from 1454–1800.* Maryknoll, NY: Orbis Books, 2012.
Jacques, André, and Elizabeth Ferris. "Migration." In *Dictionary of the Ecumenical Movement*, ed. Nicholas Losssky et al, 2nd edition, 768–770. Geneva, WCC, 2002.
Jenkins, Philip. *The Next Christendom: The Coming of Global Christianity.* Oxford: Oxford University Press, 2002.
Johnson, Carina L. *Cultural Hierarchy in Sixteenth-Century Europe: The Ottomans and Mexicans.* Cambridge: Cambridge University Press, 2011.
Jung-Stilling, Johann Heinrich. *Das Heimweh.* Dornach: Verlag am Goetheanum, 1994.
Jurgens, W.A. *The Faith of the Early Fathers Vol.1.* Bangalore: Theological Publications in India, 1992.
Kalaitzidis, Pantelis. *Orthodoxy and Political Theology.* Geneva: WCC Publications, 2012.
Kaplan, Gregory. "'In the End Shall Christians Become Jews Christians?': Franz Rosenzweig's Apocalyptic Eshatology." *Cross Currents* 53 (Winter 2004): 511–529.
Kellner, Menachem Marc. *Must a Jew Believe Anything?* Oxford: Littman Library of Jewish Civilization, 2006.
Kerwin, Donald, et al., eds. *And You Welcomed Me: Migration and Catholic Social Teaching.* Lanham, MD.: Rowman & Littlefield, 2009.
Kochan, Lional. *Beyond the Graven Image: A Jewish View.* Basingstoke, Hampshire and London: Macmillan, 1997.
Krell, Marc A. *Intersecting Pathways: Modern Jewish Theologians in Conversation with Christianity.* New York: Oxford University Press, 2003.
Kuznets, Simon E., Glen Weyl and Stephenie H. Lo, eds. *Jewish Economies: Development and Migration in America and Beyond: The Economic Life of American Jewry*, vol. 1. Piscataway, NJ: Transaction Publishers, 2011.
Lee, Jung Young Lee. *Marginality. The Key to Multicultural Theology.* Minneapolis: Fortress Press, 1995.
Lefebvre, Solange, and Luiz Carlos Susin, eds. *Migration in a Global World.* London: SCM Press, 2008.
Leonard, Karen I., Alex Stepick, Manuel A. Vasquez, and Jennifer Holdaway, eds. *Immigrant Faiths: Transforming Religious Life in America.* New York: Roman & Littlefield, 2006.
Levinas, Emmanuel. *Emmanuel Levinas: Collected Philosophical Papers*, trans. Alphonso Lingis. Dordrecht: Martinus Nijhoff, 1987.

Lodhal, Michael. *Shekhinah/Spirit: Divine Presence in Jewish and Christian Religion.* Mahwah, NJ: Paulist Press, 1992.

López-Baralt, Luce. *Huellas del Islam en la literatura española: De Juan Ruiz a Juan Goytisolo.* Madrid, España: Hiperion, 1985.

Lord, Andrew. *Spirit-Shaped Mission: A Holistic Charismatic Missiology.* Bletchley, UK, and Waynesboro, Ga.: Paternoster, 2005.

Macchia, Frank D. *Justified in the Spirit: Creation, Redemption, and the Triune God.* Grand Rapids, MI: William B. Eerdmans Publishing Company, 2010.

Maldonado, Jorge, and Juan F. Martínez, eds.. *Vivir y servir en el exilio. Lecturas teológicas de la experiencia latina en los Estados Unidos.* Buenos Aires: Kairós, 2008.

Manor, Dalia. "The Dancing Jew and Other Characters: Art in the Jewish Settlement in Palestine in the 1920s." *Journal of Modern Jewish Studies* 1 (2002): 73–89.

Manzone, G. "Le migrazione nella dottrina sociale della Chiesa." *Rivista della teologia morale* 160 (2008): 487–496.

———. "Le migrazioni umane nel magistero della Chiesa." *Nuntium* 30, no. 3 (2006): 257–263.

Martin, David. *Pentecostalism: The World Their Parish.* Malden, Mass., and Oxford, UK: Wiley-Blackwell, 2002.

Matsuoka, Fumitaka, and Eleazar S. Fernandez, eds. *Realizing the American of Our Hearts: Theological Voices of Asian Americans.* St. Louis: Chalice Press, 2003.

McClung, L. Grant. *Azusa Street and Beyond: Pentecostal Missions and Church Growth in the Twentieth Century.* South Plainfield, NJ: Bridge Publications, 1986

McDaniel, Eric Leon, Irfan Nooroodin, and Allyson Faith Shortle. "Divine Boundaries: How Religion Shapes Immigrants' Attitudes Toward Religion." *American Politics Research* 39 (2011): 205–233

McGee, B. *Miracles, Missions, and American Pentecostalism.* Maryknoll, NY: Orbis Books, 2010.

McMillan, M. E. *The Meaning of Mecca: The Politics of Pilgrimage in Early Islam.* London: Saqi Books, 2001.

Míguez Bonino, José. *Rostros del Protestantismo Latinoamericano.* Buenos Aires: Nueva Creación, 1995.

Mirzoeff, Nicholas. "Introduction: The multiple Viewpoint: Diasporic Visual Cultures." In *Diaspora and Visual Culture: Representing Africans and Jews,* ed. Nicholas Mirzoeff, 1–18. London: Routledge, 2000.

Moses de Leon. *Zohar: The Book of Enlightenment,* trans. and intr. Daniel Chanan Matt. Mahwah, NJ: Paulist Press, 1983.

Moses, Stéphane. *The Angel of History: Rosenzweig, Benjamin, Scholem,* trans. Barabara Harshav. Stanford: Stanford University Press, 2009.

Nakka-Cammauf, Viji, and Timothy Tseng, eds. *Asian American Christianity: A Reader.* Castro Valley, CA: The Institute for the Study of Asian American Christianity, 2009.

Nazianzus, Gregory. *On God and Christ: The Five Theological Orations and Two Letters to Cledonius.* New York: St. Vladimir's Seminary Press, 2002.
Newman, Aryeh. "The Centrality of Eretz Yisrael in Nachmanides." *Tradition* 10, no. 1 (1968): 21–30.
Noll, Mark. *Protestantism: A Very Short Introduction.* Oxford: Oxford University Press, 2011.
O'Reilly, Karen. *International Migration and Social Theory.* New York: Palgrave Macmillan, 2012.
Oesterly, W.O. E. *Sacred Dance.* New York: Cambridge University Press, 1923.
Olupona, Jacob K., and Regina Gemignani, eds. *African Immigrant Religions in America.* New York: New York University Press, 2007.
Padilla, Elaine. "Border-Crossing and Exile." *Cross Currents* 60, no. 4 (2010): 526–548.
———. *Divine Enjoyment: A Theology of Passion and Exuberance.* New York: Fordham University Press, 2014.
Padilla, Elaine, and Peter C. Phan, eds. *Contemporary Issues of Migration and Theology* (New York: Palgrave McMillan, 2013.
Pattison, George. *Crucifixions and Resurrections of the Image: Christian Reflections on Art and Modernity.* London: SCM, 2009.
Peters, F. E. *Muhammad and the Origins of Islam.* Albany: SUNY Press, 1994.
Phan, Peter C. *Being Religious Interreligiously: Asian Perspectives on Interfaith Dialogue.* Maryknoll, NY: Orbis Books, 2004.
Pierce, Charles. *Philosophical Writings of Peirce.* New York: Dover Publications, 2011.
Piore, Michael J. *Birds of Passage: Migrant Labor in Industrial Societies.* Cambridge: Cambridge University Press, 1979.
Poewe, Karla O., ed. *Charismatic Christianity as a Global Culture.* Columbia, SC: University of South Carolina Press, 1994.
Pomerville, Paul. *The Third Force in Missions: A Pentecostal Contribution to Contemporary Mission Theology.* Peabody, MA: Hendrickson, 1985.
Porton, Gary. "The Idea of Exile in Early Rabbinic Midrash." In *Exile: Old Testament, Jewish and Christian Conceptions*, ed. James M. Scott, 251–256. Leiden: Brill, 1997.
Rahner, Karl. *The Hearer of the Word: Laying Down the Foundation for a Philosophy of Religion.* New York: Continuum, 1994.
Ramadan, Tariq. *Western Muslims and the Future of Islam.* New York: Oxford University Press, 2004.
———. *The Quest for Meaning: Developing a Philosophy of Pluralism.* London: Penguin Books, 2010.
Raphael, Melissa. *Judaism and the Visual Image: A Jewish Theology of Art.* London and New York, Continuum, 2009.
Re Cruz, Alicia. "Taquerías, Laundromats and Protestant Churches: Landmarks of Hispanic Barrios in Denton, Texas." *Urban Anthropology* 34 (2005) 281–303.

Recinos, Harold, ed. *Wading Through Many Voices: Toward a Theology of Public Conversation*. New York: Rowman & Littlefield, 2011.

Rivera, Luis N. *A Violent Evangelism: The Political and Religious Conquest of the Americas*. Louisville, NY: Westminster/John Knox Press, 1992.

Robeck, Cecil M., Jr. *The Azusa Street Mission and Revival: The Birth of the Global Pentecostal Movement*. Nashville, TN: Nelson Reference & Electronic, 2006.

Rodinson, Maxime. *Muhammad*. New York: Pantheon Books, 1980.

Rosen, Aaron. *Imagining Jewish Art: Encounters with the Masters in Chagall, Guston, and Kitaj*. Oxford: Legenda, 2009.

Rosenberg, Shalom. "Exile and Redemption in Jewish Thought in the Sixteenth Century: Contending Conceptions." In *Jewish Thought in the Sixteenth Century*, ed. Bernard Dov Cooperman, 409–417. Cambridge: Harvard, 1983.

Rosenzweig, Franz. *The Star of Redemption*, trans. William W. Hallo. Notre Dame, IN: Notre Dame Press, 1985.

Sachedina, Abdulaziz Abdulhussein. *The Islamic Roots of Democratic Pluralism*. New York: Oxford University Press, 2001.

Sakeenah, Maryam. *Us Versus Them and Beyond*. Kuala Lumpur, Malaysia: The Other Press, 2010.

Sanneh, Lamin O. *Disciples of All Nations: Pillars of World Christianity*. Oxford and New York: Oxford University Press, 2008.

———. *Translating the Message: The Missionary Impact on Culture*. Maryknoll, NY: Orbis Books, 1989

Saritoprak, Zeki. "The Qur'anic Perspective on Immigrants: Prophet Muhammad's Migration and Its Implications in Our Modern Society." *The [E]Journal of Scriptural Reasoning* 10, no.1 (Aug 2011); see http://jsr.lib.virginia.edu/vol-10-no-1-august-2011-people-and-places/the-quranic-perspective-on-immigrants/

Schindler, Pesach. *Hasidic Responses to the Holocaust in the Light of Hasidic Thought*. Hoboken, NJ: Ktav, 1990.

Scholem, Gershom. *Major Trends in Jewish Mysticism*. New York: Schocken Books, 1954.

———. *The Messianic Idea in Judaism: And Other Essays on Jewish Spirituality*. New York: Schocken Books, 1971.

Sed-Rajna, Gabrielle. *Jewish Art*, trans. Sara Friedman and Mira Reich. New York: Harry N. Abrams, 1995.

Shapiro, Marc B. *The Limits of Orthodox Theology: Maimonides' Thirteen Principles Reappraised*. Oxford: Littman Library of Jewish Civilization, 2011.

Sharma, Arvind, and Katherine K. Young, eds. *Feminism and World Religions*. Albany, NY: State University of New York Press, 1999.

Skaggs, Rebecca. *The Pentecostal Commentary on 1 and 2 Peter and Jude*. Pentecostal Commentary Series 17. Sheffield: Sheffield Academic Press, 2004.

Smith, Margaret. *Muslim Women Mystics: The Life and Work of Rābi'a and Other Women Mystics in Islam*. Oxford, England: Oneworld Publications, 2001.
Soerens, Matthew, and Jenny Hwang. *Welcoming the Stranger: Justice, Compassion and Truth in the Immigration Debate*. Downer's Grove, IL: InterVarsity Press, 2009.
St. Teresa de Avila. *Interior Castle*. In *The Complete Works of St. Teresa de Avila*, trans. and ed. E. Allison Peers, vol. 2. London and New York: Burns & Oates, 2002.
Strack, H.L., and Gunter Stemberger. *Introduction to the Talmud and Midrash*. Minneapolis, MN: Augsburg Fortress Press, 1996.
Sujo, Glenn. *Legacies of Silence: The Visual Arts and Holocaust Memory*. London: Philip Wilson Publishers, 2001.
Swietlicki, Catherine. *Spanish Christian Cabala: The Works of Luis De Leon, Santa Teresa De Jesus, and San Juan De LA Cruz*. Columbia, MO: University of Missouri Press, 1987.
Tassello Giovanni G. and L. Favero, eds. *Chiesa e mobilità umana. Documenti della Santa Sede dal 1883 al 1983*. Rome: Centro Studi Emigrazione, 1985.
Tassello, Giovanni G., ed. *Enchiridion della Chiesa per le migrazioni. Documenti magisteriali ed ecumenici sulla pastorale della mobilità umana (1887–2000)*. Bologna: Centro Edizione Dehoniano, 2001.
Thomas, Pradip N. *Strong Religion, Zealous Media: Christian Fundamentalism and Communication in India*. Thousand Oaks, CA: Sage Publications, 2008.
Tilllich, Paul. *Systematic Theology*, vol. 3. Chicago: University of Chicago Press, 1963.
Tritton, A. S. *The Caliphs and Their Non-Muslim Subjects: A Critical Study of the Covenant of 'Umar*. London: Oxford University Press, 1930.
Turner, Victor. *The Ritual Process; Structure and Anti-Structure*. New York: Aldine De Gruyter, 1995.
Tweed, Thomas A. *Crossing and Dwelling: A Theory of Religion*. Cambridge: Harvard University Press, 2006.
United Nations. *International Migration Report 2009: A Global Assessment*. New York: United Nations Publications, 2010.
van der Leeuw, Gerhardus. *Sacred and Profane Beauty: The Holy in Art*, trans. David E. Green. London: Weidenfeld and Nicolson, 1963.
Vertovec, Steven. *Transnationalism*. London and New York: Routledge, 2009.
Währisch-Oblau, Claudia. *The Missionary Self-Perception of Pentecostal/Charismatic Church Leaders from the Global South in Europe: Bringing Back the Gospel*. Leiden: Brill, 2009.
Währisch-Oblau, Claudia. *The Missionary Self-Perception of Pentecostal/Charismatic Church Leaders from the Global South in Europe: Bringing Back the Gospel*. Leiden and Boston: Brill, 2009.

Ware, Kallistos. *Orthodox Theology in the 21st Century*. Geneva: WCC Publications, 2012.

———. *The Inner Kingdom*. New York: St. Vladimir's Seminary Press, 2001.

Watt, Montgomery. *Muhammad: Prophet and Statesman*. London: Oxford University Press, 1961.

Webb, Diana. *Medieval European Pilgrimage, C.700 – C.1500*. New York: Palgrave MacMillan, 2002.

Willard G. Oxtoby. "(Re)presenting: Muslims on North American Television." *Contemporary Islam: Dynamics of Muslim Life* 4, no. 1 (April 2010): 55–75.

———. "Confronting Misoislamia: Teaching Religion and Violence in Courses on Islam." In *Teaching Religion and Violence*, ed. Brian K. Pennington, 118–148. New York: Oxford University Press, 2012.

Willard G. Oxtoby, Amir Hussain, and Roy C. Amore, eds. *World Religions: Western Traditions*, 4th ed. Toronto: Oxford University Press, 2014.

Willard G. Oxtoby, Roy C. Amore and Amir Hussain, eds. *World Religions: Eastern Traditions*, 4th ed. Toronto: Oxford University Press, 2014.

Wolfson, Elliot. "Judaism and Incarnation: the Imaginal Body of God." In *Christianity in Jewish Terms*, ed. Tikva Frymer-Kensky, 239–261. Boulder CA: Westview Press, 2000.

Wyschogrod, Michael. *The Body of Faith: Judaism as Corporeal Election*. New York: Seabury Press, 1983.

Ye'or, Bat. *The Dhimmi: Jews and Christians under Islam*. Cranbury, NJ: Fairleigh Dickinson University Press/Associated University Presses, 1985.

Yong, Amos. *Hospitality and the Other: Pentecost, Christian Practices, and the Neighbor*. Maryknoll, NY: Orbis Books, 2008.

———. *In the Days of Caesar: Pentecostalism and Political Theology*. Grand Rapids, MI: William B. Eerdmans Publishing Company, 2010.

———. *The Spirit Poured Out on All Flesh: Pentecostalism and the Possibility of Global Theology*. Grand Rapids, MI: Baker Academic, 2005.

———. *Who is the Holy Spirit? A Walk with the Apostles*. Brewster, MA: Paraclete Press, 2012.

Yong, Amos, and Barbara Brown Zikmund, eds. *Remembering Jamestown: Hard Questions about Christian Mission*. Maryknoll, NY: Orbis Books, 2010.

Yong, Amos, and Clifton Clarke, eds. *Global Renewal, Religious Pluralism, and the Great Commission: Toward a Renewal Theology of Mission and Interreligious Encounter*. Lexington, KY: Emeth Press, 2011.

Zachariah, Mathai. *Beyond Ecumenism: A Journey into Light*. Tiruvalla, Kerala, India: CSS, 2002.

Zizioulas, John D. *Being as Communion*. New York: St. Vladimir's Seminary Press, 1993.

Contributors

Charles Amjad-Ali is academic dean of the Seminary Consortium for Urban Pastoral Education (SCUPE). Until very recently, he was the Martin Luther King, Jr., Professor for Justice & Christian Community, and the director of the Islamic Studies Program at Luther Seminary, St. Paul, MN. He was also the first occupant of the prestigious rotating Desmond Tutu Chair of Ecumenical Theology and Social Transformation in Africa at the University of Western Cape, in South Africa. Since the early 1980s, Dr. Amjad-Ali has served various departments of the Christian Conference of Asia and the World Council of Churches, including the Urban Rural Mission of the Commission on World Mission and Evangelism and the Faith and Order Commission, and worked with the Commission on International Affairs, Church and Society, and the Programme to Combat Racism, as well as Inter-Faith Unit. He has also worked with labor movements since his undergraduate days, and currently serves on the board of Interfaith Worker Justice in Chicago. He has authored and edited 16 books and over 250 articles around the world. He has a MDiv and PhD (magna cum laude) from Princeton Theological Seminary, a ThD from Uppsala University in Sweden, and a post-doctoral certificate in Islamic studies from Columbia University, and has done graduate studies in philosophy in Germany.

Nancy Bedford, born in 1962 in Comodoro Rivadavia, Argentina, is Georgia Harkness Professor of Applied Theology at Garrett-Evangelical Theological Seminary (Evanston), *Profesora Extraordinaria No Residente* at Instituto Universitario ISEDET (Buenos Aires), and a member of Reba Place Church (Mennonite). Her latest books are *Nuestra Fe* (with Guillermo Hansen; Buenos Aires: ISEDET, 2008) and *La porfía de la resurrección. Ensayos desde el feminismo teológico latinoamericano* (Buenos Aires: Kairós, 2009). Her research interests are global feminist theory and theologies, Latin American theologies, Latino/Latina theologies in North America, theologies in migration, food and theology, liberating readings of Scripture, and the rearticulation of classical doctrinal loci from the perspective of critical and poetic reason (especially pneumatology, Christology and theological anthropology).

Kondothra M. George is a professor of systematic and patristic theology at The Federated Faculty for Research in Religion and Culture, and principal emeritus of Orthodox Theological Seminary, Kottayam, Kerala. Currently a member of the board of studies of Malayalam University, he was a professor at the Bossey Ecumenical Institute in Geneva (1989–1994), and served in the senate of Serampore University in various academic capacities. George has authored books in theology and literature, and contributes regularly to secular periodicals as well. His areas of interest are theology, art, and culture.

Amir Hussain is a professor of theological studies at Loyola Marymount University in Los Angeles, where he teaches about Islam and world religions. From 2011 to 2015, Amir is the editor of the *Journal of the American Academy of Religion*, the premier scholarly journal for the study of religion. He is the co-editor for the four editions of *World Religions: Western Traditions*, and *World Religions: Eastern Traditions*, textbooks published in 2014 by Oxford University Press. He is also the co-editor for the third edition of *A Concise Introduction to World Religions*, which will be published in 2015 by OUP. Prior to those books, he wrote an introduction to Islam for North Americans entitled *Oil and Water: Two Faiths, One God* (Kelowna: Copper House, 2006).

Dale T. Irvin is president and a professor of world Christianity at New York Theological Seminary. He is the author of several books, including *History of the World Christian Movement* (3 volumes) written with Scott W. Sunquist, and numerous articles. He is also the general editor of the *Journal of World Christianity*.

Deenabandhu Manchala, a Lutheran pastor from India, Dr, Manchala has served since 2000 as program executive at the World Council of Churches (WCC) in Geneva, Switzerland. Currently, he is working in the division of Unity, Mission and Spirituality of the WCC, and is responsible for the project on "just and inclusive communities," which works with five networks of marginalized people who challenge discrimination: racism, casteism, indigenous peoples, people living with disabilities, and the migrant communities and people. For more information on this, please visit: http://www.oikoumene.org/?id=3105.

Elaine Padilla is an assistant professor of constructive theology at New York Theological Seminary. Her theological analysis interweaves current philosophical discourse with Latin American and Latino/a thought, mysticism, and religious and gender studies. She is the author of *Divine Enjoyment: A Theology of Passion and Exuberance* with Fordham University Press.

Peter C. Phan is the inaugural holder of the Ignacio Ellacuria Chair of Catholic Social Thought at Georgetown University. He has authored a dozen books and over 300 essays on various aspects of Christian theology and missiology. Among his books are *Christianity with an Asian Face*; *In Our Own Tongues*; and *Being Religious Interreligiously*. He recently edited *Christianities in Asia* and *The Cambridge Companion to the Trinity*.

Melissa Raphael is a professor of Jewish Theology and teaches theology and religious studies at the University of Gloucestershire. She has published numerous articles in the fields of religion and gender and feminist theology, specializing in the sacred/profane distinction in Western religion, Jewish theology and feminist thealogy (*sic*). She is the author of *Rudolf Otto and the Concept of Holiness*, *Thealogy and Embodiment: The Post-Patriarchal Reconstruction of Female Sacrality*, *Introducing Thealogy: Discourse on the Goddess*, *The Female Face of God in Auschwitz: A Jewish Feminist Theology of the Holocaust*, and *the Visual Image: A Jewish Theology of Art*. Professor Raphael is currently working on a study of idolatry and gender.

Devorah Schoenfeld has her doctorate from the Graduate Theological Union in Berkeley and an MA from the Hebrew University in Jerusalem. She has previously taught at St. Mary's College of Maryland, at University of California Davis, and at the Conservative Yeshiva. Her book, *Isaac on Jewish and Christian Altars: Genesis 22 in Rashi and in the Glossa Ordinaria* was published in 2012 by Fordham University Press. Her research interests include medieval Bible commentaries and Jewish-Christian relations, and she has also published on dream interpretation in the Talmud and on proofs for the existence of God in medieval Jewish philosophy.

Amos Yong is a professor of theology and mission, and director of the Center for Missiological Research at Fuller Theological Seminary, Pasadena California. He is the author or editor of over two dozen scholarly books.

Index

Abraham, 2, 9–11, 15, 29, 31, 33, 41–2, 44, 48–9, 66, 73, 77, 143, 174, 177–9, 189, 191
Abrahamic faiths/traditions, 2, 9, 17, 20, 73, 94, 109, 210, 216, 227
Alban, Saint, 71
al-hajj, 10, 15–17, 179
anamnesis, 69–70, 104

beauty, 50, 55, 71, 210–11, 214–15, 222
Benedict XV, 82
Benedict XVI, 78, 82, 87–8
Beruriah, 214
body, 41, 48–51, 54, 106, 122–3, 168, 213–14, 225
  of Christ, 104, 168
Bolshevik Revolution, 65, 71
Bonaventure, Saint, 210, 214–15, 217–18, 222, 224, 226
Braiterman, Zachary, 59
breath, 92, 102, 212–13, 215, 221, 229. *See also* soul-breath
Byzantine symphonia, 70

casteism, 157–9
Catholic theology, 3, 77–9, 83, 88–9, 94, 96, 103, 105
CCME, 156
CICARAWS, 156
Clement of Rome, 67
colonial movement, 64

constructive theology, 9
cosmos, 19, 125, 153, 165, 209–12, 214–18, 221–7, 229–30, 233n55
culturalization, 115

dance, 3, 48, 50–3, 55–8
de León, Moses (Moshe ben Shem-Tov), 213–14, 216, 218, 220–1
De Pastorale Migratorum Cura, 91
Deus Migrator, 97–9, 103, 105–6
dhimmi, 3, 195–8
diakonia, 157
diaspora, 2, 13, 27–9, 37–8, 41–2, 48, 51, 53, 65, 70–2, 74, 124, 139, 190
  Jewish diaspora, 11–13, 27–9, 37–8, 41–2, 48, 51, 53
  Orthodox diaspora, 65, 70–2, 74
diversity, 2–3, 51, 93, 112, 126, 137, 139, 157, 160, 163–6, 184, 187–8, 191, 193–4, 196–7, 200, 202, 204–5, 228
doxology, 63, 69
dwelling, 18–19, 34, 49, 102, 147, 189, 193, 211, 213, 220–1

early church, 67, 78, 137, 168
earthly existence, 64, 66–8
Eastern Orthodox, 74, 111
ecclesia semper migranda, 3, 114, 117–18, 124, 126
economy, 86, 125, 143

ecosystem, 126, 218, 226–8, 230
empowerment, 123, 139, 146
ends of the earth, 10, 12, 52, 78, 134–5, 137, 142–4
ENFORMM, 166
Erga Migrantes Caritas Christi, 87, 92–3
eschatology, 68–9, 96, 103
Ethiopia, 11, 65, 141–2, 174–5
European Islam, 204
evolution, 57, 209, 217–18, 226, 233n55
exile, 2–3, 7, 11, 15, 17–18, 20–2, 27–9, 31–42, 47–8, 51–4, 57, 66, 72, 74, 78, 86, 105, 109n18, 137, 142, 179, 183–4, 213, 225. See also *galut*
existence, 11, 19–20, 27, 29, 39, 41, 64, 66–9, 105, 112, 118, 166, 183, 216, 226–7
Exul Familia, 83, 85, 89–91

Faith and Order Commission, 157–8
familial ties, 118
fiqh, 195–7

galut, 28, 47. See also exile
gathering, 12–13, 15, 17, 72
greening, 215, 225–7, 229

Hagar, 176, 178–9
Halakhah, 36, 38, 48, 199. See also pathmaking
HaLevi, Judah, 40–1
Hellenist Jews, 139
hijra, 15, 174–6, 191–2
Hildegard of Bingen, 215, 217, 224–5
Holy Spirit, 73, 96, 102–5, 113, 120, 122, 124, 134, 137, 141, 146
home, 7–8, 11–14, 17–22, 47, 51–2, 54, 66–7, 70–3, 77, 84–5, 92–3, 99–100, 103, 105, 121–2, 126, 136–8, 141, 143–6, 156, 176, 179–80, 184, 211, 219, 221, 225, 227
homecoming, 3, 17–18, 20–2
homeland, 8, 13, 19, 21, 27–9, 41–2, 77, 213
homelessness, 18–20, 47, 52, 54, 77, 100
hospitality, 3, 72–5, 77–8, 101, 106, 116, 127, 157–8, 161–3, 189, 192, 195

Ibn al-'Arabi, 184, 211–13, 218–21, 224
immigration, 79, 82–3, 85–6, 88, 91, 106, 114–16, 119, 124, 146, 164
incarnation, 49–50, 73, 98–9, 120–2, 137, 162, 190
inclusiveness, 3, 161
indigenous peoples, 158
interculturality, 117
Ishmael, 10, 35, 174, 176–9
Islam, 2–3, 9–10, 15–17, 85, 173–4, 176, 181–4, 187–9, 191–205, 211, 218, 224, 229
Islamic history, 188, 191–2, 203
Islamophobia, 203
Israel, 3, 11–13, 27–42, 48–54, 57–8, 66, 72, 97, 100, 104, 120, 139, 141, 213

Jerusalem, 2, 10–13, 16, 28, 30–1, 34, 36–7, 39, 41, 52, 54, 67, 74, 134, 137–43, 147, 198
Jewish art, 3, 47–50, 54–8. See also Zionist art
John Paul II, 86–7
John XXIII, 84
journey, 2, 4, 7–10, 15–16, 20–2, 40, 56–7, 66, 68, 73, 77, 100, 103, 105–6, 121–2, 126, 134, 144, 155, 167, 173, 209–16, 220, 222–4, 226, 229–30
Just and Inclusive Communities, 158, 163, 165–6

Kabbalah, 213, 216, 220, 225, 234n85

latino/latina, 3, 114–15, 117–20, 123–5
Leo XIII, 80–1, 86
Letter to Diognetus, 67, 78, 105
Levinas, Emmanuel, 52–3
local church, 64, 74, 84, 91, 106
love, 4, 22, 37–9, 50–1, 67–9, 72, 74–5, 77–8, 87–8, 93, 98–9, 102, 105–6, 120, 160, 164–5, 167, 177–8, 183–4, 209–17, 219–27, 229–30

Maimonides (Moshe Ben Maimon), 12, 23n15, 27, 39–40
manifest, 50, 56, 68–9, 97, 123, 142–3, 212, 214, 221–2, 229
marginality, 117, 119, 122
Mecca, 2, 10, 15–17, 174–7, 179, 191–3, 195–6
Medina, 2, 15, 174–6, 188, 191–4, 196–7, 199
Mediterranean, 11, 78, 137–8, 143, 202, 206n9
memory, 2, 8–11, 19, 42, 69, 106, 209–10, 223–6, 229
Menocal, María Rosa, 182–3
messiah, 20, 38–9, 42, 44n23, 56, 58, 134, 137, 140–1, 143
metaphor, 35, 66, 77, 120, 123, 179, 182, 184, 210, 222
midrash, 28, 31, 33, 35, 57
migration, 1–4, 7–12, 14–18, 20–2, 27–9, 41–2, 47–8, 51, 53, 57, 59, 63–6, 70–2, 74–5, 77–96, 98–100, 102–3, 105–6, 109n17, 112, 114–21, 123–7, 133–40, 142–7, 155–8, 160–1, 163–8, 173–6, 179, 184, 188–92, 209–11, 213, 216–19, 222–3, 227–9. See also *hijra*
migration narratives, 188–92, 205n7, 206n9

millat, 3, 198–9
mirror, 210, 214, 217, 223–5, 229
mission, 14, 41, 52, 74, 78, 90–1, 93, 124, 127, 135–6, 141, 144–6, 158–60, 163–4, 166–8
missionary, 2, 14, 64, 71, 74, 78, 90, 124, 133, 135, 137, 143, 145
monasticism, 14, 66, 68, 78
Moses, 11, 66, 139, 189, 191, 214, 222
Muhammad, Prophet, 2–3, 15–16, 174–6, 178, 191, 193–5, 197–8, 218
Muslim, 3–4, 15–16, 21, 88, 93, 115, 173–6, 178–84, 187–8, 191–205, 219, 228
mystic, 4, 16–17, 97, 122, 209–12, 214–17, 219–20, 222–4, 227
mysticism, 3, 17, 47, 211, 213–14, 221–4, 229

Nahmanides (Moishe ben Nahman), 12, 40
North America, 3, 11, 42, 65, 70, 112, 179, 184, 199

oikoumene, 156, 164
Oriental Orthodox, 65
Orthodox Church of America (OCA), 65, 74
Ottoman (Turkish) Empire, 71, 81, 198–9, 204

papal teachings, 79
paradigmatic migrant, 100, 102, 105–6
pathmaking, 48. See also *Halakhah*
patristic period, 63, 71, 73, 78
Paul VI, 85–6
Paul, (Apostle), 3, 10, 121, 142–5, 159, 162, 217
Pentecost, 126, 136–7, 139

INDEX

Pentecostalism, 3, 111–12, 120, 122, 124–5, 133–7, 144–6, 166
   political dimension of, 145
   West African, 124–5
persecution, 15, 48, 51, 53, 58, 78, 81, 89, 140, 174–6, 190–1, 196, 219, 223
Peter (Apostle), 13, 77, 142–3, 167
Philip (Apostle), 140–2
philoxenia, 73, 77, 162
pilgrimage, 3, 10, 13–17, 66–7, 74–5, 179, 214. See also *al-hajj*
Pius IX, 3, 78, 80
Pius X, 81, 88
Pius XI, 82
Pius XII, 83, 85, 89
planetary coexistence, 229
   planetary love, 214–16, 223
   planetary self, 210
Protestant Principle, 113, 115–16, 124, 126
Protestantism, 71, 80–1, 111–19, 122–3, 126–7

Rābi'a (al-'Adawiyya), 17, 212
race, 12, 199, 204, 228
racism, 134, 155–9
Reconquista, 200, 219, 223
refugees, 51, 55, 73, 77, 81–2, 85–7, 89, 92, 100, 137, 156, 176, 179, 192
Rosen, Aaron, 49
Rosenzweig, Franz, 49, 51–2, 54, 57

sacred, 2, 10, 36, 38, 42, 68, 176–7, 188, 194, 202–3, 209–11, 218–20
Sacred Consistorial Congregation, 81, 90–1
Said, Edward, 184
Sarah (wife of Abraham), 9–11, 73, 77
scattering, 11–13, 15, 17. See also diaspora
Sergius, Saint, 71
shariah, 195, 197, 199, 202

Shekhinah, 34–6, 57, 213, 220–2, 225
signs, 4, 14, 68, 94, 168, 210–11, 214, 216–18, 221–3, 225–7, 229–30
Smith, Muriel, 173
Smith, Wilfred Cantwell, 3, 173
sojourners, 56, 66–7, 78, 129n23
soul, 20, 27, 30, 36, 90–1, 142, 145, 210, 213–15, 219–26
soul-breath, 213, 221. See also breath
Soviet bloc, 71
spirit, 44, 50, 70, 73, 96–7, 99, 102–6, 108, 113, 120–2, 124, 126, 133–5, 137, 139, 141–53, 175, 219, 225
stars, 209, 215

Talmud, 3, 27–9, 32–4, 36–9, 41
Teresa of Ávila, Saint, 219–21
theology of migration, 2–4, 9, 14, 18, 21–2, 27, 53, 63
   Muslim theology of, 173, 176–9
   Pentecostal theology of, 134, 136, 144–5
   Roman Catholic theology of, 78–9, 83, 85, 89, 92, 94–6, 98, 103, 105, 109n17
Thompson, Richard, 183
Tillich, Paul, 51, 53, 113
translatability, 135–6
Trinitarian theology, 63, 96, 120–1

witness, 31, 71–2, 74, 76, 95, 112, 123–4, 135–6, 151, 155, 192, 207, 226
Wolfson, Elliot, 49–50
wonder, 49, 144, 146, 209, 211–13, 215–17, 219, 221–5, 227, 229, 231, 233, 235, 237
world Christian history and tradition, 9, 21, 157, 168
World Council of Churches, 3, 156, 166
Wyschogrod, Michael, 49–51

Zionist art, 58. See also Jewish art